Deconstructing Narcissism

True Sympathy for "the Devil"

By Matt Socha

This book is dedicated to my father in spirit.

I would also like to dedicate this book to
the Millennial Generation
who has been scapegoated more than any other generation preceding it.

To my niece and nephew:
Please always honor your sacred masculine and feminine.

Contents:

Introduction

"Judge not, lest ye be judged."
- Book of Matthew 7:1

In 2014, I authored *"The Toxic States of America: And How Spirituality Can Foster a National Breakthrough,"* a socio-political analysis detailing how a large-scale mismanagement of fear resulted in economic, cultural, political, and ethical inequality and dysfunction, devolving to the point where it resembles a large-scale dysfunctional family. As described in the book, this downturn was due in part to the activity of malignant individuals who gravitated to positions of power within government, media, academia, finance, and the corporate sector. Subsequent havoc was wreaked on their constituent base by enacting policies and practices which were opportunistic, hypercritical, pathologically dishonest, manipulative, opportunistic, harmful, self-serving as well as devoid of compassion, empathy, and conscience. This book further explored how this trend was enabled by a general public with unresolved issues, an inability to set boundaries or call out bad behavior, and a tendency to over-extend themselves.

As would be expected, the remedy proposed to the reader was to cultivate enough self-love to disengage from hierarchical organizations headed by individuals affected with malignant narcissism and supported by those with enabling personalities.

While I was pleased with the outcome of this book's content, I realize now that the potential for dissolving this cultural dysfunction is even greater than I had thought, ***and this potential is based in understanding the nature of the root causes of malignant personality disorders themselves - that is, their childhood origin issues and conditions in which they were raised.***

It is my sincere hope that *Deconstructing Narcissism* will serve as a companion piece to *Toxic States of America,* allowing the healing for both "victims" and "perpetrators" alike because, as will be displayed in this book, both "empaths" and "malignant narcissists" perceive themselves as victims and the "good guys" the other party as guilty.

Before proceeding, while writing this book it needs to be mentioned that the American Psychiatric Association (APA) has recently broken up the personality disorders which were grouped under the

"Cluster B" or "dramatic" category in the *Diagnostic Statistical Manual of Mental Disorders (DSM)*. To the author, and for reasons we shall see very soon, the APA ought to be commended for doing so since these disorders vary greatly in terms of the childhood origin conditions which created them. The disorders previously grouped under this category were Narcissistic Personality Disorder (NPD), Antisocial Personality Disorder (ASPD), Borderline Personality Disorder (BPD), and Histrionic Personality Disorder (HPD).

Although there will be some material pertaining to the latter three disorders, the focus of this book will be Narcissistic Personality Disorder and "malignant narcissism" which may also arise from ASPD. Due to the varying environmental conditions and as we shall see, the "narcissism" which arises from NPD tends to be a bit different than that of ASPD. Specifically, this book will explore the potential casualty behind such hallmark characteristics such as the Grandiose Sense of Self, Lack of Empathy, Demeaning and Belittling behavior, Lack of Remorse, and Controlling Behavior.

Admittedly, I am not a licensed psychologist and understand the material presented in this book may be met with skepticism on account of this. I am more than accepting of this for three reasons:

First, the causation behind personality disorders such as Narcissistic and Antisocial has eluded many in the psychological community for an extensive period of time. This is understandable since the childhood origin conditions which create these disorders is going to vary from household to household. To date, I've heard many mental health professionals make the claim that recovery for individuals diagnosed with Cluster B disorders are slim to none; the reason for this will, hopefully, become more evident as the contents of this book progress. At best, psychotherapy may be able to modify some *behaviors* but the disordered personality will remain intact. Some professionals, because of the ruthless and abusive treatment others receive from malignant narcissists, refuse to treat such individuals at all (which I can understand.) Yet I find this both disheartening and fatalistic for both those diagnosed with such disorders and those who have close interactions with them. However, despite the material presented in this book, "recovery" for some Cluster B disordered individuals may still be difficult *if* such persons attempt to recover *on their own*. By this, I'm suggesting that for some Cluster B disorders, "recovery" is going to require not being enabled yet also involve examining the childhood conditions which enhanced the respective personality disorder. (As far as those which are narcissistic in nature, recovery on one's own is impossible since they think that nothing is wrong with them - thanks to, in part, their upbringing.) Schema therapy *is* an element of healing suggested in this book which designates the specific foundational schemas relevant to these disorders.

Second, and more importantly, whether or not the Cluster B personality is diagnosed as such or not, they will be interacting with the general public, family members, and romantic partners as opposed to a therapist. Since they rarely seek treatment until met with a life-changing event, my hope in writing this book is that the reader (as well as therapists - whom I sincerely hope would focus on childhood origin issues for Cluster B treatment as well as other disorders) will not only act as a healing conduit for the Cluster B disordered individual, but heal others who harbor any resentment or contempt toward disordered individuals due to previous interactions as well as their own "issues." In doing so, they *may* find themselves actually having compassion, ownership, and heal more quickly after an episode of narcissistic abuse or a similar interaction and reduce the frequency of such occurrences in the future.

Third, I've actually heard some mental health practitioners tell their "online community" that it's unnecessary to try to understand the psychology behind malignant narcissism. I can't force myself to be congenial here: this is stupid. As depicted in *Toxic States of America, any* organization headed by a malignant narcissist regardless of its size - whether that's a dysfunctional family, a corporation, or a country - is destined for implosion which can take the form of mass-layoffs, mass suicide or starvation, genocide, or the dissolution of the family unit; that is, no one speaks to each other anymore. By understanding the malignant narcissistic pathology, others can actually be assisting - but never a "cure" - for those with this sort of psychological make up. To me, it's astounding that a so-called mental-health care professional would be cavalier enough to overlook the root causes of this type of personality disorder for this reason alone. One practitioner even posts a video series with each video dedicated to a certain behavioral trait particular to malignant narcissism (some of which are featured in Chapter 2.) But, for whatever reason, she not concerned about such personality types gravitating to positions of narcissism and control - their drugs of choice (and they've been doing this for centuries.) Why is she not bothering to ask what might happen if such types take the reign within leadership of hierarchal organizations? Are we really to believe that malignant narcissists only abuse, lie to, take advantage of, and cheat on their wives and not *everyone* they get involved with - including their constituent bases? Not only does this "therapist" enable this potential, she enables this reality as she actively defends much of the gas-lighting this sort of malignant leadership has been imposing on the American public for decades. If it's possible to pinpoint the root cause(s) of this pathology, isn't it in the world's best interest to weed it out so that it can be healed? Or should we just watch her videos and say, "Suck it up."

That's what's happening; that's what's been happening.

And this is my appeal to the "empath community" - which, in many cases, have revealed that their empathy is limited in their rhetoric against "narcissists," "sociopaths," and "psychopaths." This is not something I judge or condemn; rather, it is something I can identify with - especially if the root cause of the disorder is due to being over-indulged or spoiled (which is quite probable.) There's no argument from me that it's never a walk in the park to be on the receiving end of narcissistic rage, a polyamorous affair, a scam, psychological or physical abuse, or deprecating comments. To me, the residual hurt, anger, and contempt is understandable and I have nothing but compassion and understanding for it. But, hopefully, this book will provide such "empaths" with insight into the conditions which create these types of disorders. For me, writing this book has substantially increased my compassion for "bullies" and "sociopaths" in particular; narcissists to a lesser extent (since, as we will see, they were spoiled.)

However, there's a meme with respect to malignantly narcissistic individuals that's been circulating for some time, referring to them as "Angels in Disguise." Personally, I find this term both awkward and morbid. What would you call a guy in a Santa Claus costume who molests children on the sly? Would you call him an "Angel in Disguise?" A "Saint in a Santa Suit?"

Please: he's a "Wolf in Sheep's Clothing." An example of an "Angel in Disguise" would be someone who resembles Hannibal Lecter but drops a pill in your drink when you're not looking and subsequently cures your cancer - pro bono. Malignant narcissists obviously do not behave this way. An angel would help to heal wounds, not rip the scab off because the wound is still there - that's exactly what a demon disguised as an angel would do.

Don't get me wrong: I understand the meaning. These individuals come across our path so that we value ourselves in areas in which we are not and manifest personal psychological protection to shield ourselves from absorbing any negativity.

But let's face it: these individuals *target* fears and "issues" which were mostly likely implanted during the early years of our childhood. An "Angel In Disguise" would help would help someone work through and *resolve* their "issues" - not reinforce or take advantage of them.

But even this isn't always the case. Some people who are raised in very healthy households try to help malignant narcissists when they come across them and it's guaranteed to be to their detriment. There really are *no* unhealed wounds in these cases so the "Angels in Disguise" metaphor really isn't applicable.

Regardless, I feel quite confident in writing this: *many narcissists, sociopaths, and psychopaths are most likely to feel the same sort of contempt for empaths as some empaths feel toward them. And this will be evident by the end of this book - perhaps even by the first chapter.*

Moreover, since the objective of this book is one of healing and analysis, I will do my best to refrain from referring to malignant narcissists as a "narcissists," "sociopaths," or "psychopaths" but I'm not making any promises. From their corner, I can assure the reader that they do not find the "empath" to be empathetic - rather, they could (and oftentimes do) consider such individuals "professional victims," "goodie-goodies," "door-mats," or overly-sensitive (the latter of which, *I'd like to emphasize now and as we shall see*, could not be more ironic since the reason narcissists have a grandiose sense of self *is due to being sensitive* to having their ego bloated by one or more parent while they were growing up. Subsequent traits like narcissistic injury, a need to control, and denigration of others all stem from this *sensitivity* as we shall see.) If applicable, I *may* use the term malignant narcissist, but my intention is to keep that limited. Regardless, the objective of this book is to catalyze a gap-closing between the two polarities therefore such labels will not be used.

So, if healing from narcissistic abuse involves tending to our own issues or under-developed areas of our life, why read a book delving into the childhood origin conditions which create malignant narcissism? The reasons are several, which will be listed here, but first and foremost:

If we do not forgive, we will relive. And we cannot thoroughly forgive a perpetrator until we - calling ourselves "empaths" - walk the proverbial mile in their shoes and understand where their behaviors originate.

First and foremost, the more we do this, the more we'll see the "hurt animal" as opposed to the "abuser." But if the actions and behaviors of the Cluster B which caused us hurt and pain are still renting space in our heads, it means we have work in one, two, or all of the following areas: 1) Developing Self-love, Self-value, and ego boundaries 2) Forgiving the perpetrator (which may involve trying to understand them; it will certainly help), 3) Having a *support system* which genuinely cares about the pain we've endured, especially as children without exploiting such systems to enable us in other areas of our lives. Note that there is a marked difference between "support system" and "support source"; the latter is used as a "cure," not a resource.

The narcissistic individual must also do the above for themselves for healing, as we shall see in Chapter 2 of this book.

Forgiving the perpetrator does not mean exonerating their behavior, but the contents of this book will help us understand *why they did* what they did as well as *understand their psychology*. And it's completely understandable that we feel hurt and anger after been victimized. But, if we continue to harbor resentment or any ill will in our minds - if our internal monologue resembles something like, "I hate that sonofabitch for cheating on me!" or "I hope she rots in hell for years!" - the very moment we hurl mental invectives at them is the moment we define ourselves as a victim. Doing so for a prolonged time will only corrode our own spirit and affect our mental health.

When we define ourselves as a victim - as we shall see - we will increase the probability of bringing out the perpetrator in others, attracting perpetrators, and/or self-secluding, which gives rise to the following cycle:

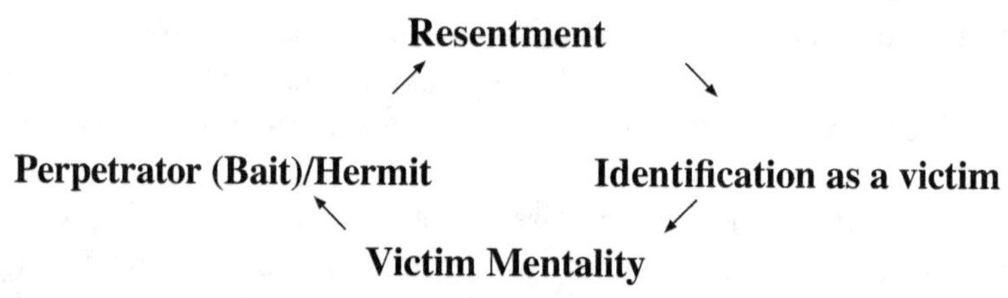

Make no mistake: malignant narcissists do exactly the same thing.

So, with empathy-based forgiveness being the first reason to read this book, here are the others:

• To gain full closure after the end of a relationship with a narcissistic individual by fully understanding their psychology. "Endings" with some narcissistic personality types are usually abrupt and leave the other party disoriented, confused, and in some cases, traumatized. The contents of this book will help the reader understand what "issues" and thought patterns were behind the Cluster B's behavior.

• To correlate episodes of narcissistic interactions to personal childhood origin mistreatment and/or abuse for personal healing.

• Become less reactive and permeable to the effects of narcissistic presence, abuse, and behavior.

• Develop a detached compassion and understanding which may condition the narcissistic afflicted individual to become vulnerable, feel safe, and to open up about their past trauma or "issues" (no, don't always count on this happening.)

• Replace contempt for the narcissistic personality with understanding, if not compassion, since the continuation of contempt will lead to the repetition and/or escalation of episodes, contempt, and altercations.

• Expedite the healing process after an episode of narcissistic abuse.

• Widen the spectrum of relationships that is inclusive of more personality types.

• Enable authentic forgiveness of those who have hurt us in the past and with whom we have conflict in the present.

• Increase emotional intelligence, wisdom, and maturity.

• To condition oneself to taking their behavior less personally, if at all.

• Reduce chances of raising a narcissistic child.

• Learn to set appropriate boundaries with equanimity.

Please note that the contents and purpose of this book are not an endorsement to "try to make things work" with someone who has this type of disorder. I'm well aware that the recommended strategy in dealing with malignant narcissists is to go "no contact" and to allow for them to work out their issues and dissolve their bad behavioral practices on their own as it is for all of us. I'm on board with this but let's be realistic: going "no contact" only goes so far. Oftentimes we are placed in situations where going "no contact" isn't an option or it's the lesser of two evils. If this is the case, the contents of this book ought to be helpful. Furthermore, if we find ourselves facing recurring scenarios where we are reenacting the same drama over and over again, it is imperative that we determine if there's a reason behind this.

This book is not in any way a suggested path to an exoneration of a malignant narcissist's behavior or worse: Stockholm Syndrome (rather, it is to serve as a buffer to any situation which may cause it) - especially if the behavior is extreme. Never should we accept a mentality that we should be okay or sympathize with "poopy-kins'" extracurricular activity such as affairs, incessant gas-lighting, drug dealing, mental or physical abuse, or hiring hit men.

It's worth emphasizing that this book is not a program for the "empath" to "fix" the malignant narcissist. To reiterate, it is to supplement the healing process, reduce interpersonal friction and animosity, and increase insight and wisdom. It's possible that you may discover some "Jedi Mind Tricks" in coping with these personality types as well.

More often than not, malignant narcissists interact with three types of people:
1) Other malignant narcissists (who either act as sounding boards, cronies, or even adversaries in some cases; this is due to similarities in childhood conditions and post-childhood life experiences.)
2) Codependent enablers (or those who provide narcissistic supply and poor boundaries); and
3) People who, after bad experiences, are fed up with interacting with them as well as their existence and try to avoid them at all costs.

Unfortunately, all three categories will inevitably meet undesirable consequences as a result.

I'd like to see both you and I in a separate category: one in which we have used the experiences we've had with these types to our benefit - to make us stronger - yet also wiser, more understanding, more compassionate, more confident, and fully-resilient in how to appropriately interact with such individuals during the course of our daily lives, especially in this materialistic day and age. I believe that being able to accurately understand the conditions in which the Cluster B personality was raised will greatly assist in mitigating our interactions with them and allow us to proceed through life not only as unscathed as possible, but as happy and alive as we have ever been.

If you consider yourself to be an "empath" and are anticipating the following material to vilify the "sociopath," "narcissist," or "psychopath," I recommend you abandon that expectation now but highly encourage you to proceed. The exception I have to this is my treatment toward the personality disorders which were over-indulged or spoiled and have subsequently developed an elitist, selfish sense about themselves, in which case the material presented is admittedly reprimanding. Some of the content will hold such personality types accountable for their behavior yet some will focus more on their early childhood environment.

Each of the subsequent chapters within Part I will focus on a behavioral trait linked to the Cluster B personality type and the childhood origin conditions which fostered the manifestation of that trait. Also, if you are an "empath," there will be recommended coping strategies regarding how to interact and respond to the particular behavioral trait focused on by the chapter.

In Part II, we'll examine organizational structures as small as the dysfunctional family and as large as cults and certain religions to examine how malignant narcissism impacts others and civilizations as a whole - potentially guiding mankind for centuries toward a grim, monopolized future. The reader should be forewarned: some of the content in this section will be considered controversial by many. However, on the basis of the material presented in Part I, my hopes is that the reader will be acclimated to sufficient objectivity by the time they reach Part II.

Especially with respect to Part II of this book, those readers aware of what's been referred to as "The Deep State," "The Military Industrial Complex," or those behind "The New World Order" (the topic of the first half of *Toxic States of America*) may find the material presented to be of utmost importance. Since, as we shall see, their collective psychology resembles that of malignant narcissism, this material may actually deactivate their proceedings - or at least the support they receive - since it shines a light on their collective "shadow self." Since shadows disappear in the presence of light, perhaps their activity will as well.

Many of us who are familiar with this takeover initiative have heard others describe this situation as a "spiritual war." Well, what exactly is "spirituality?" The word "Spirituality" has been applied to the social and existential wellbeing of the individual which, quite frankly, has little difference from "psychology." The only difference, really, is that "Psychology" - as a field of study or a "science" - didn't really exist prior to the last century and "Psychology" is more definitive and categorical. "Psychology" also takes into consideration the lack of others and categorizes subsequent spiritual disorders on the basis of such observable criteria.

Since The New World Order has been linked to self-serving

initiatives which have been based on siphoning public wealth and placing it into the hands of a few, seizing control of various types of outlets and organizations through subversive, coercive, fraudulent, and threatening tactics, and manipulating mass awareness to perceive its initiatives as beneficent (that is, brainwashing - or gas-lighting - the public to believe that various malignant objectives serve their best interest when, in reality, they couldn't be more detrimental), shedding light on the root causes on this corrupt "psychology" or "spirituality" - whichever term you prefer - can help dissipate it. So let's get started.

<u>Part I:</u>
Up Close and Personal

1

<u>Which came first: The "Victim" or The "Criminal?"</u>

"We marry our parents."
- Proverb of unknown origin

Almost a year ago at the time of writing this book, I was asked by a friend to conduct a video interview for his website about the contents of my previous book, *The Toxic States of America.* At a certain point, our conversation meandered toward the topic of Cluster B disorders, specifically those which are malignantly narcissistic, hyper-controlling, and devoid of empathy and how this character-type had ostensibly manifested itself into high-ranking positions of legislative, military, financial, and corporate power. During this portion of our talk, I expressed my disbelief at the inability of the psychological community to elucidate the root cause(s) behind the manifestation of these types of disorders and others akin to it. I don't recall my exact words, but they were something like:

"They were raised by codependent enablers!"

To me, this seemed as obvious as the day is long, and it does more so now than it did at the time I gave this interview. The term "codependent" was coined decades ago, but its use is nebulous due to a variety of reasons: the various sources on this topic, changing times, and not to mention who is using it to name a few. For that reason and for the intents and purposes of this book, it's well worth defining at this time:

By "codependent," I'm referring to *a personality who has all or part of the following:*
- Low boundaries
- A tendency to be spread thin
- A low sense of self and/or self-worth while bolstering others'

- Loving, caring, and respecting others disproportionately over oneself
- Overly considerate of others' feelings, wellbeing, or other condition while abnegating their own
- A propensity of being too kind and giving while receiving little to nothing in return
- A disproportionate prioritization of the spiritual life over the physical
- A tendency to enable or spoil others, particularly their children, with sizable
  endowments with respect to love, ego, and finances
- More supporting tendencies than asserting
- A tendency to let others occupy their mental activity
- Potential for carrying an addiction or enabling another's addiction
- A tendency to over-indulge, spoil, or enable others in some capacity

Based on the description I've just provided, however, it was obvious to me that a parent with such character would naturally raise a child with a narcissistic Cluster B personality disorder or something close to it. And this premise will be the basis of this book: *to look through the eyes of a child who was raised by such a personality type; to understand his/her experience and the impact such parenting had on his/her self-concept, values, and worldview; and why the adult version of this child has a diametrically opposing definitions of the meanings of "good" and "love" as well as behavioral traits compared to the parent(s) who raised them.*

Is this to suggest that all individuals with narcissistic Cluster B disorders were raised by "codependent" parenting? I'm not sure psychology or familial patterns are that formulaic. There's a good deal of potential that a narcissistic personality would emerge from the parenting of narcissistic parents, especially if one or both parents treated the child as a narcissistic extension of themselves. Also at play would be the birth order of the family if it was dysfunctional, with the rigidly assigned roles of Golden Child, Scapegoat, Lost Child, and Mascot, typically in that chronological order. (Refer to Page 144 of *The Toxic States of America* or simply do an online search for detailed descriptions of these roles if you are not familiar but would like to be.)

Regardless, for the sake of this book's content - which I strongly believe will be applicable to the vast majority of those affected with disorders under this categorical umbrella - we will focus on how the codependent parenting style as define above led to the emergence of theCluster B personality type.

Parents Tend To Give That Which They Didn't Receive

Have you ever noticed that success typically skips a generation within a family? Or being "kind" and "good-natured" or compassionate for that matter? A generation which was raised in financial depravity (money, clothing, food, financial instruments, higher education, etc.) will oftentimes ensure that their children will be well provided for, sometimes more than enough. To ensure that (they and) their children won't have to face the hardships (or worse: trauma) which accompany such scarcity, respective parents may even resort to measures regarded as unconscionable to ably provide to their children that which they didn't receive in the name of love - and oftentimes with the expectations that their children will appreciate such endowments and love them in return for it.

However, if in such families the children's psycho-spiritual needs (such as praise, positive reinforcement, and constructive feedback) were routinely neglected or disregarded, the financial support received by this successive generation may go unappreciated and unacknowledged as a source of love. Such a generation is likely to eschew or downplay all things related to physical and material wellbeing as a result. If this generation's need for psycho-spiritual care was *abused,* they'll likely become rebellious and antagonistic with respect to their own *physical and financial* needs. This is often seen in adult versions of such children who fail to provide for themselves (and their children) because they hold a grudge against their parents for damaging their psycho-spiritual needs instead of caring about them. Such self-inflicting children will oftentimes "grow up" and tap their parents' finances as a result because they feel some form of unlovability and are entitled to financial handouts. Any money given to them actually serves as an ineffective surrogate for the "issues" inherited as children and carried on into adulthood.

If this subsequent generation proceeds to have children of their own, its members are likely to prioritize the psychological and spiritual wellbeing of *their* offspring, thus providing that which they not only did not receive, but experienced significant lack thereof while being raised. If this generation of parents have carried a lack of gratitude for or inability to create the same material prosperity provided by their parents, they are unlikely to endow their own children with such provisions, and so the cycle continues. Instead of providing the material and financial prosperity to *their* children, they will endow (probably lavish) their kids with that which they didn't receive: the psychological and spiritual attentiveness that was lacking or absent in *their* lives growing up. *Their* children are likely to be the recipients of copious amounts of verbal and physical affection, empathy, positive reinforcement, loving comments, praise, ego-elevation, emotional attentiveness and so on. *These* parents are the "codependents" as described earlier (or "empaths") and their children are likely to be groomed as future Cluster B's or someone having some of these traits. Because of the lack of material support (which may result in trauma), this generation may refute the moral, ethical, altruistic, empathetic, or spiritual components of *their* upbringing, catalyzing the traits common to the malignant narcissistic prototype.

And the cycle continues…

Of course, real-life is hardly this cut and dry. But, again, for the sake of understanding the narcissistic personality, we shall see how it is likely these conditions which have served as a cocoon for it to emerge.

Entitled Lineage

In contrast to the previous subheading would be some bloodlines who perceive themselves (or are perceived) as superior due to amassed wealth and/or social status. These "upper-class" families or "old money" lineages not only pass down substantial wealth to their progeny, but their narcissism and sense of entitlement as well. Their children - regardless of any inherent intellectual shortcomings - will still make in into the best schools because of the ties their relatives have. Despite not having the scholastic acumen, they'll manage to get good grades due to their parents' status or bribery and subsequently land "good jobs" after they graduate for the same reason. Unlike the description of the previous generational dynamic, material care does not leapfrog over emotional care. Instead, subsequent generations will consistently provide expansive material care to their children since it's been the family's assets, shares, real estate, trust funds, and culture for decades if not centuries. In place of emotional care, narcissism and entitlement may also be an inheritance as is a lack of empathy for those less fortunate. Believing they are "special" and endowed with financial abundance by God (perhaps they are? I don't know; Part II of this book might provide some insight into this), they develop a respective complex. Here, the only victims to be made are the "peasants," "the help," and the proletariat who exist to serve if not adulate them. The reliable heirloom within such families is the belief that they are special and entitled to the social and economic status they were born into.

I suppose the lineage doesn't need to be from extensive wealth or "old money" either. Sadly, some generations of families of a more "common" background also subscribe to the "monkey see, monkey do" way of life. Because a son saw malignantly narcissistic behavior in his father, he mimics this as an adult. Personally, I find this pathetic.

Mother!

In the 2017 film *Mother!*, writer/director Darren Aronofsky presented us with a storyline involving a "May/December relationship" with the wife being considerably younger than the husband. The plot line starts with the young wife engaging in home improvements while her middle-aged poet husband embarks on penning his magnum opus. As the story progresses, outside influences which poo-poo the husband's ego increasingly prevent the wife from living a peaceful and productive existence. Because of a lack of boundaries and ability to say "no," the self-abnegating wife meets a crescendo of mayhem to the point where her reality morphs into a living nightmare. The self-sacrificing wife, believing she loves her husband, finds that her catering nature not only disrupts the very sanctuary, marriage, and home life she wished to create, but her mental and physical health as well.

I'm sure many readers are aware that with certain Cluster B personality disorders (particularly Narcissistic and Anti-Social Personality Disorder, the latter commonly referred to as "psychopathy"), men are more commonly diagnosed than women. Although many believe this is due to a genetic component (and there could be some truth to this), as a former biochemist, I'm reluctant to attribute this entirely - if at all - to "nature." Rather, it is my belief these disorders are manifestations of "nurture" and cultural and gender roles; that is, environments in which the parent/child relationship respectively parallels the husband/wife dynamic illustrated in Aronofsky's film. As I'm sure most readers will agree, men are not exclusively diagnosed with narcissistic personality disorders. Any time a child's will and needs for love, care, and respect are either eclipsed by a parent's ego and demands or found to be irksome, that child - regardless of gender - is being conditioned to become codependent. However, since the estimated percentage of men occupying the NPD category is roughly 80%, it is my sincere belief that this is not due to a series of sex-linked genes but rather the parenting of a codependent mother.

"Loving Fathers"

Years ago when I was an actor, I was friends with a well-known regional playwright who asked me to perform a role in a stage play he had written called "Loving Fathers." Part of the theme of the play was how we as adults are attracted to other adults with the same personality traits and characteristics as one of our parents, and that this is due to the proto-sexual attraction we felt for that same parent as a child growing up.

Apparently, this was going to be the second time "Loving Fathers" was going to be produced. During a conversation with the playwright regarding its first production, he recalled how nervous he was in displaying this work to the general public considering how taboo the subject material was. And who can blame him? Who the hell wants to admit - let alone publicly display - the fact that they had an attraction toward one of their parents of that nature while growing up?

He recounted how uncomfortable he was while sitting in the audience during the first performance, fearful of how the audience might react to the controversial content. He described how the hour and a half long production seemed to last a day and a half...

Much to his surprise and relief, he was astonished at the audience's positive reception at curtain call and even more so at the feedback he received from audience members in the atrium following the performance. One-by-one, he either heard audience members discuss between themselves or confide in him directly that they thought they were the only ones who experienced this sort of phenomenon as a child growing up. The play turned out to be a medium of catharsis and relief for the audience members since they realized they weren't "freaks" or "weird" for having these sorts of feelings when they were little.

As shame-based as it seems to admit on the surface, when you think about it...how could this not be the case? Why are we to believe that, as children, we're only developing physically and mentally but not sexually? And, just with learning curves and and physical development, each of us develop at different rates. The same applies to sexuality and sexual orientation. Just as some of us knew "which side our bread was buttered" before others, some of us hit puberty sooner than others. Have you ever seen a small child who seemed a little shy but curious and perhaps a bit flirtatious? This is just as natural as losing baby teeth.

And why should we burden ourselves with shame that this attraction was toward one of our parents? For the most part, they were the only ones available. Who else were we to direct this experience toward?

Right now, I want to be emphatically clear that observing the fact that some children develop a sexual curiosity at a young age is not a green-light for ANY sort of molestation or sexual abuse. Period.

But it is precisely this sort of attraction which creates "the cord" commonly discussed in New Age literature that shapes our relationships as adults. If this "cord" was attached to a malignant narcissist, the "drama" continues of wanting to receive love, care, and respect **in the form of attentiveness, nurturing, and support** from a narcissistic individual - who *demands love, care, and respect but returns the opposite, because* **they** *never received love, care, and respect* **in the form of dutifulness and efficacy**. This drama will play out far, far longer than any production of "Loving Fathers" ever will. And it will continue to play out until "the cord" is broken. For the adult version of such a child, relationships will probably resemble an attempt to suck air out of a vacuum followed by the appliance's explosion. Until this "cord" is broken, not only will such a child continue to attempt to draw water from a dry well, they may go through excruciating measures in trying to do so. Such measures include overworking their body image, changing their body type, altering their authentic personality, modifying their mannerisms, downplaying their gifts and talents…the list goes on.

This is going to be the same experience for the narcissist: *their* cord, as we shall see, was most likely attached to a parent with a Cluster A (odd), Cluster C (anxious), some variant of a depressive disorder, or even a Cluster B - and they have their own cord to mend.

With these sorts of cords, both parties were hoping for some quality to emerge from the other to fulfill a certain need or desire. If/ when the other party did not fulfill these expectations, the other party would usually retaliate in a passive or aggressive manner out of spite. If the parent was highly punitive (and this could be passively or aggressively) with the child when they failed to measure up to their expectations - especially if the child was young and the learning curve was not honored - the child is not only likely to resist developing that very quality as an adult, they are likely to vilify it.

An example of this is a child who lacks confidence in performing his schoolwork despite having the intrinsic aptitude to complete it. His mother may have the wish that her child be better at his scholastic performance (for the reason, say, to feel like a competent mother.) If instead of being attentive when her son struggles with getting the correct answers and provide words of encouragement, she flies off the handle and screams at him for "being stupid," this child is liable to rebel against any sort of achievement as an adult out of resentment. But, here, the son will eventually have to forgive his mother and resolve his own issues of incompetence if he's ever to rise above it and succeed in life. Regardless, the qualities this mother/son combination was hoping would emerge in the other in this scenario were confidence and attentiveness, respectively.

As an adult, the hypothetical son in this example is likely to not only rebuke those who seem volatile to him, *but the qualities of confidence and success as well.* He is likely to perceive these qualities as "evil" while he regards attentiveness and caring (that which he needed and didn't receive) as "good" and proceed through life personifying these qualities in order to perceive himself as "good." In actuality, however, this "goodness" is somewhat contrived: it's based on compare-and-contrast and has the foundation of resentment. Not that being caring and attentive are bad qualities - not at all; the fact that the son came away from this episode bearing the qualities of be caring and attentive is truly a silver lining on the grey cloud. However, the inability or unwillingness for the son to forgive his mother will *inhibit* other good qualities such as being confident and successful.

The son in this example will likely emerge as the "empathic codependent," always caring and attending to others while succeeding very little in life and possessing little confidence. He will probably be passively rebellious and retaliatory toward those who are discontent with his lack of confidence and success and resemble a similarly volatile nature to that of his mother, viewing them as "evil." I write this with 100% confidence: the emergence of a narcissistic personality type is based on similar trauma, only their experiences involve parental neglect and abandonment or being spoiled as opposed to verbal, physical, and psychological abuse. The adult version of the son in the previous example, because of his lack of success and confidence, will trigger the ire of narcissistic types due to trauma based in the lack of success and confidence present in one of their parents and subsequently perceive this son as "evil.

However, in order for anyone to manifest the ideal, healthy, and harmonious relationship they've been hoping for, *they are going to have to cultivate the very qualities that their parent of interest saw a lack of in them when they were a child. Similarly, the ideal partner is also going to have to possess the very qualities the child was hoping would emerge in their parent of interest but did not.*

Before we leave this topic, it's worth mentioning that we're liable to get involved with partners who resemble the *other* parent as well, despite the absence of the proto-sexual feelings the child had for the other parent, if applicable. This just means we also have unfinished business with the other relationship as well.

Esoteric Abuse

Before proceeding to the next chapters, I want to address what many people have experienced in relationships with malignant narcissists; that is, the abusive and manipulative behavior is almost always sequestered behind closed doors without any witnesses. This is precisely due to the intimate upbringing these types experienced with their primary caretaker while growing up and it's simply history repeating. Because the core issues behind the narcissistic personality arose within the intimate confines of the home, they're going to be triggered in similar environments as they grow older. Many readers can relate to trying to raise awareness of or receive support for their partner's physical and/or psychological abuse from others who also know the narcissist personally. Whether or not they receive such support will depend on the psychological health of the individual they're trying to receive support from. Here, it's important to understand that "fake people believe fake news." Especially if the sought-out party is also narcissistic, I wouldn't expect much credence or support for that matter. Others may simply find it "too hard to believe" especially if the treatment is severe and highly contrary to the perception they have of the victim's partner. Although the person seeking assistance may actually lose friends if it's the case that they and their partner have friends in common, it's important for such persons to understand that it's a blessing that such "friends" be lost in this scenario. True friends - and I mean "true" in every sense of the word - will support you and believe you, and that is because they have empathy and integrity.

Those involved with narcissistic Cluster B personality types may even feel like they're living in *The Twilight Zone*. The dichotomy between the Cluster B's home versus public life may be so divergent, *nobody* may believe the victim when he/she goes to others for help. Again, this is something the Cluster B is accustomed to due to their upbringing within a dysfunctional home, which is usually a home that looks decent on the outside but is hell on the inside.

2
Defining the Terms

Since the term "codependent" was described in the previous chapter with respect to the remaining material to be presented in this book, it's imperative to define and describe the former Cluster B nomenclature as well. Per previous versions of the Diagnostic Statistical Manual of Mental Disorders (DSM), four categories of Cluster B personality disorders were grouped under this category: Narcissistic Personality Disorder (NPD), Borderline Personality Disorder (BPD), Histrionic Personality Disorder (HPD), and Antisocial Personality Disorder (ASPD.)

Presently, there's has been much material presented in the form of books and videos regarding "Narcissists," "Psychopaths, " and "Sociopaths." The interchangeability of these terms often cause confusion, yet usually refer to persons with a sense of entitlement, a grandiose sense of self, a lack or absence of conscience, a lack or absence of integrity, exploitative behavior, attention seeking behavior, disregard for moral and ethical behavior, and manipulative characteristics. For the purpose of this book - and for the purpose in designating that not *all* of the characteristics described in this book will apply to *all* of the Cluster B disorders - it is necessary to precisely define and describe the traits of each personality disorder. In the chapters which follow, the Cluster B disorder relevant to the subtopic will be designated by use of its abbreviation.

First, I'd like to list the *ten schemas - or fears or "issues" -* which induce poor mental (and subsequent physical) health; they are: *Unlovability, Abandonment, Deprivation, Subjugation, Vulnerability,Mistrust, Failure, Perfection, Exclusion, and Entitlement.*

Let's get started:

Narcissistic Personality Disorder (NPD)

The characteristics of NPD are as follows:
- Grandiosity with expectations of superior treatment
- Continually demeaning, bullying and belittling others
- Exploiting others to achieve personal gain
- Lack of empathy for the negative impact they have on the feelings, wishes, and needs of other people
- Fixation on fantasies of power, success, intelligence, attractiveness, etc.
- Self-perception of being unique, superior, and associated with high-status people and institutions
- Need for continual admiration from others
- Sense of entitlement to special treatment and obedience from others
- Intense envy of others, and the belief that others are equally envious of them

It is the author's sincere and tested belief that **in one case scenario,** the origins for this disorder arise from a child being over-indulged, spoiled, or enabled during their upbringing in one or more capacities while being subjected to little discipline and structure. The over-indulged, structureless child simply grows up to be an over-indulged, controlling adult. The subsequent adult is, of course, a grown version of their childhood self who is accustomed to being over-indulged yet in need of structure.

The core "issue" or schema behind NPD is *Entitlement* - the belief that one is special, deserving of preferential treatment or status, or the belief that the rules do not apply to oneself.

The **other causality** behind this disorder arises from an upbringing involving *Abandonment* - that is, one or both parents subjected the child to episodes where the child was abandoned, neglected, betrayed, or even rejected in some capacity. For the sake of this book, I need to make a distinction between these two potentials by using two separate categorizations. The first, involving an upbringing which conditioned the child with a schema of Entitlement, I'm going to continue to refer to as NPD. The second, which will be discussed in greater detail in a bit, I'm going to refer to as **Maternal-based ASPD**

(M-ASPD) for the sake of distinction. Note that these two scenarios can coexist in a child's upbringing - that is, their condition arises from a childhood environment involving both *Abandonment* and *Entitlement*.

With NPD, when the individual ceases being over-indulged and enabled by others, the subsequent, secondary "issue" they experience is *Abandonment (it's actually Entitlement)* which is actually *withdrawal.* The issue of *Abandonment* gives rise to the issue of *Unlovability*…which requires most NPD's to revert back to their objective to seeking to be over-indulged and enabled.

There are five ways in which a sense of entitlement can be instilled in a child during their upbringing. They are: **Ego-spoiling, Attention-spoiling, Empathy-spoiling, Freedom-spoiling, and Material-spoiling.** It's all done in the name of "love" by one or both parent or primary caretakers.

First, a child can be spoiled with respect to their self-concept or "ego" while growing up. This involves one or both parents over-indulging the child with over-the-top messaging with how cute, talented, "good," smart, *special,* etc. they are. Of course, there is nothing wrong with loving your child and programming them with a healthy self-concept when they are young - *especially* when they're young - but the parenting described here is excessive, inapplicable, or inexplicable and bloats the child's ego way out of proportion and far past the age where it's developmentally appropriate.

Since men are more likely to develop Narcissistic Personality Disorder than women (though not exclusively), this dynamic is undoubtedly a factor in the codependent mother/son relationship. The grandiose sense of self the son will develop as a result of his mother placing him on a pedestal is likely to continue throughout life since the psychological programming during childhood is consistent and therefore both indelible and expectant. What may be intended as "love" being given from parent to child is received by the child as an inflation of his/her ego. The child has next to no chances of avoiding this; s/he is defining his or her self-concept based on the feedback the environment is giving. However, the end result is a child who truly believes they are "special" or "the greatest" - akin to believing themselves to be a demigod or something along those lines - and they don't grow out of it. The child, programmed for years with this conditioning since their birth, carries with them an "elite" sense of self and oftentimes over-confidence. Giving the child the impression that they're "Mommy's hero," a "Chip-off-the-old-block," or "Daddy's Princess" and other narcissistic extensions from parent to child can contribute to this, too. This usually leads to hubris and the hallmark grandiose sense of self.

The NPD adult will expect to be adulated, admired, ogled over, favored, and lavished with excessive praise, admiration, attention, and status. They will expect you to view them as being on a pedestal (higher than your own if yours is acknowledged at all) since this is precisely the impression they were cocooned in during their upbringing. This also conditioned the NPD not only to expect to be seen as "greater" by others, but also overlook their peers, partners, and associations as being worthy of having talents, gifts, or aptitudes. Not only was the NPD conditioned not to honor the "specialness" in others, it's liable to be considered a threat to their own "greatness" if they or others recognize the attributes in anyone else other than themselves. To them, the "spotlight" can only shine on one person: *them*. The above bullet-points which arise out of this are:

- Grandiosity with expectations of superior treatment from other people
- Continually demeaning, bullying and belittling others
- Self-perception of being unique, superior, and associated with high-status people and institutions
- Fixation on fantasies of power, success, intelligence, attractiveness, etc.
- Self-perception of being unique, superior, and associated with high-status people and institutions
- Need for continual admiration from others
- Intense envy of others, and the belief that others are equally envious of them

Next is "attention-spoiling," that is, the parent(s) over-indulging their child's need for "look at me!" long after the need has been satiated, listening to the child excessively without being heard, indulging the child's self-directed vernacular, not conditioning the child to provide others with attention or consideration, abdicating one's own need for alone time and attention long after the child is developmentally ready for greater autonomy. The narcissistic adult will thus engage in self-directed monologues as opposed to conversations when "talking" to others and continue verbal content which has a high personal pronoun density ("I," "Me," "Mine," "My," "Myself") and an apparent lack or inability to speak in the "second-person" or "third-person" (using words like "You,"

"Yours," "Ours," "Him," "Her," "He,""She," "They.") Any deviation on the NPD's part from this behavior can be seen as obligatory and/or necessary. The NPD adult will also find it foreign, burdensome, and even disdainful to provide others with attention, consideration, or support. Due to the elation over being spoiled with attention, they are prone to self-market and self-promote by publicly broadcasting information about themselves or engage in other attention-seeking behaviors. *Any publicity is "good" publicity.* They are also prone to expect, if not, demand attention with instant gratification when they see fit; otherwise, they will throw a tantrum if a phone call or text isn't replied to within ten minutes (but it's *understandable* if it takes them weeks to return yours.) The above NPD traits which emerge from "attention-spoiling" are:

- Fixation on fantasies of power, success, intelligence, attractiveness, etc.
- Need for continual admiration from others
- Sense of entitlement to special treatment and to obedience from others

"Empathy-spoiling" involves the child's feelings and emotional state becoming something akin to a centerpiece on the table which everyone talks about all night long. The child's wants, needs, opinions, perspectives, feelings, beliefs, likes, dislikes, preferences, etc. take center stage and, as an audience member, undivided attention is mandatory.

Due to this sort of upbringing, and especially if ego-spoiling also took place, the NPD adult-toddler behaves the same way: it's a one-way street here - "Do Not Enter" - and the wants, needs, opinions, feelings, likes, dislikes, preferences, etc. of the NPD adult *cannot* be challenged. Nor can they be disagreed with. Nor can you agree to disagree. Nor is it open for mature, rational discussion in many cases. Nor is there any cooperation or "meeting in the middle." Mature, grown adults will welcome and consider other people's perspectives, opinions, and viewpoints provided they are supported by logic or facts. They will keep an open mind without losing their own mind while it's open.

Not the malignant narcissist. Their wants, needs, perspectives, opinions, etc. are basically to be regarded as facts - even when they're not

supported by facts. In fact, the fact that facts *are facts* matters little to how the NPD formulates opinions, viewpoints, beliefs (even "religious"), perspectives, and the "feelings" they perceive as facts - even though the facts don't support them. Logic doesn't matter either.

Failure to comply with, indulge, poo-poo, concur with, or agree with the NPD adult's opinions, needs, feelings, wants, preferences, beliefs, and tantrums, etc. results in one or more of the following: more tantrums, escalated tantrums, and being regarded as offensive, blasphemous, detracting, dishonest, rebellious, insubordinate, stupid, naive, ignorant, unloving, unsupportive, and being subjected to a host of epithets.

Moreover - and perhaps worst of all - because they were always empathized *with* while never being required to *employ empathy toward others or entertain their point of view,* this too is likely to become apparent in the NPD adult-toddler phase (which may never end.) Any draws for support, care, or empathy from the NPD adult-toddler can and will be seen as a nuisance, burden, or an irritation. After all, *you're* supposed to "baby" them. In some cases, they may actually seem to be confused - not knowing what to do or how to react; a kind of a state of anomie. That's because it is. Otherwise, they're liable to redirect attention to themselves and start to extract support from the person originally seeking support (and actually needing it) almost instantaneously.

Bullet-pointing the "Empathy-spoiling" aftermath as designated by the DSM, we have:

- Continually demeaning, bullying and belittling others
- Lack of empathy for the negative impact they have on the feelings, wishes, and needs of other people (We could probably throw in opinions, beliefs, perspectives, and *knowledge* of others as well, but I didn't write the DSM.)
- Sense of entitlement to special treatment and to obedience from others

Then, we have "Freedom-spoiling," which entails the parent(s) allowing their child to do what they want, when they want, how they want, how often they want, where the want, and *get* what they want too much, too often, with little to no restrictions or repercussions. It also involves **no boundaries** or discipline with respect to amoral behavior, disregard, and mistreatment of other people. Thus, the child who is to become an NPD adult-toddler will become accustomed to and exhibit the following behavior for years to come: pathological lying, extortion, (emotional) blackmail, manipulation, bullying, whining, humiliation (public or private), nagging, theft, blame-shifting, gas-lighting, scapegoating, exploitation, abandonment, exclusion, ostracizing, self-exoneration, future-faking/carrot-dangling, entitlement, cheating, infidelity, bribery, sabotage, Machiavellianism, deprecation, false victimization - I mean, really: the list is endless. I'm not saying we're all angels (in disguise) and haven't been involved in some of the behavior previously, but for the NPD it's routine.

Note that in the NPD adult-toddler's mind, it's acceptable if they engage in the above laundry list of bad behavior, but if you do it, it's "wrong."

As far as **no boundaries,** this also applies to the parent(s) directly as well. By abdicating their own needs, inability to say "no" to their child, and giving too much, the parent(s) can allow themselves to wear down to the point of exhaustion and illness, which the spoiled child may interpret as abandonment or neglect since they're accustomed to more from the parent(s.) Suffice it to say, the effects of Freedom-spoiling are the following:

- Continually demeaning, bullying and belittling others
- Exploiting others to achieve personal gain
- Lack of empathy for the negative impact they have on the feelings, wishes, and needs of other people
- Fixation on fantasies of power, success, intelligence, attractiveness, etc.
- Sense of entitlement to special treatment and to obedience from others

"Material-spoiling" is probably the most self-explanatory of the five methods of spoiling. It involved providing the child(ren) with surplus money, material goods, status symbols, financial instruments, automobiles, accessories, real estate, etc. despite the child(ren) not deserving let alone earning such endowments. Material-spoiling is usually the surrogate form of attention and love which spoiled children receive. The characteristics which emerge from Material-spoiling are:

- Grandiosity with expectations of superior treatment from other people
- Exploiting others to achieve personal gain
- Need for continual admiration from others
- Sense of entitlement to special treatment and to obedience from others
- Intense envy of others, and the belief that others are equally envious of them

As mentioned before, the core "issue" or fear behind NPD is *Entitlement*. Many of you may be wondering how "entitlement" may be a fear. The fear arises when their expectations of some sort of preferential treatment go unfulfilled, whether that is to their ego, being the center of attention, a solipsistic mindset, or excess liberty. The realization that one isn't "special" leads to the "issue" of *Abandonment* which gives rise to *Unlovability* or that their "greatness" is an illusion. "My [fill in the blank] isn't here like it *usually* is, therefore I must not be "special" or loved [more than I deserve.]"

Oftentimes with this disorder, an expectation exists to be given undivided attention - where, when, and how often and on *their* terms - to be catered *to,* to be perceived as "better" or "special" or "more deserving," to be the center of attention, to never be required to consider anyone other than themselves, and to be able to get away with anything *because this is precisely how they were raised and they haven't done much to mature out of it.*

Even if you were to call out their bad behavior, narcissists are so entitled, *they attack their victims for "making them feel bad" about how badly they behaved.* Any contrition they experience is as self-involved as they are: they do not feel sorry for what they did to *you;* they feel sorry for themselves for "being made to feel bad" for what *they* did to you. Ever see how one reacts to finding out their infidelity has been discovered? They react with the same anger, rage, hurt, disbelief, and sense of betrayal that the cheated party *ought* to feel. See how that works?

Welcome to bizarro world. Or George Orwell's *1984.*

Empathy is handled by those with NPD the same way as they handle contrition: *it's for themselves, about themselves, and only themselves.* It's due to the Empathy-spoiling described earlier. For example, an individual with NPD who comes across an indigent, homeless person will feel *sorry for themselves* for having to have seen such a person rather than feel an iota of compassion for the person living in rock-bottom squalor and strife.

With narcissists like this, who needs psychopaths? Actually, I think I'd rather be around a psychopath - we'll see why in a bit.

Some literature makes the claim that "narcissists" don't love themselves. No, they actually think they're wonderful and perhaps even superior (they were raised to think this was the case) and believe others should support this belief. If they don't, the grandiosity can't be maintained because a diva can't be a diva without an audience. In their eyes, there's something *wrong* with *you* for not doing so: you're rupturing *their* world because it no longer *favors* them. Also, it's called cognitive dissonance.

Narcissists believe *others* should do their self-loving *for them*. *Others* are responsible for their negative feelings, *not they*. They also believe it's *your fault* when they don't take responsibility - again, the empathy-, ego-, and attention-spoiled toddler mentality comes into play.

It's possible that NPD can be rightly perceived as a "First-World Problem" which may account for the prevalence of this "disorder" within nations exhibiting higher GDPs. It may very well be what's regarded as a "boutique illness" or a condition which arises within a population once conditions on a mass scale have changed, such as food production or technological advancements.

I've come across some rhetoric making the claim that the parenting described in this subheading qualifies as a form of abuse. Do I personally agree with this? Sort of. The over-indulging upbringing - especially with the sense of self - can produce a high self-expectation that may lead to disappointment and cognitive dissonance if reality reflects back a contrary narrative.

The same rhetoric claims that this enables the child in some fashion. Here's the thing: the NPD individual actually *is* aware that they're being spoiled and/or placed on a pedestal. They're *not* unconscious that this is going on; they *know* there's preferential treatment taking place. But at any given point - and this includes during the childhood years - the child could have disengaged from this. What's worse, if the NPD individual has siblings and *knows* that he or she is *preferred, loved more, or placed on a higher pedestal than his or her siblings, it is actually both the parent and the NPD individual who are engaging in abuse with respect to the other children, not the other way around - and despite what the NPD individual would likely have you believe.*

Regardless and provided the individual is an adult, the recommended strategy to deal with these types is to go "no contact." Many professionals also recommend that no second chances should be given either.

In closing, it's worth noting that the repercussions for the NPD continuing this pathology later in life involve cycling through friends, partners, and acquaintances much like a toxic work environment produces high turnover. Like the unreasonable working conditions, no sane, mature, self-loving adult will stand it. Otherwise, their relationships are as deep as a puddle. Or, they actually *do* land a partner/spouse/friend who they run into the ground like a pair of sneakers. Involvement with narcissists - whether in the workplace or in relationships - usually have an adverse effect on the others' mental and physical health. Or, if it's another narcissist they get involved with, their "union" is not going to be stable.

Another narcissistic trait involves the expectation that someone else apologize for things the narcissist has done wrong - ironically, it's often the person who's been *done* wrong. They'll also expect you to chase after them or "fight for" the "relationship" - despite the fact that the "relationship" is really a situation where you're inappropriate blamed, the lop-sidedness favors them, your hand gives while theirs receives, manipulation is a non-stop pastime, they talk about themselves and not you, and covert infidelity is a hobby for them. Yes, they expect you to "fight for" this…"prove your love"…*for this…*

Regardless, the NPD individual will spend the majority of their life expending energy - *completely in vain* - attempting to obtain *meaningfulness* while simultaneously (and perhaps subconsciously) repelling it. All the dates, interviews, training,paperwork, courtships, marriages, employees, associations, etc. will otherwise come and go while the NPD individual remains an adult toddler unless and until they decide to grow up. The more pathological the narcissist, the more fleeting it will be.

If control issues accompany this disorder, again, it is likely that the individual with NPD was exposed to periods of abandonment or neglect. However, these issues might be rooted in the fact that the individual was so spoiled as a child, the parent who did so could not keep up the "going above and beyond" all of the time and the child, accustomed to the parent doing more than he or she should, regarded these periodic "breaks" as betrayal rooted in abandonment or neglect. In short, the child was given the expectation that the parent would be capable of "giving themselves" more than they were humanly capable of and this was interpreted otherwise by the child while he/she was growing up. When 110% wasn't 100% of the time, the "minus 10%" was considered by the NPD to be neglect.

Again, if control issues and a lack of empathy born out of *genuine* episodes of abandonment and neglect are present, I would not classify the individual as having NPD; I would say they are either "co-morbid" or have a different disorder entirely.

Common pathological NPD behaviors include the following:

• Gas lighting: Attempting to warp another's sense of reality by altering facts, distorting present circumstances, or reinventing history, much like a mischievous toddler does to avoid getting caught or being held accountable

• *Narcissistic Rage:* The adult version of a temper-tantrum where the adult NPD exhibits excessive, disproportionate, and immature ego-based anger for reasons which are behaviorally age-appropriate for the human infant and toddler developmental stages, such as: being presented with a contrary opinion or disagreed with, not having someone at their beck-and-call, not getting what they want, imaginary hurt or mistreatment, inability to be alone for short periods of time, and having to consider someone else besides themselves.

• *Objectifying others* and subjecting them to cycles of *idealize, devalue, and discard*, much like a toddler or child would do with a toy that's lost its novelty. This is most commonly performed in romantic relationships, friendships, and workplaces.

• *Bread-crumbing: aka: Intermittent Reinforcement.* The act of issuing intermittent, sporadic messages of feigned interest to another person, usually to keep the other person interested. The purpose of this is speculative: perhaps it's for attention-seeking or to keep the other party as an option to satisfy an objective. Toddlers do this with toys they stash just in case they might want to play with them again someday; maybe not.

• *Future faking:* Formerly known as "Carrot Dangling" (why the new, revised label is beyond me; the first one worked just fine. Actually, by now, the carrot's probably rotten so a new, fresh label is probably for the best), this activity involves giving another party the false impression that compliance to their objectives will bring about results which never manifest, most often performed in romantic relationships, "religious" institutions and cults, pre-schools (ironically), and the workplace.

• *Projection:* The act of superimposing one's fears, flaws, or insecurities onto someone else with the intent of making the person engaging in this behavior feel better about themselves.

• *Selfishness:* This occurs due to the NPD's victim-mentality rooted in Abandonment (whether or not real abandonment, neglect, or deprivation took place or expectations just fell short due to the drop in being spoiled.) The NPD feels they're "owed" something and subsequently proceeds to engage in behavior which is self-involved, self-absorbed, self-prioritizing, self-ingratiating, and at the expense of others.

The NPD's selfishness can and will involve *anything:* time, goods, money, attention, freedoms, care, food, shelter, women, men, etc.

- *High personal pronoun density* in conversational discourse: again, much like a toddler who's just mastered the art of speaking yet defunct in the art of *conversing.*
- *Love-bombing:* The act of bombarding a new romantic interest with messages of self-directed excitement, reminiscent of a toddler who's expressing their anticipation to play with a new toy that's not right in front of them at the moment.
- *Mirroring:* Or "Mimicry." This is a rapport building (more like a "bait trapping") technique employed by NPD's where their true self is disguised by imitating and reflecting back the other party's personality, appearance, and demeanors with the hopes that the other party will find them palatable, normal, or appealing. (Authors note: This is actually *the best part* of a relationship with an NPD because, here, you actually get to see how you come across to other people and you like what you see.)
- *Scapegoating:* This practice involves singling out an undeserved party to be the recipient of negative treatment. This can also involve blaming someone or something else for one's own misfortunes.

Many sources claim that those who are diagnosed with this condition have low self-esteem/self-love, depression, anxiety, and so on. Let's explore this in greater detail.

What's regarded as "low self-esteem" with NPD is the following: from a very early age - the latest starting in the teens - the NPD was programmed to believe that they are "special," "better," or were entitled to preferential treatment. Whether or not this was pre-ordained or childhood-ingrained makes no difference. The NPD individual believes they're special and entitled to a life of attention, special status, or the focus of adoration and accolades.

Thus, narcissistic supply is actually like "candy," "comfort food,"or even "vitamins" for the NPD. When that sort of "fuel" isn't there, they come to the harsh realization that they've always relied upon others' attention, praise, compliments, adulation, arrogance-enabling etc. as a surrogate for true self-love and, like a bratty toddler or teen, throw a fit when it isn't there. So, if you don't call them, don't respond to them immediately, don't shower them with attention and praise, don't regard them as the center of attention, do what they want, when they want, *how the want* - they're going to act like a toddler having a tantrum. Psychologically speaking, this is because they are.

Some high profile actors got into "the business" because they love to act and wanted to be successful; *not* for the reason to become famous and to be adulated at large. The same applies to some high-profile athletes. Some politicians got into politics and policy making *out of the interest of serving the public; not* due to fantasies of power, a status symbol, a wish for continuous admiration and attention of others, and a sense of entitlement. Some famous singers pursued their dream because they love to sing and perform; *not* to have an extensive fan club or become a "diva." Some people appear attractive and beautiful because they have a genuine desire to preserve their health and strength; *not* to attract the attention of hosts of oglers as they walk down the street or to be broadcasted on a magazine cover to garner nationwide attention.

Consider all those in the latter categories of the above paragraph. Now, please revisit the characteristics of NPD listed earlier. *This is who these people are*.

If it's a high-profile politician in Washington, they do not give a lick about you or your quality of life. If it's an obnoxious "diva" who sells millions of albums, same thing - only your money, worship, attention, and adulation.

This is basically the case with anyone who has NPD. They do not care about you, only what you can give them - which, in a nutshell, is everything you have.

Potential Maternal-based ASPD (M-ASPD)

Before proceeding, it's also the case that some people who bear traits resembling NPD actually *were* raised by at least one parent who was ineffectual. That is, the parent - whether being spread thin, lacking in a strong sense of self, addicted, or facing some sort of incapacitation or impairment such as severe depression - was unable to be fully psychologically present and efficacious for the child. *In such cases, genuine neglect or abandonment may have occurred*. The effects of which may have ranged from mild to detrimental health-compromising conditions. If this is the case, an upbringing where parenting reflected neglect, poor boundaries, an inability to ably provide, a lack of attention and availability, and a disconnect with reality *could* have a basis in the manifestation of NPD. For the sake of the material presented in this book, **and since *Abandonment* is the root issue of this disorder and not *Entitlement*,** this condition will be referred to as *Maternal-based ASPD or*

M-based ASPD and will be described in greater detail in the next section. If this is the case, the child may have learned how to manipulate, exploit, demean, and developed a lack of empathy for anyone displaying addicted, depressive, or even overly kind demeanors. It's vital to emphasize that the ***Abandonment*** behind this condition can take a variety of forms: abandonment for one, of course, but also neglect, rejection, and betrayal amongst others.

While this hypothetical parent may have *appeared* to have spoiled their with child respect to freedom, the other four components - ego, attention, material, and empathy - may or may not have been spoiled or even indulged. Such a parent may not have had many if any boundaries with respect to their child or for themselves; almost as if they were a shell of a person. Such a child in this case - while having no restrictions to behavior or activity - is liable to have "picked up the slack" and became pigeonholed to take up responsibilities which belonged to their ineffectual parent. The grown-up child is liable to hold anyone in contempt who doesn't "pull their weight" with respect to personal responsibilities as an adult.

It's likely that the child born to such a parent *also* has a parent who had NPD or ASPD (more likely the former) and their parents' union was an acute Narcissistic/Codependent relationship. In this case, it's likely that such a child *most likely* developed ASPD due to the above treatment coupled with abuse from the narcissistic parent. (See below.)

NPD + M-ASPD

It wouldn't surprise me in the least if those diagnosed with Narcissistic Personality Disorder experienced elements from *both* sets of conditions described earlier corresponding to NPD and M-ASPD (which will be described in greater detail in a bit) to some degree or another. That is, the child was exposed to both Entitlement and Abandonment while growing up.

So, in a nutshell, here what is most likely behind Narcissistic Personality Disorder: **When the spoiling stopped, they felt abandoned (neglected) and if/when actual abandonment *did* occur, they felt *entitled* to be spoiled as a result: the parent needed to "make up" for abandoning them and/or ceasing to spoil them.**

Whether or not feelings of "Abandonment" arose from the cessation of Spoiling (Entitlement) or Entitlement to being Spoiled arose from being Abandoned, the end result is a feeling of "Unlovability." But, this "Unlovability" is actually "Un-preferential Treatment" in the case of spoiling-cessation. In the case of *real* Abandonment and neglect, however, it's understandable why the child would feel unloved: they have a *reason,* not an *excuse.* It's for this reason I've made a distinction between NPD and M-Based ASPD in this book.

This distinction is actually *imperative* for those of us who have been verbally,physically, or psychologically abused while growing up in order to *really empathize* with those having M-Based ASPD. Whereas those of us who internalized the message by our parent(s) that we were "unlovable," "unworthy," "didn't matter" etc. through what appeared as *aggressive abuse at the time*, those with M-Based ASPD internalized the exact same messaging from their parent(s) from what appeared as *passive abandonment or neglect at the time due to depression.* Because of the age of the child at the time, this is very difficult *not* to do: the child based his self-concept directly on the parent's behaviors and reactions. It's also very difficult for either child to see their parent's behavior as stemming out of *their own issues, with the first parent(s) having Abandonment issues and the second parent(s) having, as we shall see, issues of Unlovability. Ironically, the parent(s) with Abandonment issues subsequently felt Unloved whereas the parent(s) harboring issues of Unlovability subsequently felt Abandoned.*

Yet, as mentioned earlier, since the child's self-concept is extremely impressionable during his or her early years, the rage and abuse stemming from a parent's unhealed Abandonment issues condition the child to believe he or she is unlovable, whereas the depression behind a parent's unhealed Unlovability issues conditions the child to believe he or she will be abandoned, neglected, and therefore unloved.

Welcome to the truce between dysfunctional partners: When the Abandoned party feels empathy and compassion for the abuse behind their spouse's Unlovability issue and the Unloved party feels empathy and compassion for the neglect behind their spouse's Abandonment, this should be a huge game changer. **The thing is, one of you needs to admit you *do abandon because* you feel unlovable and/or the other needs to admit you *do hate* because you feel *abandoned or neglected.***

However, if *Entitlement* replaces *Abandonment* as the core issue and the disorder resembles NPD over ASPD, forget about it. When things go sour, those who are narcissistic (whether NPD or NPD co-morbid) will expect you to "fight for" the "relationship" or "chase after" them even after they've been selfish, rude, self-involved, manufacturing contrived victimhood, controlling, avoiding accountability, and blaming *you* for things *they've* done wrong while offering *you* nothing in return. They'll expect you to pick them up in a magical horse-drawn carriage made out of a giant golden pumpkin after they've made Pol Pot look like Princess Diana. When you stop "chasing" them you're liable to witness a one-man (or woman) pageant showcase where the Narcissist (literally) parades themselves in front of you, attempting to induce you into chasing them once again. If you *were* to "chase after" them as they perform at "the pageant," they'd run away again until you've decided to stop, in which case they're likely to recycle the process all over again. That is, until it's become suitable *to them* that you've "fought for" the relationship enough - that you've "proven" your love…which won't be reciprocated… *ever*.

If it's more of a case of M-ASPD you're involved with, you *might* have something to work with *if* they're able to be vulnerable to their past episodes of abandonment and neglect. Otherwise, they *are* unlovable. Well, you *can* love them, but the love will be taken advantage of and you won't receive anything in return.

Unlovability/Perfectionism

Since I went on a tirade before, I'd though I'd end this section with some compassion. With or without "ego-spoiling," oftentimes the love a parent provides their child is conditional - which of course means the love the child receives is contingent on the parent's *approval rather* than with respect to *boundaries*. This, of course, prevents the child from growing into an adult living a life of authenticity, and "You can't be completely happy if you can't be yourself completely." Right? Of course right.

Since a grandiose sense of self usually emerges from "ego-spoiling," this sense of self is often a "false self" since traits and attributes heralded by the parent(s) are not only accentuated, but a sense of obligation and shame emerges as well. Here, the individual "hides" or "downplays" any traits, preferences, or characteristics which the parent(s), the outside world, and *even they themselves* might regard as being undesirable, unlovable, or running the risk of shattering their "perfect child" image.

Such is the case with homosexuals growing up where

homosexuality is eschewed, sinful, or taboo. Homosexuals growing up in homophobic households which hold the potential for repercussions for homosexuality are likely to hide or disguise their sexuality for as long as possible. Some may even commit or attempt suicide for fear they may not be loved and accepted for who they are. The "ego-spoiled" closeted homosexuals will not only downplay the gay, but "straight-the-gay-away" and convince themselves and others that they are, in fact, heterosexual. To maintain the ego-spoiling - because even though it's conditional, it comes with *privilege and clout* - the child goes along and barters their authentic self for the grandiose/false one.

Thus, we can see how *Unlovability* as an "issue" could be germane to NPD as well: the "false self" that was a byproduct of ego-spoiling prevents the true self from being seen and loved.

This sort of ego-spoiling can actually set the child up for a lot of distress as an adult. Spoiling a kid's ego, perhaps unbeknownst to the adult who does, can create a cocoon of *conditional* love the child's has for himself. The child may deem the praise, accolades, and other ego-endowments as *expectations* which are to be met and maintained. Because the child was made to feel "perfect" and *loved on account* of being "perfect, fears of not maintaining this *perfection* may lead to the manifestation of a *Perfection* schema. He may go through life going through great and diligent effort to maintain this "perfection" fearing that "dropping the ball" means "dropping anchor." Otherwise, even if the efforts the adult puts into being "perfect" - with intelligence, appearance, personality, etc. - are sufficient to stave off his fears of needing to be perfect, if his efforts don't solicit the appropriate feedback from his environment *despite* his efforts, the cognitive dissonance can cause a great deal of frustration:

"Why aren't my efforts paying off?' or "Why isn't my best good enough?" can be defeating inner-monologues which result from such a situation.

Antisocial Personality Disorder (ASPD)

The characteristics of Antisocial Personality Disorder are as follows:

- Disregard for right and wrong (Maternal)
- Persistent lying or deceit to exploit others (Maternal)
- Being callous, cynical and disrespectful of others (Maternal)
- Using charm or wit to manipulate others for personal gain or personal pleasure (Maternal)
- Arrogance, a sense of superiority and being extremely opinionated (Paternal if the arrogance is out if defiance or Maternal if the arrogance is grandiose)
- Recurring problems with the law, including criminal behavior (Paternal)
- Repeatedly violating the rights of others through intimidation and dishonesty (Maternal)
- Impulsiveness or failure to plan ahead (Paternal)
- Hostility, significant irritability, agitation, aggression or violence (Maternal)
- Lack of empathy for others and lack of remorse about harming others (Maternal)
- Unnecessary risk-taking or dangerous behavior with no regard for the safety of self or others (Paternal)
- Poor or abusive relationships (Paternal - poor; Maternal - if the subject is abusive)
- Failure to consider the negative consequences of behavior or learn from them (Paternal and/or Maternal)
- Being consistently irresponsible and repeatedly failing to fulfill work or financial obligations (Paternal)

Symptoms include:
- Aggression toward people and animals
- Destruction of property
- Deceitfulness
- Theft
- Serious violation of rules

I intentionally chose ASPD as the condition to discuss after NPD because, although there might be some seeming overlap and similarities in characteristics, the part of the causation behind this disorder is, in my estimation, very close to being the diametric opposite of the upbringing those with NPD experienced; in some cases, it's similar. That is, instead of being spoiled with respect attention, empathy, freedoms, and their ego, the child who grows up as an adult (or even before) exhibiting the traits of ASPD was subjected to abuse by *one or both of the dysfunctional set of conditions:*

    1) **Dysfunctional "Paternal" Parenting:** Here, the child was subjected to *severe abuse and draconian "boundaries"* that, in reality, were punitive, violent, irrational, and trauma-inducing - not to mention extremely disproportionate to the child's actions or developmental needs for correction. The abuse, torture, or maltreatment inflicted was physical, emotional, or psychological in nature. Note that it is typically the dysfunctional father figure who behaves this way, but it not always the case - the biological mother could have behaved this way. The characteristics parenthesized as "paternal" in the previous list correspond to this set of dysfunctional conditions.

    2) **Dysfunctional "Maternal" Parenting:** Here, the child's mother most likely had symptoms resembling codependency, BPD, or some sort of depressive disorder and/or lacking in self-love. The child's mother was overly empathetic - usually due to the wish that the empathy she bestowed upon others would elicit love in return since she never received this as a child. In short, because her "pedestal" was low due to a lack of self-worth, her child's was higher by default. Chances are, the pedestal her child was placed on was elevated thanks to her overdosing his ego - creating the Messiah complex in her child earlier.This parent - whether male or female in real life - instilled an issue of Entitlement, Abandonment, or both in the child.

Paternal ("P-based ASPD"):

    Whereas NPD was put on a pedestal, the Paternal-based ASPD was kicked down a hole - much like "It places the lotion in the basket" from *Silence of the Lambs*. If this sounds extreme, I doubt it's a stretch in some cases.

    Whereas NPD diagnosed individuals are spoiled and deserve less love, those with *Paternal* ASPD symptoms *are gravely deprived and deserve more*. It's quite probable that an individual with ASPD was raised by a "Paternal" who had NPD, if not Maternal-based ASPD themselves or both.

The challenge these individuals are going to have later in life if they are to recover is:

• They must learn to value themselves and cultivate self-respect.

• Engage in some sort of reparenting (both with respect to healthy environments and boundary setting) with the objective of self-reprogramming in mind.

• Revisit childhood episodes of psychological, physical or emotional abuse, torment, torture, trauma, etc. with calmness and objectivity with the intent of training the adult-self to react to future situations differently (that is, boundary setting even in extreme situations.)

• Regularly practice self-praise and direct positive reinforcement to the self.

• Employ a stress-relieving activity such as meditation on a regular basis.

• Forgiveness of the perpetrator for the abuse and trauma they had subjected them to.

The last item is imperative for alleviation from symptoms of Paternal-based ASPD. Otherwise, the *only* consequence such residual anger, resentment, desire for revenge, etc. is going to procure is detrimental effects to their own mental and physical wellbeing - and this not only must be made clear to the Paternal-based ASPD individual but *they have to fully understand this is true.*

If the ASPD individual is experiencing difficulty in doing this, they need to revisit the second item listed above which may involve being able to vent or receive support from an outside party. It would also be helpful if the Paternal-based ASPD individual realizes that a "victim mentality" is completely understandable in this case, but only harms oneself over time. If thoughts of revenge, resentment, or ill-will persist, all they have to do is look at the perpetrator and realize that they live, have lived, and continue to live their own hell and a different path is better for them. Understanding the conditions in which their abusive parent was raised is extremely helpful as well.

Homo sapiens can be an arrogant species at times since many of its own do not perceive it as an animal due to its intelligence. This mistaken thinking inhibits the healing process for Paternal-based ASPD or any psychological disorder for that matter. If a dog, say, is abused, it's going to display skittish or aggressive behavior - usually it would alternate between both.

The human animal is not much different from this which can be seen in Paternal-based ASPD affected individuals. If a child is raised with psychological abuse - accosted with verbal assaults against their intelligence, appearance, or another quality - the child is either going to personify the abuse or attempt to defend itself against it. For example, a child told that she is "fat and ugly" is either going to continue to appear this way, look like they're trying to avoid appearing this way with results that involve backlash, or even develop an aggressive, hostile exterior. Like an abused dog, it's going to succumb, defend, and have the propensity to be violent toward others. In some cases, however, this could possibly strengthen the dog somehow.

However, being the recipient of extreme physical abuse and torture is most likely the causality behind acts of violence (either to animals or other children if a child; other adults or children as an adult) or damage to property. Since the child cannot sufficiently defend himself against such abuse let alone express his anger, the violence against other people or things becomes the only outlet for the pent up rage outside of exercise. Otherwise, it is unfair and unkind to expect the child to "brush it off" and turn the anger and resentment off; the stockpile of frustration and anger builds until the child *requires some kind of* outlet for the abuse he's been subjected to. At the very least, this would require allowing the Paternal-based ASPD child a support system with whom they can vent.

Alternatively from appearing angry or rebellious, Paternal-based ASPD affected individuals may actually appear timid, skittish, sensitive, withdrawn, or shellshocked. *If the child appears "sensitive," this is because they were not loved.* If they appear timid, skittish, or shellshocked, this is because *they internalized fear due to the abuse*.

Since the abuse such children face during their upbringing came from at least one of their parents, a resentful, rebellious stance against authority (actual or perceived) will continue throughout adulthood. This underlying resentment - regardless of how subconscious it might be - is liable to influence and sabotage their performance at work or their relationship with law enforcement. Paternal-based ASPD individuals may feel this consistent, inexplicable battle with authority - at the same time both fearing it and harboring resentment toward it. (This antagonism is, in part, also catalyzed in the perceived authority figure since they can sense the underlying rebelliousness and uncooperative demeanor present in the Paternal-based ASPD individual.) As far as the Paternal-based ASPD is concerned, this is no doubt this is due to unresolved issues with respect to parental abuse. The criminal behavior, theft, and disregard for right and wrong bullet-pointed above all become more obvious products of such abusive early childhood environments.

The arrogance and sense of superiority displayed by some Paternal-based ASPD individuals is often mistaken as narcissism. *It is not, unless they were simultaneously Ego-spoiled.* More likely, the "arrogance" based on the "paternal" causations of ASPD are rooted in the resentment toward the authority figure(s) who abused them and the residual disdain they have developed toward others per the "defense" mechanism that was conditioned in them. Instead of the "air of bravado" and grandiosity seen with NPD arrogance, the Paternal-based ASPD's is more of a "chip on the shoulder" grandstanding against others who either don't try to or haven't tried to understand them or are perceived as having it easier than they. It's the resigned, bitter demeanor which is way past the cry for help; it a flippant, "go fuck yourself" attitude. It's not hubris; it's *defiance*. And who can blame them? They're mad at the world because the world has not been good to them whatsoever. Enduring a past that includes things like getting burned with cigarettes, being forced to eat garbage, beaten with blunt objects, and being locked in basements or closets for prolonged periods of time certainly contribute to this. Continuing on with life with others not giving a damn about this - or even finding it irritating - makes things worse. Even if others make the attempt or actually *do* have some idea what their hellish history has involved, it may not be enough to the Paternal-based ASPD because it's either too little, too late or the Paternal-based ASPD feels their background was so extreme, very few, if any, could possibly empathize with it to a suitable extent.

They may very well be right about that.

If the Paternal-based ASPD individual finds the lingering resentment too difficult to release, it is likely due to the severity of the abuse itself. Forgiveness is the real challenge for these individuals, but this cannot take place until they have healed themselves first, and this can only be accomplished by *care* - whether they are willing and able to receive that from someone else (which requires vulnerability) or if their capable of providing that to themselves. Yet it is the author's belief that wounds which have a social origin be healed by means of a social solution; that is, since the condition arose from abuse at the hands of someone else, the "cure" lies in *care* from someone else.

However, this must be applied to themselves first before any other healing can happen; the Paternal-based *ASPD MUST make themselves top and the foremost priority.*

Also, this cannot be forced or have a deadline set on it; improvements will be contingent of diligence and effort. But this "ego attachment" to the perpetrator based in resentment and ill-will will need to be dismantled in order for the Paternal-based ASPD individual to avoid regression.

Another obstacle these individuals will face is the reluctance to relinquish the "tough guy/inner victim" identity. Many wear their pathology as a badge of honor and, in a sense, they *should*. They *are* survivors. Being "raised" by an abusive monster and expected to live a continuous and productive life after being damaged during a vulnerable life period is no simple task by any stretch of the imagination. The real heroes with this disorder will find a way to rise above the hell and become a strong, healthy presence and a functional mentor and guide for others.

However, part of the Paternal-based ASPD's recovery (and part of the contribution they *can* impart on the world at large) is engaging in reparenting exercises, both where they are raised by caretakers who love, care, value and respect them but *more importantly,* ***exercises where they reparent themselves where they challenge and effectively counteract the abusive parent they had growing up who most likely had NPD or was co-morbid for this disorder.*** This is actually imperative for them, otherwise similar versions of these scenes of abuse will present themselves later in life.

They must also learn to set appropriate boundaries when facing mistreatment. This is going to be difficult especially if the abuse during childhood occurred early in their development and/or if the abuse was extreme.

Otherwise, the residual effects up the upbringing linked to this disorder include abusive behavior (or being abused), substance abuse, homicidal and suicidal behavior, homelessness, incarceration, low economic status, and comorbidity with other disorders involving depression and anxiety.

Also, the inability to forgive their perpetrator(s) and heal themselves will be behind their propensity to engage in manipulative behavior to exploit and deceive others, use charm or wit to manipulate others for personal gain, display disrespectful and haughty behaviors toward undeserving others, and to lack empathy when harming or hurting others. It is in their best interest to do so for their own sake and for those who they come across; it *will* come back to bite them in the ass at some point if they do not.

The Paternal-based ASPD will have to acknowledge that the core "issues" behind their condition are *Vulnerability* and *Unlovability* and understand that the childhood-origin causes which manifested these fears often caused BOTH of them to manifest at the same time - *precisely* from the the abuse, torture, and maltreatment which compromised their physical, emotional, and, psychological well-being while growing up. *The very moment* their impressionable, childhood self was subjected to abuse by their supposed "caretaker" is the moment such individuals incorporated the beliefs that they are fundamentally both unlovable and vulnerable. *Understanding and challenging these core beliefs about the Self is crucial for their healing.*

For the Paternal-based ASPD, understanding this should be quite easy. The child's experience was to see an angry, hateful face which threatened them and, in some cases, actually caused them harm. The face was not only unloving, *it threatened their safety* **at the same time.**

For this reason, they will often suffer from what appears to be low self-confidence, which is precisely the result of Vulnerability and Unlovability issues gone unattended to.

Also, it will be required for the Paternal-based ASPD to heal their "issues" of Vulnerability and Unlovability if they are ever able to be successful. Adopting a mantra of "I value myself and will not tolerate harm" may be helpful.

It's also likely the reason that **shame** *is also an underlying factor since Vulnerability plus Unlovability equals Shame - which will plague their life until these issues are identified and resolved.*

It should be brought to the attention of the Paternal-based ASPD that they were most likely never given positive reinforcement or told they were "good" at anything in any sort of capacity. In light of this, plus considering Vulnerability and Unlovability were the core issues instilled in them due to the abuse inflicted upon them, the "being set up to fail from the start" was most likely the perpetrating parent projecting their own issues of vulnerability, unlovability, and/or failure onto the child, just like the child is subsequently prone to inflict on animals or property.

Moreover, the abusive parent was likely to perceive their child as a "threat" in some capacity, most likely due to the child receiving

attention. *The "contest" or "competition" between abusive parent and child is likely to influence other dysfunctional and abusive parental behaviors as well, such as "teaching" their kid to "love themselves" - not through positive reinforcement and defense training - but by becoming their "sparring partner." Here, the parent inflicts emotional, psychological, and physical torture and distress upon the child with the supposed "objective" to "make the child stronger."* There are plenty of other ways to "strengthen" the child without *bullying* or abusing them.

Also, because of the anger and resentment toward their respective parent for making them feel Unlovable and Vulnerable and their inability to express this anger toward said parent that the Paternal-based ASPD will "act out" in violence or be prone to self-sabotage or self-inflict - that is, hurting oneself is the **only** *way to retaliate against the perpetrator and release pent up hurt and anger. It is also due to this lingering sense of being unloved and compromised that they will harbor a fear/contempt hybridization of feelings toward perceived authority, whether that is law enforcement, employers, bosses, etc. despite their wish for acceptance.*

It is also likely that being required to become keenly aware of un-forewarned episodes of abuse conditioned some Paternal-based ASPD's to become "empathic" - or hypersensitive to other people's energies as well as losing themselves.

Since the various types of abuse jeopardized their well-being *while simultaneously* causing them to feel unloved, the "issues" of Vulnerability and Unlovability can and should be equally regarded. **Secondary "issues" which affect those with this "disorder" are *Mistrust, Deprivation, Subjugation, Failure, Perfectionism, and possibly Exclusion.*** The one "issue" which may not effect these types is "Abandonment" since being alone is preferable to being in the company of another or others who mistreat them. As such, they may take on "loner" lifestyles and, unfortunately, be judged accordingly.

<u>*Maternal ("M-Based ASPD"):*</u>

The characteristics of ASPD designated as "Maternal," as described previously, are liable to be linked to the entitled, conscienceless, glib, controlling, manipulative, intimidating, selfish, degrading, exploitative and callous use of others, disrespectful, and remorseless and abusive behavior so often associated with ASPD, "Psychopathy," "Malignant Narcissism" or NPD itself. If the "mother" (again, this *could be* the father or another caretaker in real life) was depressive, lacking in self-worth and care, spread thin, anxious, etc. or had symptoms related to BPD, it is highly likely that the "mother" did not possess sufficient *and consistent* efficacy in caring for her child logistically, financially, psychologically, and/or materially which is liable to catalyze resentment and disdain within the child as they grow older into adulthood. As an adult, this child is prone to harbor resentment toward said parent as well as mistreat anyone resembling the parent's depression, inefficacy, overt kindness, empathy, and/or lack of performance with respect to personal obligations and responsibilities.

(The worst case scenario would appear as such: a child who was left in the bathtub and almost drowned or a child who was left alone for days without food or attention. In this case, the adult version is likely to become a domestic abuser. Otherwise, their propensity to control their external environment is going to be immense as an adult.)

Symptoms of the child's lack of empathy toward individuals with psychological states similar their dysfunctional parent tend to manifest in other ways as they get older. Rather than having compassion or empathy for them, they're prone to despise, manipulate, denigrate, humiliate, bully, violate, and take advantage of such persons. Genuine episodes of childhood abandonment and neglect afflict Maternal-based ASPD individuals who have not healed from such events and, much like BPD's, will often display frantic, even violent behavior during situations of perceived or real episodes of abandonment or neglect in the future.

Because the Maternal-based ASPD bore the brunt of the "Mother's" "issues" and was subsequently abandoned, neglected, or required to "grow up" at an earlier stage than was age appropriate, he will resent, ridicule, humiliate, take advantage of, denigrate, bully, and abuse others later in life who show signs of depression, low self-worth, and low confidence. Again, it reminds him of the neglect he experienced as a child which planted the seeds for present-day resentment and animosity not to mention the negative self-concept he developed as a result of this sort of upbringing. Since the latter characteristics were present in his parent during his childhood for which he bore the brunt of, it's possible that the Maternal-based ASPD will regard and prioritize cheerfulness, high self-worth, and high confidence as attributes - much like his "Mother" regarded empathy, compassion, patience, understanding, and altruism. Both prioritize the qualities that were lacking in their parent which caused them suffering. Both are liable to vilify the qualities in the other since it reminds them of the qualities of their parent which caused them a painful childhood.

But, in both cases, the displayed attributes each party deems as "good" **are actually contrived** *since they are based on compare and contrast with the parent they perceived as defunct.* Thus, the "mother" displays meekness, humility, overt kindness, altruism, selflessness, leniency, and overt supportiveness because she perceives these qualities as "good." "She" perceives these as "good" because she perceived one of her parent's narcissism, degradation, self-involvement, hyper-control, selfishness, strictness, and overt aloofness - the opposite - as "bad." The Maternal-based ASPD will do the inverse: they will prioritize self-worth, self-care, self-interest, firm boundaries, and self-containment as "good" since they found their parent's lack of self-worth, lack of self care, lack of structure, and tendency to be spread thin to be an infringement upon their own upbringing.

But, again, the attributes both parties display because they're regarded as "good" are phony: they're only displayed because of unhealed wounds and resentment toward the part whom they deemed as "bad." "Yin" gives rise to "Yang."

Thus, the boastful, flaunting announcements of self-promotion commonly perceived as narcissism or arrogance in the Maternal-based ASPD *may* be perceived by *him* as being as *dutiful* despite others finding it arrogant and irritating - and not to mention *superficial:* **because it is.** (Actually, it's also probable that this involves attempts to extract narcissistic supply since the likelihood that they were also spoiled - at *least* with respect to ego - is there.) The same applies to the ostensible referencing to the Self: the lack of self care (and care for the child) and focus in the "Mother" was seen as "bad," so the Maternal-based ASPD perceives excessive self-care and self-focus as "good." The problem is, in relationships, other parties will find this irritating especially if it "was never about them" growing up. However, the Maternal-based ASPD is most likely going to be impervious to this.

In truth, and as we'll see in a moment, the primary objective for the Maternal-based ASPD's propensity to self-showcase is to stave off abandonment - the core "issue" behind this disorder; that is, if they appear lovable, their hopes are that they won't be left. Even if the self-showcasing simply attracts attention or accolades, this is used as a surrogate for authentic self-love.

This doesn't negate the potential, however, of the "Mother" over-indulging the child's ego while growing up. *This compounds it*. Again, "she" never received praise, adulation, attention, compliance, acquiescence, focus, etc. while growing up; instead, she *gives* it with the hopes that it might be reciprocated (because she was subjected to intermittent reinforcement or "bread-crumbing") and/or the belief that doing so makes her "good."

This affects the Maternal-based ASPD in two ways. First, they're not taught to love themselves; they become dependent on others to feel good. Second, they're not taught to empathize with others since such a "Mother" never made it about "her." Also, because the "Mother's" depressive state impacted them in a negative fashion while growing up, they're liable *not* to feel much if any empathy or compassion for other individuals who resemble "her" psychological state going forward.

If the abandonment and neglect the Maternal-based ASPD individual was detrimental, this would account for any hostility, significant irritability, agitation, aggression, violence, or abuse when similar episodes appear in the future, whether real, reminiscent, or imagined. (And if the ASPD individual is involved with a depressive personality, they most certainly will - often by unconsciously created *by* them.)

Otherwise, the lack of the "Mother's" psychological efficacy is the likely culprit behind the Maternal-based ASPD characteristics of disregard for right and wrong; persistent lying and deceit to exploit others; being callous, cynical and disrespectful of others; using charm or wit to manipulate others for personal gain or personal pleasure; and repeatedly violating the rights of others through intimidation and dishonesty. All are reminiscent of a child raised by a parent who was not fully psychologically present for the child, with each characteristic representing a childlike behavior of obtaining what they needed, whether that be care, attention, moral structure, or other needs.

While writing this, the unfortunate thought came to mind that the rise in single parenthood *might* be a causality behind the increase of children and adults bearing symptoms of Maternal-based ASPD. The child does not understand the taxing, demanding role of single-parenthood - being the sole breadwinner and/or caretaker - is guaranteed to wear their parent thin. Otherwise, if the "Father" in such a household was largely absent or unavailable, the "Mother's" over-extension of herself may be the reason her psychological efficacy was depleted, unbeknownst to the Maternal-based ASPD child(ren) at the time.

Whatever the case may be, therapy for alleviating Maternal-based

ASPD symptoms is going to be two-fold. First, the Maternal-ASPD individual is going to have to manage their abandonment and neglect issues with holistic methods involving mindfulness and reparenting. Second, it is essential that the Maternal-based ASPD individual "walk a mile in the shoes" of the "Mother's" upbringing, **empathizing** and imagining what it was like for "her" to be raised in the way she was - that is, to be raised in an overly strict household which eclipsed her wants, needs, preferences, and sense of self in addition to being the recipient of negative reinforcement and content as opposed to praise, attention, and love. (It would be helpful for the ASPD - and especially the NPD - to read the BPD section of this chapter for this reason.) They will benefit from understanding the early childhood environment which caused such a "Mother" to internalize self-messaging such as not being lovable, competent, worthy of attention, worthy of preferences, worthy of having things, worthy of privacy, worthy of respect, needing to be perfect, and unable or disallowed to set boundaries or defend. Not doing so will guarantee the adult Maternal-based ASPD a series of grave disappointments in future relationships. He or she must realize that "Mother" did not feel loved by one or both of "her" parents; quite possibly just the opposite: hated.

As we shall see later with BPD, the core issue behind that disorder is Unlovability which quickly catalyses the secondary issue of Abandonment. With Maternal-based ASPD, it's the reverse: the core issue is **Abandonment** (often in the form of neglect) which *may* subsequently catalyze the secondary issue of Unlovability! The reason I write "may" is because after Abandonment (or neglect) takes place, the Maternal-based ASPD *may* hold their neglectful parent accountable for any subsequent feelings which *may* arise after being Abandoned. "Because *you* abandoned me, it's *your* fault I feel unloved (or unlovable.)" Or, in the child's mind, it's: "*You abandoned me, so **you're** bad*" with "bad" being anything the child feels negatively about themselves as a result of being abandoned. ***And this is precisely where the mechanism of "projection" kicks in.***

As we shall see in the content going forward, it is from this issue of Abandonment that a sense of Entitlement arises in the Maternal-based ASPD. From this, Unlovability arises.

Because the Maternal-based ASPD feels neglected or abandoned (whether they truly have been or not), they feel *Entitled* to partake in the following: control, violate, demean, exploit, manipulate, coerce, engage in selfishness, hoard, abuse, self-exonerate, abandon, humiliate, subjugate, sabotage, exert unrealistic expectations, and ostracize. These behaviors all have origins in childhood and are reminiscent of a child reacting to situations where they felt abandoned or neglected.

Since Maternal-based ASPD is likely to be co-morbid with NPD - that is, enduring past episodes of both Abandonment/Neglect and being Spoiled (Entitled) respectively - their Abandonment "issue" will give rise to a sense of Entitlement and their Entitlement "issue" will give rise to a sense of Abandonment.

The Maternal-based ASPD both craves love but fears it will leave them *precisely* because they have an ingrained belief that they will be abandoned. This subsequently causes them to feel unlovable and it's a cycle that's been repeating since childhood. Often, they fear they are "leave-able." Once prospective love they've craved so desperately for *leaves* them (quite possibly because their unhealed abandonment issues self-fulfilled this prophesy), the unlovability issues kick in. Subsequent frantic efforts to maintain the "loving" presence cause the Maternal-based ASPD to make the other party feel *unlovable* when they sense they are about to be abandoned.

Moreover, this fear of accepting the love they so desperately crave is *born out the culmination of the resentment and anger the Maternal-based ASPD feels toward the gender of the respective parent for abandoning them while they were growing up, the litany of antagonistic thoughts they've had against the respective gender, the refusal to forgive the respective parent for their behavior, and the acknowledgement of the lack of empathy they employed to the respective parent's upbringing and subsequent judgement they've dispensed against said parent up until then.*

For healing, the Maternal-based ASPD needs to forgive their parent's treatment, forgive the parent's lack of presence and availability, love themselves and become more at ease with being alone, forgive themselves for any animosity they've held and the duration for which they've held it, be willing to love the gender they're sexually attracted to, and do their best to empathize with their parent's childhood conditions which caused them to behave the way they did. The material presented elsewhere in this chapter should help with the latter (see BPD below if you're M-ASPD and reading this.)

This desperate yearning for the love from the gender of the parent of conflict stalemated by the fear of receiving it due to the Maternal-based ASPD's long-held resentment and anger toward said parent and subsequent guilt and shame *is what is behind behavior such as sexual promiscuity, aversion to intimacy, preference and addictions to pornography, and intermittent, short-term, and unstable relationships.* If the Maternal-based ASPD's parent of conflict is female and women are their sexual preference, *the vagina represents the maternal love the ASPD wishes to be embraced in but is adverse to succumb to due to the hurt of not being embraced by such parent at an early age, continuing to blame the parent for their feelings abandonment and unlovability, the rage and animosity for any neglect and lack of love the ASPD still harbors, and any shame they have accrued.*

With this in mind, ASPD resembles not only codependency to the extreme, but also prototypical "Mommy issues" as well and I hardly mean this pejoratively.

When the term "Mommy issues" is used, it usually refers to a person's primordial or even seemingly congenital *Abandonment Issues*. It is precisely because of this that some of the behaviors usually associated with NPD are seen in ASPD. The core issues of abandonment is likely the reason why discarding and "ghosting" occur: the Maternal-based ASPD *abandons* the other party to make them feel how *they* feel but also the subsequent *unlovability* they feel - which the other party, especially if they have a self-love deficit up to and including BPD, *is* going to feel *deeply* since, as we shall see in the next section, Unlovability is the core issue for this disorder.

The "love bombing" often associated with NPD is also likely to be seen in the Maternal-based ASPD. Bearing in mind that abandonment/ neglect issues are at the core of this pathology, it's understandable why this happens: the ASPD feels the rush or the high of having their abandonment insecurities alleviated through such activity since it's *projected.*

It is also no surprise that M-Based ASPD's with abandonment issues are going to place significant effort into their personal appearance ("somatic narcissism"), intelligence ("intellectual narcissism"), or status ("financial narcissism.") In these cases, it becomes obvious that such "preening" serves to counteract the core issues of abandonment and neglect at the archive of the M-Based ASPD's pathology. That is, the primping serves to *appear attractive* and *attract* others in order to accommodate for their the underlying fears of abandonment and neglect and the subsequent fears of unlovability and inadequacy. Even if the primping simply attracts *attention* from others, *this very attention* serves as a drug to soothe the primary *abandonment* and secondary *unlovability* fears within the ASPD individual. It was mentioned earlier that this sort of preening is often apparent in conversations with such individuals, who resort to charm (which comes across as superficial and self-involved; that's because it is) and self-promotion when conversing with others, especially with those whom they are interested in. The principle is the same: "If I appear lovable and attractive, I'll attract the attention which counteracts my fears of being abandoned, neglected, and not worthy."

It's also worth mentioning that the pathological lying, cunning and manipulative behavior, deprecating and demeaning comments, and aversion to moral character most likely originate during their childhood years, where such behavior came from acts of antagonistic rebellion against an ineffectual or spread-thin parent. "If you don't give me attention, I'll be a bad boy," is the child's mentality which, unfortunately, progresses into adulthood.

The lingering resentment and animosity Maternal-based ASPD individuals harbor against their "Mother" will negative influence their relationships with others as a result unless healed. As mentioned earlier, the more the ASPD empathizes with their "Mother" and the closer this empathy reaches *sympathy,* the more healthy their relationships will be with others since they will cultivate a more authentic capacity to be empathetic, compassionate, caring, and loving - all the traits considered "spiritual" by many.Recovery/alleviation from Maternal-based ASPD includes the following:

• **The ASPD must acknowledge their core issue of *Abandonment and secondary issue of Unlovability.*** Otherwise, this will have a negative impact on all other areas of their life, including work, family, relationships, *health,* friendships, finances - *everything.* Prioritizing their primary Abandonment issue will permit other "issues" such as Unlovability, Deprivation, Subjugation, Vulnerability, Mistrust, Failure, Perfectionism, Exclusion, and Entitlement. Specifically, the symptoms most likely associated with "Sociopathy" and their tendency to cause *others* to feel deprived, subjugated, vulnerable, mistrusting, failing, needed to be perfect, excluded, while indulging their own sense of entitlement (that is, the rules apply to me, *not* you) will continue. In short, others will regard them as "psychopaths" or "toxic" when, in truth, is very much their "inner child" with unattended fears of abandonment and neglect... ***The more the Core Abandonment Issue and secondary issue of Unlovability are healed and dissolved, the more of a game changer this will be for the ASPD since Abandonment is the keystone for*** *everything wrong in their life.*

•　　　The ASPD **MUST FORGIVE THEMSELVES** and **NOT HOLD THEMSELVES ACCOUNTABLE FOR HAVING THE CORE ISSUE OF ABANDONMENT AND SECONDARY ISSUE OF UNLOVABILITY**, yet expecting others to accommodate for it is not fair to them - they didn't create it nor should they be held accountable for it. As frustrating as it might be for the ASPD to read or hear this, *it is not their fault, but it is their responsibility to tend to this issue.* However, by pinpointing *abandonment* as the seed which causes *all* other distress in their life, the ASPD *can rightfully regard this knowledge as a "silver bullet."*

•　　　Cultivating the ability to empathize by engaging in practices where the M-ASPD experiences the conditions someone else experiences, particularly their depressive parent's.

•　　　If their caretaker(s) and others *had* exposed them to excessive praise, adulation, and placed them on a pedestal while growing up (not all of them had, mind you), considering that they were not only over-indulged, but gravely unappreciative of the excess positive reinforcement *which they have greatly benefitted from and that not all children have received this growing up; in fact, just the opposite.*

•　　　If they are selfish, demanding of others' time, and lacking in empathy toward others, realizing the potential of this being due to being parented by someone who was *selfless* and *provided them with surplus and undeserved consideration, attention, and availability - which was, after all this time, taken for granted.*

•　　　Most importantly: If life-threatening or health-compromising episodes of abandonment or neglect are a part of the subject's history, they *will* need to forgive the negligent parent - or at least the situation - *after* healing themselves by reparenting and revisiting their inner-child. No, it's not going to be easy to do, but considering *why* said parent was ineffectual may be helpful.

　　　Now, it's possible that an individual was exposed to an upbringing which involved both the Paternal-based ASPD and the Maternal-based ASPD conditions described as above, that is, each parent dispensed the respective treatment upon the child while growing up. A mild example of this would be a child born to the stereotypical Malignant Narcissist/ Codependent relationship which typically heads a dysfunctional household. If multiple children are born, the rigid, prototypical roles the children inhabit in chronological order are as follows: The Golden Child/ Hero; the Rebel/Scapegoat; the Lost Child; and the Jester/Mascot. As mentioned earlier (and nowhere else in any material I've come across), it

also the
case that children in dysfunctional households *will inhabit a secondary dysfunctional role with respect to each parent.*

For example, a "Rebel/Scapegoat" with respect to the dysfunctional family at large may be the father's personal "Golden Child" yet the mother's "Lost Child."

I'm digressing here. A child who was subjected to a Paternal-based ASPD upbringing from one parent and a Maternal-based ASPD upbringing from another is liable to turn out like the following:

Psychopathy

First, it must be made clear that "Psychopathy" is not a disorder listed in the DSM nor has any psychological or psychiatric organization sanctioned "Psychopathy" as a diagnosis. I've decided to write about "Psychopathy" since much published material references this psychological label.

"Psychopathy," since employed by psychiatrist Hervey Cleckley, has been a term that has apparent interchangeable use depending on the source. "What's the difference between a 'psychopath' and a 'sociopath?'" is a commonly asked question. So is "What is the difference between a psychopath, sociopath, and a narcissist?" I hope to answer these questions thoroughly in this section.

Below is the "Psychopathy Checklist Revised," or "PCL-R" as devised by psychologist Robert D. Hare in the 1970s [1]:

Factor 1: Personality Aggressive Narcissism
1. Glibness/superficial charm
2. Grandiose sense of self-worth
3. Need for stimulation/proneness to boredom
4. Pathological lying
5. Cunning/manipulative
6. Lack of remorse or guilt
7. Shallow affect [i.e. superficial experience and expression of emotions]
8. Callous/lack of empathy

Factor 2: Socially Deviant Lifestyle
9. Parasitic lifestyle
10. Poor behavioral controls
11. Promiscuous sexual behavior
12. Early behavior problems

13. Lack of realistic long-term goals
14. Impulsivity
15. Irresponsibility
16. Failure to accept responsibility for own actions
17. Many short term marital relationships
18. Juvenile delinquency
19. Revocation of conditional release
20. Criminal versatility

Now, parlaying the traits in this list back to the characteristics of ASPD, we can see some ostensible similarities. Essentially, the PCL-R is a paraphrasing of the list of ASPD characteristics and separated into two categories: Factor 1: Personality Aggressive Narcissism and Factor 2: Socially Deviant Lifestyle. Notice how the PCL-R Factor 1 traits corresponds the the ASPD characteristics I designated as "Maternal" while those in Factor 2 correspond to the ASPD's labeled "Paternal."

So, what we actually have here is both the PCL-R and the DSM's diagnostic ASPD characteristics involving the combination of two potential personality disorders! In fact, it seems the PCL-R "sensed" this by by separating the symptoms into two categories.

What both the PCL-R's Factor 2 traits and the ASPD characteristics designated as "Paternal" in this book accomplish is describe someone often referred to as a *"Sociopath:"* that is, someone who ignores social norms; displays criminal behavior and problems with the law and authority; displays arrogance (which is really defiance); displays deceitfulness such as repeated lying or using aliases; cons others for personal profit or pleasure; is impulsive and fails to plan ahead, is irritable, hostile, and agitated; aggressive, such as repeated physical fights; involved in abusive relationships; unable to learn from negative consequences; has a reckless disregard for safety for self and others; fails to hold down a job or honor financial obligations; and displays a lack of remorse. Factor 2 traits represent an individual that leads a **"chronically unstable, antisocial, and socially deviant lifestyle,"** which is the lifestyle most commonly regarded as "Sociopathic."

If this isn't the product of a physically and psychologically abusive parental figure who's historically been the father, I don't know what is. Think of a repeat blue-collar offender, automobile thief, thug, drug dealer, rebellious proletariat, or the "six pack," papa-was-a-rolling-stone, perennial underachiever with no career path, broke-as-a-joke, deadbeat dad as examples.

On the other hand, the person bearing the PCL-R Factor 1 traits and/or the ASPD characteristics designated in this book as "Maternal" is going to appear to be what is usually referred to as a "narcissistic psychopath"; that is, one who engages in **"selfish, callous, and remorseless use of others."** Hypothetical examples of this would be: a charismatic religious or cult leader who manipulates and exploits his followers for money, power, and authority; a handsome politician (usually male, certainly not always) who engages in things like maintaining a charming yet surfaced public presence with an air of grandiosity, insider trading, off-the-books campaign record-keeping, a litany of extra-marital affairs, child molestation, drug-trafficking, pathological lying, and hiring hit men to execute anyone who attempts to expose his criminal behavior; a sleazy yet well-manicured coke-sniffing lawyer who engages in bribery, blackmail, and extortion; a pretty up-and-coming actress who sabotages her competition by stealing their scripts and tarnishing their public images with false information so that she can get ahead; a boss who "manages" a department but only works two hours and day and collects $100,000 per year despite his contract specifying 40 hours per week while he fires underserving people due to the department's poor performance - because of his mismanagement; and an attractive, outgoing, and charming suitor who love-bombs you, manipulates you, and ridicules you as he's having a slew of affairs.

Basically, a phony, selfish, self-absorbed, conscienceless, often well-maintained, materialistic, power-hungry, fame-seeking individual who believes in an ends-justify-the-means sense of entitlement with no sense of remorse or compunction over the detrimental, harmful, traumatic, or lethal treatment they subject others to.

What are we to diagnose such a person with? NPD? ASPD? Maternal-based ASPD?

Factor 1 is basically Narcissistic Personality Disorder (and/or M-Based ASPD) to the extreme, courtesy of a caretaker (usually the mother) who set no boundaries with their child but instead spoiled them with praise and adulation and never correction and, at times, subjected the child to abandonment or neglect.

The proposal I'm arriving to is this: If Narcissistic Personality Disorder is its own disorder, then both "Psychopathy" as described by the PCL-R and Antisocial Personality Disorder as defined by the DSM *need to be regarded as co-morbid disorders* if either are to be used as diagnosable personality disorders. The reason for this is both Psychopathy as described by the PCL-R and ASPD both contain the very criteria used to diagnose NPD as part of their diagnostic criteria: with the PCL-R, it's lumped in a separate category (Factor 1) whereas it's embedded with ASPD.

The question I have is this: How are we to diagnose someone who exhibits some, most, or all of the criteria presented in the PCL-R's Factor 2 category and *none* from Factor 1? That is, some, most, or all of the characteristics *except* those also represented in the NPD diagnostic list? Also, is it appropriate to have traits of NPD cross-pollinate and also appear under the ASPD categorical umbrella? Why not create a dichotomy and diagnose co-morbidity if applicable?

I'll answer my first question first. "How are we to diagnose someone who exhibits someone who exhibits some, most, or all of the criteria presented in the PCL-R Factors 2 category and *none* from Factor 1? That is, *someone who displays a parasitic lifestyle, poor behavioral controls, promiscuous sexual behavior, early behavior problems, lack of realistic long-term goals, impulsivity, irresponsibility, failure to accept responsibility for own actions, many short term marital relationships, juvenile delinquency, revocation of conditional release, criminal versatility but lacks glibness and superficial charm, a grandiose sense of self-worth, a need for stimulation/proneness to boredom, pathological lying behavior, cunning and manipulative behavior **yet has the ability** to experience (excess) remorse or guilt, deep experience and expression of emotions, and a surplus of empathy?*

Factor 2 is essentially a variation Borderline Personality Disorder (see below) - or *"female sociopathy." With men, it's commonly seen as "Sociopathy," but any differences which exist are differences in the forms of abuse.*

It's no wonder "Psychopathy" and ASPD receive more male diagnoses than women; provided they display symptoms from *both* PCL-R "factors" and ASPD characteristics which fall under *both* "Maternal" and "Paternal" labeling as designated in this book. Males are more likely to be raised by one parent who abuses them (typically a malignant father) and one who enables them, spoils them, and/or is depressive (typically the mother.) **As such, "Psychopathy" and ASPD are both co-morbid disorders: both contain characteristics associated with BPD and either NPD and/or what I've described as Maternal-based ASPD in this book.**

In light of this, to answer the questions I posed earlier: "What's the difference between 'Psychopaths' and 'Sociopaths'?" The answer is "nothing whatsoever," that is, if you define "psychopathy" as described by the PCL-R and "sociopathy" as equivalent to ASPD. If you define "sociopathy" as equivalent to *BPD or the contents of the PCL-R's Factor 2*, the answer is "Sociopaths aren't narcissistic and have the ability to experience guilt, remorse, deep emotions, and surplus empathy."

"Are all psychopaths narcissistic?" The answer would be "yes," so long as "psychopathy" is considered as described in the PCL-R and they have traits from the Factor 1 category. "Are all sociopaths narcissistic?" "Yes," if "sociopathy" is considered to be the same as ASPD. If it's considered synonymous with *BPD,* not at all.

[1] http://www.psychopathicwritings.com/2011/04/pcl-r-psychopathy-check-list.html

Borderline Personality Disorder (BPD)

Borderline Personality Disorder is characterized by the following characteristics:

- Markedly disturbed sense of identity
- Frantic efforts to avoid real or imagined abandonment, and extreme reactions to such.
- Splitting ("black-and-white" thinking)
- Impulsive or reckless behaviors (e.g., impulsive or uncontrollable spending, unsafe sex, substance abuse, reckless driving, binge eating)
- Intense or uncontrollable emotional reactions that are disproportionate to the event or situation
- Unstable and chaotic interpersonal relationships
- Self-damaging behavior
- Distorted self-image
- Dissociation
- Frequently accompanied by depression, anxiety, anger, substance abuse, and rage

With Borderline Personality Disorder (BPD), sometimes referred to as "female sociopathy" as mentioned earlier, women are three times more likely to develop this condition than men. In addition to the above criteria, individuals with this disorder tend to display sensitivity to rejection or criticism, alternating between idealization and devaluation, as well as a lack of empathy. Like ASPD, BPD may involve a disregard or confusion for what is "right and wrong" as well as dangerous and impulsive behavior.

BPD affected individuals often experience emotions with greater depth, ease, and duration than others. These emotions tend to take on amplified states: mild embarrassment turns into extreme shame and humiliation, rage instead of irritation, and panic over worry. This disorder can involve extremities between positive and negative emotions as well. The BPD individual may be caring, outgoing, vivacious, exuberant, and fun-loving in certain stages while being bogged down with excessive worry, depression, anxiety, shame, and rage in others. Also, sensitivity to perceived feelings of rejection, failure, abandonment, isolation, and criticism accompany BPD. Extreme emotions, self-destructiveness, absent or fragmented sense of identity, and a feeling of victimization are also associated with BPD. Extreme emotions tend to accompany extreme reaction with respect to how they are treated: positive treatment tends to elicit intense feelings of joy and appreciation while negative elicits anger and sadness.

A sad statistic regarding BPD is the tendency to self-harm, with 50-80% self-inflicting ("cutting" is common) while 10% of those affected succumbing to suicide. Men diagnosed with BPD are twice as likely to die by suicide in comparison to women.

In relationships, the BPD's strong desire for intimacy is coupled with heightened anxiety and fear. As such, they tend to avoid intimacy and gravitate to indiscriminate sex with multiple partners. If intimate relationships are initiated, the BPD affected individual is prone to idealize their partner too quickly as well as form strong emotional attachments. Doing so can have disastrous consequences if the partner is not mentally healthy. The BPD individual may sustain mistreatment and abuse and attempt to continue pursuing their quest for intimacy despite the maltreatment.

Like ASPD, those affected with BPD inspire compassion from me. Most literature regarding this disorder makes the claim that Abandonment issues are at the root cause of this disorder. Personally,I think this is only part of the story. It's more likely that issues of Unlovability are coupled with Abandonment as far as this disorder is concerned. That is, they were yearning to be loved and, when that didn't happen, they felt subsequent Abandonment. I doubt it's "Abandonment" itself because you can have someone *present* for you and not love you. You *can* be in the company of people but not be or feel loved. That's pretty much the core story of the "Lost Child" in dysfunctional families.

Since BPD is more commonly diagnosed in women than men and

is regarded as "female sociopathy," it's possible that such women are the product of a disconnected, controlling, suffocating, or abusive mother.

I imagine a young child - the "Lost Child" or perhaps even the "Scapegoat" of dysfunctional families (this could actually be the first born "only child" as well) - and quite possibly as young as an infant or toddler who does not receive love from one or both caretakers and subsequently feels abandoned on top of it. The core issue is *Unlovability:* the BPD both craves love but fears it will leave them *precisely* because they have an inculcated belief that they are defective, not lovable for who they are, and unworthy of being the recipient of attentiveness - and this is something they were trained to believe during and since childhood. Once prospective love they've craved so desperately for *leaves* them or shows signs of doing so, the abandonment issues kick into high gear. Subsequent behavior involves frantic efforts to maintain the "loving" presence or being placed in a horrible pit of despair and desolation once this occurs.

Moreover, this fear of accepting the love they so desperately crave is born out of an amalgamation of the Unlovability issue itself, resentment and anger the BPD feels toward the gender of the respective parent for not loving them (if not, abusing them) while they were growing up, the litany of antagonistic thoughts they've had against the respective gender, the refusal to forgive the respective parent for their behavior, and the acknowledgement of the lack of empathy they employed to the respective parent's upbringing and subsequent judgement they've dispensed against said parent.

To reiterate without sounding like legalese, the BPD needs to forgive their parent's treatment, forgive the parent's lack of love, love themselves, forgive themselves for any animosity they've held and the duration for which they've held it, be willing to love the gender they're sexually attracted to, and do their best to empathize with their parent's childhood conditions which caused them to behave the way they did. The material presented elsewhere in this chapter should help with the latter.

They should also seek out the company of those who truly show them love, care, and respect.

This desperate yearning for the love from the gender of the parent of conflict (or both) stalemated by the fear of receiving it due to the BPD's long-held resentment and anger toward said parent and subsequent guilt and shame *is what is behind behavior such as sexual promiscuity, aversion to intimacy, preference and addictions to pornography, and intermittent, short-term, and unstable relationships.* If the BPD's parent of conflict is male, *the penis/sperm represents the parental love the BPD wishes to receive but is adverse to take due to the hurt of not being loved by such parent at an early age, continuing to blame the parent for their feelings of unlovability, the rage and animosity for any abuse, lack of love, and abandonment the BPD still harbors, and any shame they have accrued.*

With this in mind, BPD resembles not only codependency to the extreme, but also prototypical "Daddy issues." I hardly mean this pejoratively.

While we're here, and whether or not you have BPD or not, if you're a woman you need to consider the following as far as the dichotomy between your upbringing with that of men's: it is more culturally acceptable for a mother to dote on her son than it is for a father to dote on his daughter - unless said daughter is "Daddy's Little Girl" and grows up to be "Men's High-maintenance Annoyance." It's fine if a mother tells her "sweetie" how cute, handsome, adorable he is, but for a father to tell his daughter how "pretty," "cute," and "adorable" she is… well, that would be considered to be weird by some. The thing is, from a very early age, boys are endowed with this sort of ego-boosting which girls are less likely to be the recipient of. Also, it need not be the mother: *any* older woman can lavish this sort of praise on a boy (it happened to me all the time when I was a boy; I was a cute kid), but if an older boy or man does this with a girl, he's likely to be seen as a pervert (and he might be; maybe not.) Regardless, *this alone* is part of the reason boys grow up with more confidence than girls. I may very well be one of a handful of males willing to acknowledge this.

However, *if* abuse - whether verbal, physical, or psychological - is experienced with being made to feel unlovable, the BPD also inherited an issue of *Vulnerability,* in which case reading the above section designated *"Paternal-based ASPD"* would be applicable to them as well.
Chances are, the BPD individual had at least one parent who had ASPD, NPD, or had NPD and was co-morbid with another disorder. In this case scenario, the young child - instead of receiving love, care, and respect - was tapped for those very qualities. He or she may recall a childhood where their focus was continuously on the parent and hardly the other way around. That is, he or she was programmed to be highly attuned to the wants and needs of their caretakers while the BPD's "self" was rarely

accounted for by such caretakers.

As such, the fact that these children grow up to have a difficult time with their self-identity would be understandable. They are liable to have difficulty differentiating their own wants, needs, preferences, and activities of enjoyment especially with respect from others since theirs were routinely eclipse by their parent's (which would be a *Subjugation* schema.) This would explain the BPD's aversion to intimate relationships despite their craving for such relationships. A healthy, intimate relationship would involve the BPD's partner to show them love, care, and respect - a situation which the BPD individual is hardly accustomed to: it would put them in a state of anomie. They would falter and the healthy relationship would have difficulty getting off the ground. Otherwise, the BPD individual is liable to "get lost" or "feel like they're losing themselves" in relationships due to their disturbed sense of identity since it was rarely honored during their upbringing. Because of this, they're liable to be controlled and exploited by controlling personalities. They may not know "where they end and the other person begins" which will ensure psychological chaos and relationship instability.

However, because of this deep inner yearning for interpersonal intimacy due to being starved for love, respect, and attention throughout their childhood (actually, being sapped for those three qualities by their own caretakers), the BPD individual will sometimes engage in frantic efforts to avoid real or perceived abandonment even with others who are not mentally healthy. The may tolerate or exonerate maltreatment since "poor love" is better than no love at all. Otherwise, the types will often push others away even if they genuinely care about the BPD individual.

Since their "self" was never honored growing up, they may have a weak ego and subsequent issues with setting boundaries. Since they were never if rarely allowed to honor their selves or speak their wants, needs, and preferences, we can see how this would be the case.

As with Paternal-based ASPD, success in life is liable to be out-of-reach for the BPD individual due the Unlovability and Vulnerability issues at its core. Thus, the *Failure* schema becomes a factor. Shame is also liable to effect those with BPD for due to the same "issues" since Unlovability plus Vulnerability equals Shame.

Persons affected with BPD would benefit from reparenting exercises, starting from as early as they can remember. Imagining one or both parents treating them with love, patience, mutual respect, praise, positive reinforcement, fun, encouragement, constructive feedback, and care would be beneficial if practiced continuously and consistently over time. The BPD individual needs to be reminded that this exercise is not an endorsement or program to become narcissistic. Narcissism involves siphoning the praise, adulation, attention, and accolades from others in order to feel good about oneself; it is *not* self-love - it is parasitic and dependent. And not that there's anything wrong with receiving compliments, respect, and praise from others; it's when it's *elicited, solicited, or demanded or obtained through degradation of another party*. The goal of this exercise is to condition the BPD individual to generate self-love on their own even if the catalyst in the exercise is imagining another person loving them. They need to understand they are actually *reversing* the negative programming done by their caretaker(s), that their low self-worth programming *wasn't of their own doing either*. That being said, the BPD individual must commit to being

permeable to the love, care, and respect the improved yet imagined version of their parents are giving them. Again, the BPD absorbing messages that he or she is "beautiful, cherished, appreciated, wonderful, valued, loved, protected, good, talented, smart, etc." and more from an imagined second party is *not* narcissistic.

Boundary setting is also imperative for individuals affected with this disorder. Because their physical and psychological self, wants, needs, and wellbeing were often disregarded, violated, or abused while growing up, the adult BPD will have to develop this ability. Another reparenting exercise would help with this as well which involves the BPD individual canvassing their childhood for episodes when they were mistreated, humiliated, abused, unloved, isolated, alienated, neglected, etc. and set appropriate boundaries *with appropriate emotions* with those responsible - that is, they need to disintegrate any issues of vulnerability they inherited as well.

Like the ASPD with forgiveness, the BPD may find this difficult, especially if the mistreatment was severe - and most likely it was (or was interpreted as such by their child self.) They may be of the mindset, "I shouldn't have to set boundaries with someone who loves me!" They're absolutely right to think this way. The thing is, since their boundaries were violated when they were vulnerable children and most likely later on in life, this affected their self-worth, self-value, and self-concept. When boundaries are crossed, the person absorbs conditioning that they are unlovable, unworthy, guilty, responsible (for things they aren't), and more.

If these psychological wounds are not healed, they will be targeted later on by predatory individuals. If the BPD does not learn boundaries, their inner self will be vulnerable to other's abuse and mistreatment.

Initially, engaging in this practice may induce anxiety and fear, but the BPD needs to be reassured that doing so will bring about empowerment within them. They also need to be reminded that the offending parties deserve to be reprimanded and that doing so makes the world a better place.

With relationships, BPD affected individuals need to understand that they are entering a situation where they are both to love and be loved. Since a deep rooted primary schema of unlovability is at the hallmark of this disorder (because they did not receive love from one or both caretakers) that is likely to have been instilled while a toddler, they need to conditioned themselves to know that they are lovable and deserve attention, regard, and respect. The lack of love, attention, regard, and respect was that was consistent throughout their childhood needs to be deprogrammed so that the BPD understands they are to be loved, regarded, and respected. In short, they need to undo the childhood conditioning.

Before this can happen, the BPD must also *find themselves*. Since their sense of self was eclipsed by one or both parents wants, needs, opinions, desires, beliefs, preferences, etc., they need to reclaim this for themselves. Part of the reason BPD individuals have a nebulous sense of self is due to never being allowed to individuate from one or both parents. For this reason, they need to reclaim their ego. This going to require them to assess and cultivate their talents, gifts, preferences, life path, hobbies, personal style, weaknesses, strengths, and what they are willing and unwilling to put up with. They need to build the strength of character of knowing who they are.

Moreover, since they were perceived as chattel by one or both parents, the BPD individual needs to learn to distinguish self from non-self in order to build their ego and retain their energy. Throughout their childhood, individuals with BPD often have no sense of self because their entire awareness was superimposed onto one or both parents; that is, it was always about *them, never themselves*. Thus, they may not know where "they end and others begin" with respect to romantic and interpersonal relationships going forward. As such, this will be draining for them as it will feel like their energy is being sapped from them when dealing with others. Because of this, they may consistently try to present a jovial or kind demeanor with the belief that, since it's going to be absorbed anyway by others, they may appreciate it.

The sad fact is, no: the other parties are not going to appreciate it; rather, they're liable to take advantage of it or take it for granted due to the rise of narcissism in our culture. If the other party has a history of being over-indulged or has a victim mentality rooted in abandonment, this is guaranteed to happen. Also due to this, such persons have perceive themselves as "empaths" due to their keen ability to sense others' energy for good or for bad, not to mention absorb such energy. This, again, is due to the fact that they were trained to be like this during their childhood: to be hypersensitive and keenly aware of Mom and/or Dad's moods since everything revolved around them. This is draining beyond belief. And they're not "empaths" - they've been trained to lose themselves when interacting with others and need to work on changing that, for themselves yet also for the Adult-toddlers who don't deserve an iota of their love, care, respect, regard, and attention. Otherwise, they're like a pitcher of water that gives water away to every empty pitcher they come across. After a while, their own pitcher becomes empty. BPD's need to realize that they're not responsible for filling up others' pitchers despite what their upbringing tried to have them believe.

But it is because of this dislocation of self with respect to others that gets taken for granted and advantage of that BPD individuals themselves are hypersensitive to how others treat them. They're liable to feel a surge of elation and gratitude when treated with kindness or the off-chance that *they* were actually *considered* - "Wow! Someone cared about *my* pitcher! That *never* happens! Thank YOU SO MUCH!" Conversely, they are liable to feel great sadness and anger after being hurt or criticized. Who can blame them? Their entire existence serves to serve others with their attention and kindness: to have this sort of literal self-abnegation and sacrifice be taken for granted let alone criticized or mistreated is a slap in the face to the unabashed and extensive psychological charity they impart to others.

Again, this is a relic of the dysfunction that was present in their childhoods. "If I do what Mommy or Daddy wants - actually do what they want because I've tried so hard to be keenly *aware* of it and even *expect* what they want before they *demand* it - maybe at some point I'll be loved for being a good kid."

No, especially if Mommy or Daddy was an adult-toddler themselves. What the BPD doesn't realize is that they were expected to parent their toddler-parents while growing up. Being *expectant, anticipatory, and hyper-aware* of another's needs, moods, and state of well-being as a full-time job *is only appropriate when the receiving party is actually a toddler!*

On top of this, if the emotional and psychological needs likelihood of this *not* happening is slim to none - the BPD never learned how to self-soothe! Thus no one - including themselves - is going to heal their "issues" - certainly not *they* since they were never trained to do so! *No one ever asked the BPD "How are you doing?"* with the intent of gleaning an honest answer let alone being attentive to it. If the BPD doesn't know "how they're doing" since their focus was always on Mom and Dad and Mom and Dad never asked or cared...*BPD's are never going to have a clear, defined, and stable sense of self!*

Because the BPD individual has been programmed to always hold others in consideration rather than themselves, the likelihood that they'll go throughout life constantly replaying interactions they've had with others in the past over and over and over again is highly likely, especially if the BPD was mistreated. This is understandable. For most of their life, the locus of their awareness was usually on others - *their* wants, needs, moods, happiness, well-being, etc. Thus, the BPD's conditioning to always consider others becomes a habit; a habit formed due to the expectation that, if they just "consider others" enough, one day they'll be loved and that all the self-sacrificing consideration they've been doing will somehow pay off, being told this is "good karma." If you've been diagnosed with BPD or suspect you are diagnosable, I'm here to tell you that the carrot you've been chasing was rotten years ago and to stop running.

However, this habit of constant consideration of others can make forgiveness extremely difficult since forgiveness - which is for the self and *not* the other party - involves no longer letting the situation "rent space in one's head." Part of the BPD's reluctance to "forgive" as defined here is due to the resentment over all the mental of the BPD went ignored or disregarded as a child - and the consideration the BPD has involved themselves in and *not* being appreciated or taken for granted for doing so.

Here, it must be emphasized that *forgiveness* is *not* the same as *reconciliation.* The latter involves reuniting ties with a party with whom ties were severed in the past. BPD's *should never, ever seek to reconcile with parties which have mistreated or abused them unless and until the other party or parties can demonstrate <u>by actions, behaviors, and character</u> - <u>not</u> by words alone.*

This trend is exacerbated by the fact that the BPD is highly sensitive. Actually, *everyone is sensitive.* For instance, NPD's have a grandiose sense of self because they were sensitive to the excessive adulation they received as children. They're also "sensitive" to supposed "abandonment" even though that "abandonment" was due to the 110% that they were being given dropping down to 100% or a more appropriate 50%. ASPD's are sensitive to the abuse and/or abandonment they endured as children and manifest a "victim mentality" later in life. The brandishing of BPD as "sensitive" is merely those of other psychologies projecting their own insecurities about being sensitive onto others in order to feel better about themselves *(see the above subtopic entitled "Narcissistic Personality Disorder")* since a weird stigma against being sensitive has been circulating for years from God-knows-wheredespite it being a necessary component of human socialization.

The reason BPD is perceived as "sensitive" in the conventional sense - that is, overly thoughtful, impacted, and sympathetic to the moods and feelings of others as well as being very *feeling* themselves - is due to the core "issue" behind this disorder which is *Unlovability*. The BPD's inner child - as young as an infant or toddler - still awaits that consistent, smiling adult face to tell the child it is loved and cherished; that it is "good, it is kind, and it is important" and to be consistently loving as the child gets older. Anyone who does not receive love from a developmental stage *this* early onward is absolutely, 100%, no-way-out, balls-to-the-walls, going to appear "sensitive." Period. This is utterly unavoidable. By "reparenting" themselves or engaging in meditative practices where the BPD feels a loving presence - or if someone else actually *loves them* - this "sensitivity" should dissipate.

The BPD's supposed "sensitivity" is merely he unloved inner-child doing the only thing he or she knows to do in order to receive that love and that is to love and empathize with others in the hopes that the recipient will appreciate and reciprocate the love back. Again, if this is done with an NPD or Maternal-based ASPD, it will taken for granted and even expected since the they had the opposite problem: *their* child was over-dosed with love from the start and it kept going *way* past the developmental phase where self-reliance on self-love ought to have been the focus; they're also liable to have *abandonment* issues so any attention the BPD *provides* them with is liable to be sucked up like an ungrateful sponge. Thus, the BPD *gives;* the NPD/M-Based ASPD *takes. Always. The BPD "gives" with the hopes of "receiving" someday by doing so; the NPD/ASPD "takes" with the hope of someday being "satisfied."* Yes, it's a bum deal if there ever was one.

With this in mind, the BPD should not abort their ability to provide love to their partner or abandon the expectation that they will need to love their partner; they need to understand that love, care, respect, and regard need to go both ways.

Their pendulum should not swing the other way and expect others to cater to them out of resentment for not receiving reciprocation in the past.

However, just as the Maternal-based ASPD employs the attention-capturing behavior described earlier to counter fears of Abandonment (which usually backfires), the excessive caring, nurturing, empathy, availability, and self-sacrifice the BPD employs to counter *their* issue of Unlovability (which also usually backfires.) The constant empathy, focus on others, consideration, appeasement, awareness, selflessness - the constant loving in order to be loved back - which leaves the BPD drained, confused, and frustrated eventually leads to anger and resentment. The BPD cannot understand why their "giving-ness" not only did not yield results, but went unappreciated, taken for granted, and taken advantage of. After all this effort, the BPD may actually develop the "go fuck yourself" arrogance similar to that of Paternal-based ASPD albeit not as defiant. The BPD may become so frustrated that they'll never be good enough or loved enough, they'll begin to self-inflict which is why things like "cutting" and other forms of self-harm and the propensity to jeopardize their own health - physical, financial, emotional, *and* psychological - become a factor.

This sort of self-infliction, at it's core, is the inward-directed resentment and hatred the BPD feels toward the parent who hurt, abused, or did not love them. The fact that the BPD has "issues" is blamed on the parent; it's almost as if the inner child is saying, "I'll kill myself because you hated me" or "I'm going to die because you didn't love me." The blame *is* understandable - the fears they have did *not* create themselves nor were they tended to by their parent. But the propensity to self-inflict is likely to continue until the wounds are healed.

Also, because of the BPD's gravitation to exhibiting "good" behavior such as the consideration, care, attentiveness, and laser-sharp focus on being mindful of and how their actions effect others, it's possible they may develop contempt for those who do not. The BPD also needs to develop the ability to say "no," especially within relationships and with potential suitors. Akin to the Maternal-based ASPD, individuals with this disorder can oftentimes indulge the advances and interests others may have in them without having genuine reciprocal feelings. They must learn that other's happiness is not their responsibility nor are their feelings of rejection or disappointment.

If anything, the BPD should realize that consideration should only be given to those who are considerate. The extremities in the behavior arise when the excess consideration, attention, and self-abnegation the BPD has given goes unappreciated. This sort of heightened disappointment will hopefully serve as a deterrent for such individuals going forward. Abandonment in relationships can hit hard to these types, especially if discarded by an NPD since it rips off the scab that is their Unlovability schema. The lesson here is to learn never to give your *self* in a relationship let alone so quickly. A better lesson to learn is actual thanksgiving if and when discarded by a narcissist - the sooner, the better. Recovery/alleviation from BPD includes the following:

- **The BPD *must* address their core issue of *Unlovability (possibly Vulnerability as well) and secondary issue of Abandonment.*** Otherwise, this will have a negative impact on all other areas of their life, including work, family, relationships, *health,* friendships, finances - *everything*. Prioritizing their primary Unlovability issue will permit other "issues" such as Abandonment, Deprivation, Subjugation, Vulnerability, Mistrust, Failure, Perfectionism, Exclusion, and Entitlement. Specifically, the self-inflicting nature stemming from the belief that they are unlovable will manifest a lifetime of being deprived, subjugated, vulnerable, violated, failing, needing to be perfect, excluded, while being hyper-mindful of and abiding

 by rules, morals, which others systemically disregard. In short, others will regard them as deviants or delinquents when, in truth, it is very much their "inner child" with unattended fears of not being lovable. *The more the Core Issue of Unlovability and secondary issue of Abandonment are healed and dissolved, the more of a game changer this will be for the BPD since Unlovability is the keystone for everything wrong in their life.*

- The BPD **MUST FORGIVE THEMSELVES** and **NOT HOLD THEMSELVES ACCOUNTABLE FOR HAVING THE CORE ISSUE OF UNLOVABILITY AND SECONDARY ISSUE OF ABANDONMENT**. It is truly not their fault! - and this *will* be proven in the chapters which follow. Yet expecting others to compensate for it is not fair to them - they didn't create it nor should they be held accountable for it either. As frustrating as it might be for the BPD to read or hear this, *it is not their fault, but it is their responsibility to tend to this issue*. However, by pinpointing *unlovability* as the seed which causes *all* other distress in their life, the BPD *can rightfully regard this knowledge as the "silver bullet" which kills all other psychological and spiritual strife **they will*** *ever face in life in the future.*

- Practicing the mantra *"I love you, and I am here for you"* or even just *"I love you"* as though coming from themselves or a second party - whichever works - during times of anxiety and seclusion or as a regular, meditative practice. *"I respect you"* is another mantra which will counteract any dysfunctional childhood-origin programming.
- Reminding yourself that you are lovable for who you are.
- Reclaiming your sense of self.
- Meditating/Practicing Guided Meditation.
- Becoming aware of tendencies to over-extend in the workplace and relationships; never "lose yourself" in anything.
- Learning to set boundaries (the sooner, the better) when "losing yourself" becomes apparent.
- Practicing mindfulness, becoming aware of how often personal mental activity revisits past events and situations with others.
- Loving/Reparenting the Unloved Inner Child by whatever means necessary.
- Understanding forgiveness is for oneself, *not* the other party.
- Learning to distinguish self from non-self, or "where you end and others begin." Or, "This is *you,* not *me.*"
- Learning to enjoy disciplining and setting boundaries with narcissists; celebrate the times when they leave your life even after you've set a boundary. The boundary is for your self-worth and to weed out "weeds." If the narcissist leaves, know it's a blessing.
- Setting personal goals and dreams: Who do you want to be? What sort of attributes would you like to cultivate in your appearance and personality? What do you want out of life? What kind of partner would you like to have? What do you *want?* How do you want to *feel everyday?* "Sexy?" "Smart?" "Confident?" "Masculine?" "Feminine?" "Carefree?" "Responsible?" "Non-reactive?" "Self-loving?" "Mature?" Hash it out and make your lists - *find yourself.*
- Absolutely understanding that *you're much better off at the present time than you think.* I've watched numerous interviews with BPD afflicted individuals and they are grossly underestimating themselves for *who they are at the very moment they're giving the interview - saying they look ugly, etc. - and they don't whatsoever!*
- If you feel like you're settling, that means you are. If you get the feeling that you're compromising, settling for less, or "could do better" - the answers are: "you are," "yes, you are," and "yes, you could," respectively.
- If you could feel like you could improve in some areas you can

and you should - *for you*.

Histrionic Personality Disorder (HPD)

The last "personality disorder" belonging to the Cluster B category is Histrionic Personality Disorder or HPD. Curiously, little research within the psychological community has been conducted to determine the root causes of this disorder. Like BPD, women are more likely to be diagnosed than men - roughly four times as often.

Like potential NPD and Maternal-based ASPD, HPD involves excessive attention-seeking behaviors including an excessive need for approval as well as flirtatious, provocative, and seductive measures which tend to take on a maternal or paternal role as the individual gets older. Those with HPD are often vivacious, outgoing, dramatic, and enthusiastic.

Other characteristics for HPD are as follows:
- Exhibitionist behavior (NPD)
- Constant seeking of reassurance or approval (BPD)
- Excessive sensitivity to criticism or disapproval (BPD)
- Pride of own personality and unwillingness to change, viewing any change as a threat (NPD)
- Inappropriately seductive appearance or behavior of sexual nature (NPD)
- Using factitious somatic symptoms (of physical illness) or psychological disorders to garner attention (BPD)
- A need to be the center of attention (NPD)
- Low tolerance for frustration or delayed gratification (NPD)
- Rapidly shifting emotional states that may appear superficial or exaggerated to others (NPD)• Tendency to believe that relationships are more intimate than they actually are (BPD)
- Making rash decisions (BPD)
- Blaming personal failures or disappointments on others (BPD)
- Being easily influenced by others, especially those who treat them approvingly (BPD)
- Being overly dramatic and emotional (NPD)
- Influenced by the suggestions of others (BPD)

Like NPD, HPD also involves ego-centricity, self-involvement, and persistent manipulative behavior. Looking over the list of HPD characteristics, I find it remarkable that psychology cannot determine the core causes or issues behind this "disorder.

What we have with HPD, just as with ASPD earlier, is a co-morbid disorder: HPD is a hybrid of NPD (or Maternal-based ASPD) and BPD. Above, I've correlated the associated characteristics with their co-morbid counterparts using the co-morbid disorders' abbreviations.

That being said, the core schemas behind HPD are as follows: *Entitlement* and/or *Abandonment* (depending on whether or not the co-morbid disorder is NPD or Maternal-based ASPD, respectively) or both and *Unlovability* (BPD.) The "Unlovability" may also be present in tandem with *Vulnerability* and reinforce the "Abandonment" already present.

In short, whereas BPD has been considered to be "female sociopathy," HPD could be regarded as "female psychopathy."

What I personally glean from the HPD description is, like BPD, this condition develops, in part, from a paternal relationship - one where intermittent reinforcement and sporadic attention was provided to the child. The fact that this "disorder" effects women four times more than men reinforces this. This would account for the issues of *Abandonment* and perhaps *Deprivation* (if neglect is considered "deprivation"; typically, this schema refers to the deprivation of "things" or material goods) being present in the child. The intermittent positive interaction a father may have had with his daughter would account for the attention-seeking character this "disorder" displays as well as the aversion to delayed gratification. The withdrawal from love, like BPD, would also account for the propensity of this "disorder" to perceive relationships as more intimate than they are. The exaggerated emotions play into this as well: the dramatic, almost theatrical persona, like the behaviors just mentioned, are attempts to gain attention from others.

The co-morbid component - akin to BPD - has its roots in an *Unlovability* schema as mentioned earlier. Although speculative, it wouldn't surprise me if this component was inherited from a maternal figure; one who was hyper-critical and withheld approval or approving comments from the child. This would manifest the traits of constantly seeking approval or reassurance, sensitivity to criticism or disapproval, being over-influenced by others or by those who *do* treat them with approval, and being easily influenced by the suggestion of others. Again, attributing this to the maternal figure is speculative; it's possible either parent could have impose "Unlovability" onto their child.

Also, the fact that the child was *objectified,* that is, perceived as the parent(s)'s chattel as well as being starved for attention and love (or given this sporadically) would account for the adult's inappropriate seductive behavior. Because the child was objectified, the HPD-adult is likely to self-objectify and, instead of considering their *psychology* as themselves, regard their *physical bodies* as themselves and subsequently self-somaticize.

Personally, I'm reluctant to suggest that HPD is a co-morbid disorder incorporating NPD since it doesn't seem like this "disorder" arises from being spoiled; I think it's much more likely due to sporadic exposures to and withdrawals from attention and love which develops an Abandonment and Unlovability schema in adulthood.

In closing, it is my sincere hope that the previous has presented a sharp contrast amongst the "personality disorders" formerly categorized as "Cluster B." In certain cases, some disorders not only have radically different childhood-origin "upbringings" and environments, but the psychology between some appears to be the inverse of others. While some harm others, others self-inflict. Some appear dishonest while others are honest to the point of their own detriment. Some are narcissistic while others are sadistic. And, whereas some are highly manipulative, others are overly trusting and naive. Apparently, the only thing they have in common is being "dramatic" in character and that the "issues in common" within these "disorders" are *Abandonment* and *Unlovability* - but, even this, one "issue" gives rise to the other in some cases whereas it's vice-versa in others.

Before proceeding to the next chapters which examine the causes and dynamics behind behaviors most associated with malignant narcissism, we have to address the Cluster B category itself. As mentioned earlier, the four previously discussed personality disorders - Narcissistic, Antisocial, Borderline, and Histrionic - are no longer grouped together under the same category. Recently, the American Psychiatric Association (APA) dismantled this group from being categorized together in the Diagnostic and Statistical Manual of Mental Disorders which, from the author's perspective, was a wise and appropriate decision considering the only common thread with these disorders is the propensity to be "dramatic." Ungrouping these disorders removes this superficial similarity and, hopefully, reveals the root childhood-origin causes behind these disorders (which is part of the objective of this book) which, as we've seen in this chapter, varies greatly.

Since many readers are accustomed to these disorders being grouped together, I figured I would describe each one in detail in this chapter. It's worth observing since it supports the APA's decision to de-categorize these disorders considering their extreme differences in some cases. In the chapters which follow, however, the focus will be on primarily on the characteristics most commonly associated with NPD and ASPD or even "malignant narcissism," although some content will apply to BPD and HPD as well.

Now that we have the "disorders" understood and described, let's look at the characteristics in greater depth:

3

<u>Grandiose Sense of Self</u>

"I wanted somebody to love me."
- A mother of an unplanned pregnancy on a late-90s talk show

Pre-programmed Ego (NPD, potential M-Based ASPD)

I'll start this chapter with the simplest reason a malignant narcissist has the hallmark characteristic of the grandiose sense of self: _they were programmed from a very early age that they were special in some capacity - "entitled" to an inflated sense of self._ This may or may not have been due to the actions of a _codependent_ parent who placed the child on the proverbial pedestal for too long, too often. It is possible that the child was perceived as an extension by a _narcissistic_ parent whose over-inflated ego was extended to the child since the child is seen by such a parent as an extension of themselves; that is, since the child _came from_ the parent, the child _is part of the parent_ which means the child must be special if the parent is (or perceives him/herself to be.) In short, if the "old block" is narcissistic, so will any "chip" which comes off it. Regardless, whatever psychological state effected the parent, the child received the message early on that he or she was "better" or "special" and it is likely that this message continued on for years. If they child received such egotistical elevation from a _codependent_ parent, see _"Messiah Complex"_ below.

Messiah Complex (NPD, M-Based ASPD)

Many readers will be familiar with something akin to the above quote at the heading of this chapter. During the late 90's and early 2000's "talk shows" would often feature "guests" who learned about their partner's cheating as well as the subsequent physical altercations when they met the involved third party. Other guests learned whether or not they were their girlfriend's "baby daddy."

Other times, the topic was unplanned pregnancy, typically featuring a young mother who provided something akin to the above quote as a reason for giving birth to a child before she was ready or prepared.

However, whether it is starting a pregnancy or pursuing a relationship going into either with the mentality *"I need someone to love me"* will almost guarantee a union with an NPD or M-Based ASPD. If any unhealed wounds or ill feelings toward an NPD or M-Based ASPD parent growing up are present before going into the relationship, the greater the chance will be of this personality being abusive.

Note that *it is this very lingering childhood-origin void of needing/ wanting to be loved in the form of attentiveness, nurturing, and/or support with respect to self-worth that the codependent wanted and needed from their NPD or M-Based ASPD parent that they are looking to their newborn child to fulfill.* Because this child will grow up resenting this burden, they will resent providing attentiveness and nurturing to others as they grow older - and a residual lack of empathy will manifest in their interactions with others, especially in romantic relationships. Depending on the severity (and especially if the child was exposed totraumatic abandonment), the child may do the opposite and *sabotage or even attack others' needs for attentiveness, nurturing, and support with self-worth* as they get older.

But it is because of this void that the parent's ability to adequately care for the child's physical, material, and financial needs is impaired. Such a child may have to learn to provide for himself or at least take on a level of elevated competency to compensate for the depressive parent's (or even family's) lack of efficacy. Moreover, this elevated competency taken on by the Cluster B-to-be will be fueled by the depressive parent's heaping doses of praise and adoration upon the child for doing so.

And thus begins the bartering cycle: "If you take on extraneous (and inappropriate) responsibility, I'll fuel your ego."

The one thing such a parent is *likely* to provide to their newborn is love in the form of attentiveness, nurturing, and support with self-worth. This, again, is due to the parent's belief that if they bestow upon their child the type of love they did not receive, this means that they love their child. That is, they're filling this child's "void" when it actually is their own. But, especially when over-dosing the newborn with support with respect to self-worth, ***this is precisely the causality behind the*** *grandiose and/or false sense of self the child is bound to incur.*

Again, it is because of this extraneous endowment of self-worth that the child will develop grandiosity as well as a high level of efficacy - the high "self-confidence" also linked to narcissistic Cluster B disorders - as an adult. Yet, because of the parent's still unattended self-worth void and resulting lack of efficacy, the child's surplus will be tapped to maintain the logistical management of his physical and material upbringing.

Before I proceed, I want to apologize to any and every reader for using the above "talk-show" source as an illustration. This is by no means an attempt to belittle, denigrate, or judge you if this resembles your state of mind prior to having a child or getting into a relationship. We all experience this and pursue relationships because we want to be loved. There's absolutely nothing unreasonable about that whatsoever. It's when the other party is perceived as a "cure" for pathological loneliness that this becomes a problem.

However, from the very start of his or her existence, a child born to a parent with this sort of mantra as an imperative for giving birth is guaranteed to adopt the identity that he or she is "special" - they are, after all, being cast in such a role from an extremely early age that they are the "cure" to the void of love his/her parent possesses in whichever form that may be - whether it is pathological loneliness and isolation, low self-worth, an absent support system, or another source of love that was absent in the parent's household growing up. *They were born to save mommy - mommy's "hero."*

This sort of role is bound to be calcified as the child grows and, if the child is relied upon as a surrogate spouse (called "emotional incest"), a mock therapist, an outlet for depression, or a support system for the codependent parent far greater than the child can (and should) provide (if they are able to), the child is likely to develop a disdain for such "neediness" and *the hallmark lack of empathy emerges which the NPD or M-Based ASPD personality types are known for.* This will be discussed in further detail in the next chapter.

Of course, it is neither unrealistic nor inappropriate that the wish to be loved be abandoned when pursuing parenthood or a relationship. What makes a codependent a codependent involves two things: *1) A tendency to give without receiving or care excessively with the expectation that it will be appreciated and reciprocated and 2) The expectation that an outside source* *be the sole, reliant solution to personal issues or tribulations. In other words, that the solution to one's own life problems is **solely** another person used as a sounding board, surrogate, or support source.*

Most importantly: They love others more than they love themselves with the hopes that others will love them.

This is not to suggest that we as human beings should not have support systems, friends and family, and relationship partners with whom we can vent and act as periodic "shoulders to cry on" when needed - it is when these types of support outlets are used *exclusively* in coping with personal life difficulties - *"dependently" is the appropriate word to describe this* - with little to no self-sufficiency on the part of the person seeking it. In other words, they seek others to "carry their cross" *for* them without putting any effort into carrying it on their own. They may even ask others to keep carrying their cross after it's reached its destination. Alternatively, they may "carry others' crosses" with the hopes and expectations that these others will carry theirs - and not that there's anything *wrong* with this other than when taken to excess.

Excess Emotional Care/Incest/Emotional Incest As Support for False/ Grandiose Self (NPD, M-ASPD, HPD)

Furthermore, it is because of *this sort of attachment involving the parent bestowing excess attention, nurturing, and self-worth upon their child in order to elicit it in return (since they're not receiving it elsewhere or from within) the child will develop a disdain for anything resembling "emotional incest."* Emotional Incest is **a dynamic that occurs in parenting where the parent seeks emotional support through their child that should be sought through an adult relationship**, particularly their spouse's.

This "emotional incest" is prone to condition the "false self" in the child's early ego. (If actual incest did take place, this is bound produce and influence the "false self" in the child well into adulthood, not to mention objectify the child as in the case of Histrionic Personality Disorder and possibly Narcissistic.)

If emotional incest *was* the child's experience, the respective imprint of discomfort and irritation is likely to show itself later during adulthood when others mimic the parent's behavior. That is, any requests the adult-version receives for attentiveness and nurturing elicits an off-putting response due to the history of emotional incest as a child.

The Hero/Golden Child

More often than not, and because love is a finite quantity within the dysfunctional household, the Messiah will emerge as "The Hero" or "The Golden Child" within the family if subsequent children are born. As described on Page 144 in *The Toxic States of America*, The Hero is typically (but not always) the first born and tends to outshine their younger siblings in performance, recognition, acceptance, career, and quality of life as an adult. If this child was the first born, this is most likely due to the fact that is was "first come, first serve" when it came to receiving the family's limited supply of love, care, and respect and there was little to none available at the buffet for subsequent children when it was their turn. The needs of subsequent children born into the family are thus seen as burdensome or inconsequential by dysfunctional parents. And, let's face it: stress arises due to a lack of resources available to satiate increasing demands.

Plus, there's also the "novelty effect" to consider. Since the first born is a new, unprecedented experience - and therefore a "special" experience - for the parent(s) (as is the pregnancy itself), the attention and perception of the child is unique in comparison to additional children born in the future. Subsequent births are "charted territory." If subsequent children are provided with "hand-me-downs" from the first child, you can imagine how this "second-hand" trend will effect these kids' sense of status, which undoubtedly will be lower.

Regardless, since the identity of the child was inflated (possibly as early as birth), this grandiose self is also a *false self*, since their "special" status is contingent upon inhabiting the Messianic role as they get older. This is liable to condition the adult to enter into career fields the later-in-life adult considers "Messianic" but not authentic to the individual's interests or talents, taking on additional responsibility with respect to the household or the other children (which is likely to generate resentment and a future disdain for those who appear "weak" or "needy": *thus fortifying the characteristic of lack of empathy)*, and abnegating authentic personality traits, thus reinforcing the "false self."

If other children are born to the dysfunctional family, they will adopt the following roles, usually assigned chronologically as: The Scapegoat (or Rebel), The Lost Child, and The Mascot (or Jester.) See pages 144-145 of *TSOA* or simply do an online search for more detailed descriptions of each role. Because of this, the Messianic Role is not only strengthened (due to compare and contrast) but, as we shall see, other narcissistic traits are likely to emerge or be strengthened. But, with this role, certain perks most certainly come with it: think "Marcia, Marcia, Marcia" Brady.

One element I regret not including in *TSOA* is the fact that the previous list of dysfunctional roles children take on in the family *may not* be the extent of the dysfunctional conditioning. By this, I mean that the children inherit a dysfunctional role with respect to the family as a whole, but also *two supplementary roles with respect to each parent* in dysfunctional two-parent households.

I'll use myself as an example of this: Being the third born (and youngest) in my family, my overall role was a combination of The Lost Child and The Jester growing up. With respect to my father, I was a pronounced version of the Scapegoat; with my mother, I was raised as a Golden Child (and proceeded into an educational/career path in biochemistry which, if you knew me personally, was like jamming a square peg in a round hole.)

Regardless of my mini-bio, if the Hero/Golden Child role is the one assigned with respect to the family as a whole, not only is the Messianic quality likely to be reinforced, but also a disdain for sympathy and lack of empathy as well, which itself is reinforced if the Messiah has been sapped by a codependent during their "poor me" parades.

Responsibility (M-Based ASPD)

Whether or not a child was placed in the Hero role within a dysfunctional family, he or she may have been given responsibilities that were extraneous or considered burdensome. Being given responsibilities can often build self-confidence and efficacy but, if it is the child who is given responsibility over other children, it can often build a sense of superiority over others, not to mention a sense of resentment. Regardless, if the child was raised by a codependent, depressive, or dysfunctional parent, being required to take on operational responsibilities within the family is almost a guarantee. Being given the responsibility to take care of younger siblings or the family as a whole when such a child feels it's unfair or an infringement on their own life, a tendency to adopt a tone with others that talks "at them" rather than "to them" can emerge. Otherwise, they may carry an underlying sense of resentment toward others who are "needy." Regardless, despite the underlying feeling of resentment (most likely toward others), children being held accountable for duties which may have involved caring for other children will tend to present a grandiose sense of self as an adult - often regarded as "bossy." Other M-Based ASPD characteristics which are likely to emerge are a lack of empathy and entitlement.

Additional inappropriate responsibilities need not require taking care of siblings either. Other household duties or operational functions which are inappropriate for children to be held responsible for fall under this umbrella. Essentially, it requires the child to be more "grown up" than age-appropriate. An example of this would be a child who has to drop out of school and take a job due to the family's poor household income.

It needs to be mentioned here that - instead of the "grandiose" sense of self seen in NPD, the self-important demeanor is more out defiance and irritation born out of obligation rather than willingness.

Addictions to Narcissistic Supply/Ego Inflation (NPD, M-Based ASPD)

Harkening back to this book's introduction, it was discussed how parents tend to give that which they didn't receive growing up.

For the narcissistic child of a codependent parent, this comes in the form of being psychologically amplified and placed on a pedestal. The child is "so cute!", "so smart!", "so talented!", "so wonderful!", "so good!", as so on. The problem is, if it's over-the-top excessive, such positive reinforcement is like crack to the child. Imagine walking into a room and watching everyone stop what they were doing to adulate you. To an adult it might feel strange, but to a child who knows nothing different, life's a party. Only a very precocious child would be saying to themselves, "Ehhh…that really ain't me…not so much."

But when raised in an early environment where this sort of party doesn't stop (and the first seven years are the most formative of a person's life), it's easy for the child to accept this as reality. It *is* their reality, in fact, and such a reality will assist them greatly in life as they get older. When they enter school and the workplace, the self-concept that they are "wonderful," "preferential," or belonging to a higher status will likely be perceived by others as being true. There's a high probability that success, popularity, recognition, and/or accolades will be in their future.

The problem is, this grandiose (or, at least, elevated) sense of self is like a car that needs gas, but here the car is the ego and the gas is narcissistic supply. Without the gas, the car most likely is not going to go far.

Questions then arise such as "how many octanes is the car used to?" "How many miles per gallon for the particular vehicle?" Or, "Is the narcissistic supply the narcissist accustomed to akin to worship?"   More importantly, "Do all of our 'vehicles' *need* gas?" They probably do to some degree. Perhaps some us are "electric" and require less "fuel."

The answers to these questions, I suppose, are purely subjective. However, rest assured: if a narcissist stops at your "gas station" and the quality and/or quantity of "gas" available isn't enough, it's going to be a while before they visit your station again, if at all. This is part of the reason behind the prototypical "Idealize, Devalue, Discard" cycle so many of you are aware of that is commonplace to narcissistic behavior. This cycle will be discussed in a later chapter in greater detail.

Make no mistake, though: codependents run on their own fuel source, which is *sympathy and attentiveness*.

They, too, are likely to embark on their own version of Idealize, Devalue, and Discard cycling sprees if their stations run out of feeling sorry for them or aren't overly attentive.

Whereas the narcissist would benefit from providing their own self-worth, the codependent would benefit from providing their own self-compassion. Actually, I'll correct myself here: *Both parties would benefit from providing themselves their own self-worth and self-compassion and ween themselves off from others as supply, but not cut themselves off completely - this would make them anti-social.*

"I'm trying to save you!" (M-Based ASPD)

Because the narcissist-to-be child was seen as a savior to their parent's woes, this is both a blessing as a curse for the young one. On one hand, they're provided with the sense of
being special which benefits them as they proceed in life; on the other, it's highly possible that a feeling of inadequacy is planted since the child is being tapped to be *the* source of support for the adult.

The latter is devastatingly heartbreaking when you think about it. Imagine the disappointment and alarming sense of futility a little kid would feel if they were asked to lift a hundred pounds off the ground to save mommy - or at least to make her happy - only to feel an immense sense of disappointment, frustration, anger, panic, and inadequacy when they're unable to do so. Only the "weight" in this case may be mommy's depression that, in some cases, may be so acute she may be struggling with her will to live. In such cases, the only way a young child - who was given the expectation that they were special by that same parent - would be able to cheer the parent up is to act out the cute, sunny, charming, playful kid role they were cast in rather than mitigate their parent's psychological distress, which they would have had no chance in hell in being successful at doing.

To the small child in this scene, the source of love (albeit excessive in some cases) is fading and the child is taking it personally. In truth, this is an impossible fate for the child since *every* child from ages zero to seven has *no choice but* to rely on the responses (or lack thereof) from other people in their lives as feedback for their sense of self. It is actually crucial for their survival and growth.

Have you ever been on a date or met someone who was interested in you and the "conversation" between you was more like a monologue or a "Me spree" on their part? Either they kept talking about themselves or steered the conversation back to them? If they *did* ask you a question about yourself, did they start talking about themselves before you could answer or while you were answering? If so, it's possible that it's a childhood relic behavior of the tragic dynamic described above. It's a panic-driven response to their fears of being abandoned and unloved. At the very least, this sort of behavior is an attempt by the adult to receive love or be seen as lovable *because they were loved conditionally as a grandiose self while being raised.*

I'm sure many of you have heard that narcissists have poor self-esteem. Oftentimes, the reason a M-Based ASPD puffs up their grandiosity is fear-based, and the above is an example of this. Usually, this display of grandiosity is due to the addictive tendency of the excessive self-worth disposed upon them by one or both parents. When feeling low-self worth (usually because the false self is waning), the M-Based ASPD may default on grandiosity in order to conjure the "narcissistic supply drug" to anesthetize the feelings of inferiority (which, in truth is usually mediocrity, but this is a harmful realization to
the narcissistic mindset.)

Offense Mechanisms (NPD, M-Based ASPD)

<u>This subheading is of utmost importance, because this is probably the most important information contained in this book:</u> In *The Toxic States of America,* I discuss how malignant narcissists use what I refer to as "Offense Mechanisms" to mitigate their "issues." *Because their codependent parent showered them with extraneous spoiling and empathy-spoiling - to the point where the love in the form of* *attentiveness, nurturing, and support with self-worth - or ego-child never learned to develop any of this or manage this on their own, the malignant narcissist will subsequently blame the "parent" when their "self-love" (or "self-image" or "self-concept") erodes, falters, or needs repair and/or requires the "parent" to fix it.*

This is also compounded during times when the codependent parent - experiencing any bouts of depression - "dropped the ball" and neglected the needs of the child.

The "parent" in this case is anyone who provides this sort of care or "narcissistic supply," be it a close friend, an actual parent or, most importantly, a romantic partner.

Again, the "issues" or schemas we face as human beings are as follows: *Unlovability (or Defectiveness), Deprivation, Subjugation, Mistrust, Vulnerability, Abandonment, Failure, Perfectionism, Exclusion, Entitlement.*

*Because the codependent parent took it upon themselves and "self-loved" the child for them too much for too long instead of weening them off and teaching them how to "fly solo" (that is, learn how to love themselves and "self-sooth"), the adult child will blame **others** for their feelings of Unlovability, Deprivation, Subjugation, Mistrust, Vulnerability, Abandonment, Failure, Perfectionism, Exclusion, Entitlement.*

Not only does this condition *- provided it was overinflated by the original parent -* **require external support in the form of Narcissistic Supply to maintain, but also Scapegoats when it breaks down.**

The reliance on the Grandiose Sense of Self (and need for Narcissistic Supply) and a Scapegoat source to mitigate unresolved "issues" emerge as the narcissist's "Offense Mechanisms." Offense mechanisms involve "Over-compensating" (defaulting on the Grandiose/False Self), "Projecting" (superimposing the issues onto others), or both.

So, with Over-compensation, they will do something like boast about their IQ when they feel weak in their intelligence (in order to implant the "Oh, Honey! You're so smart!" inner-monologue within a second party so that the other party is groomed to be a source of narcissistic supply.) They'll attach and control when they experience feelings of abandonment. They'll broadcast about past accomplishments when they feel like a failure, and so on. *The Over-compensating Component is born out of either the codependent parent's over-indulgence of the child's self-concept (Grandiose Self) or the inability for such a child to be self-reliant in generating self-worth or both. (Most likely, it's both.) "Mommy (or Daddy) told me I was over-the-top wonderful, so I need you to agree or make me feel that way because I don't right now. If you don't, you're 'no good' and it's your fault."*

As mentioned before in Chapter 2 under the Maternal-based ASPD subheading, this is also due to stave off potential Abandonment. That is, "if I 'appear attractive,' that means 'I won't be left and will be loved.'" It also means that the "love" in the forms of ego- and empathy-spoiling they derived so much benefit from during their childhood years will continue. But the "loving" comes from someone else, not from the self, because the ego was spoiled to the extent to which it *requires* others to prop up in the future.

With *Projection*, if the Cluster B feels stupid, they'll make other people feel stupid. If they feel incompetent, they'll make other people incompetent. If they feel betrayed, they'll betray others, and so on. Causing others to feel worse "helps" them "feel better." Also,it's someone else fault they feel bad about themselves. Consequential smear campaigns toward the "parent" who "made them feel bad" are likely to ensue since they consider someone else responsible for the appearance of their "issues" or at least not being "attentive *to* them." The Projection Component arises out of *withdrawal* from the Grandiose Self (the enhanced "self-image" the mother or father created and enhanced) because they faced periods of neglect and abandonment during their childhoods which have not yet been healed.

"No! It's you who's stupid because you're not here to make me feel smart!" "It's YOU who's ugly because you're not here to tell me I'm pretty." "You're not here for me, so I'm not here for you!" "It's YOUR fault I don't feel better."

Basically, it's "Fuck you Mommy (or Daddy) for not being here to make me feel better." But, again, this is an *adult* we're talking about.

Here, it's easy to see the Abandonment schema at play.

This mechanism was articulated earlier in Chapter 2 under the "Maternal-based ASPD" section; it's worth reiterating here since it's a keystone of this pathology. Once the child feels Abandoned, any subsequent negative feelings which arise become the neglecting parent's fault: "*You abandoned me, so **you're** bad,*" with "bad" referring to any negative feelings the child feels as a result of being neglected or abandoned, whether or not neglect or abandonment actually happened. Mentally speaking, this "projection" is essentially automatic *precisely* because of the close bond the child feels with said parent, and the close bond itself is due to being overly pampered, preferred, spoiled, etc. by said parent for too long. Psychologically speaking, the child may not have been permitted to "distance" themselves from said parent, especially when considering the parent may have been highly codependent themselves.

As adults, NPD's and Maternal-based ASPD's will crave a sort of reenactment of this tight, intimate, and proximal "bond" since it *was* and *felt* so loving (and it *was, albeit spoiling)* which is precisely what codependents *crave* (since they've went so long without being loved and have been essentially *starved.*) However, anytime "Abandonment" enters the picture, whether it is real or perceived reasonably or unreasonably (the latter due to being *spoiled)*, the narcissist will lash out at the codependent by means of projection.

With this, it's easy to understand why the typical "Idealize, Devalue, Discard" cycle Cluster B's subject their partners to takes place. *They feel neglected, abandoned, and betrayed by their source of love and they're retaliating. This is more like a parasite who realizes that there's nothing left for them to feed off from the host. They meant nothing to you (because you didn't spoil them), so now you mean nothing to them.*

In truth, this is hardly the case, but the wounds of resentment certainly help to convince them otherwise.

In light of this, it's easy to see why some narcissists are heartless and ruthless when they "discard." If they assault you with a salvo of insults, invectives, or character assassinations during this stage, this is representative of the same psychological state the child had when they were abandoned. It's worth mentioning here as well that this "tight, intimate, and proximal" bond may not have been there and that the "Abandonment" was so extreme it was traumatic. Most likely, the"projection" in this instance is going to take the form of some sort of *abuse.* Such would be the case behind spousal abuse, where the abuser *did* experience acute abandonment or neglect at the hands of a parent with whom a close bond *was not* well formed during their childhood. Episodes in their adult years where similar or reminiscent scenes appear are likely to trigger such acute reactions. In short, with *Over-compensation* and *Projection,* they'll *either deny their inner hell by pretending they're in Heaven and having you agree* or *project their inner hell onto you or others to feel better, respectively.*

Codependents face the same issues but, instead of the over-compensating and projecting character of Offense Mechanisms, they default on Defense Mechanisms which involved internalizing and/or avoiding such issues. This will become more clear in a later chapter.

What's for Dinner? (NPD, M-Based ASPD)

To help out with the material presented in the preceding subheading, think about "love" in the form of attentiveness, nurturing, and provisions to self-worth to be like food. Try to see how things like praise, compliments, accolades, and mental and emotional and soothing to "issues" are like different kinds of nourishing food. You've got protein-based foods of "praise" to build self-confidence, "complimenting" fruits and vegetables to provide "vitamins" and "minerals" to nourish self-worth, healthy soups to sooth "issues," and "desserts" in the form of accolades.

Growing up, many narcissists never went without this kind of "food." In fact, the "meals" they were given were probably pretty big and hearty. As time went on and they got older, they were still getting great meals - *feasts* in some cases.

If and when breakfast, lunch, or dinner *didn't* appear on the table [abandonment or neglect] they were probably thinking, "What's going on? Where's my food?" If, per chance, they went without for the day or more than one day, "What the hell? I thought you loved me?" If it's been a week and they're literally starving, "I hate you, mommy! [Literally] Die!" (or trauma-based abandonment and neglect.)

If they're grown-up children and can't "cook" for themselves, they're always going to be looking for the next great "cook." Plus, if "mommy" falls short in her "culinary abilities," he's going to seek out a better chef and, hopefully, one who provides a delicious breakfast, lunch, and dinner everyday in every way for the rest of his life - but *that* chef is going to burn out pretty quickly.

They will go through life seeking out others to prepare their meals for them (their "self-worth," "self-confidence," "self-love," etc. (all in quotes because there's nothing "self-generated" about it) until they learn to "cook" for themselves.

They may respond to this angrily by saying, "I need that fuel and nourishment so I can be strong enough to go out into the world and earn a living so I can buy the damn food for you to make my meals as well as other things!"

They're right in a sense: this sort of "nourishment" in the form of self-worth, self-confidence, and efficacy *is* absolutely needed in order to be successful let alone survive. But again, for the Narcissistic personality type there's nothing "self" about it - it's always "prepared" by someone else. And not that there's anything wrong with this whatsoever. In fact, it's very difficult to proceed through life without having people in our lives who love us and give us that boost. We'd be antisocial if we didn't. But, part of the problem behind the Narcissistic personality type is they never "cook" for themselves - or for others.

And this could very well be a reason there is animosity on codependents' behaves toward narcissists: they're resentful of the fact that narcissists received "food" while growing up and they did not.

If they have reoccurring issues of unlovability, failure, deprivation, abandonment, subjugation, perfectionism, exclusion, vulnerability, mistrust, and entitlement, they're going to need to be "fed" a lot. (To understand why these issues arise, please revisit Chapter 2 and the descriptions for NPD and Maternal-based ASPD.) If they're "hungry" and these "hunger pains" aren't "fed," they're liable to make others "feel their pain" - usually through narcissistic rage or projection. Perhaps worse than this is when they *are* fed ample food but insist on more and more and more.

They may even "steal other people's food" and engage in "self-worth vampirism." Making other people feel stupid when they feel stupid becomes the source of their diet, just as a vampire sustains himself off of the blood of people.

The codependent has the opposite problem. Growing up, nobody "fed" them. Or, they were fed food with no nutritional value whatsoever.

Instead of being told they were "good," "smart," "handsome," "pretty," "talented," "lovable," "strong," "adequate, "precocious," "wise,"or "a pleasure to be around," it was radio silence.

Worse, the food was junk food or poisonous: they were fed that they were "stupid," "bad," "gullible," "flawed," "weak," "ugly," "no good," and "a nuisance." If they had older siblings who fed them this in addition to their parents, their health was liable to deteriorate more as a result unless they learned to protect themselves and refuse to eat this crap.

Such codependents are susceptible to provide nutritious food to others later in life with the hope that they'll be grateful, reciprocate, and nourish them back. There's nothing wrong with this whatsoever, but if they're used to being around narcissists, they're going to wind up disappointed and malnourished if not poisoned.

Worse, if and when the codependent *does* receives nutritious food from someone else, they may be so accustomed to going without, receiving it puts them into a state of confusion. Moreover, they may have developed a disdain for receiving such nutritious food because of their association with malignant narcissists, who not only expect such food but even demand it while not appreciating it and, subsequently, don't reciprocate it because of a history of being overindulged. Because of this, many codependents have adopted a persona of humility because, to them, receiving or even expecting or demanding such nutritious food is equivalent to being the quintessential asshole - shaped by their perception of the narcissistic personality type because of the reason just given in the sentence preceding this one. What most codependents don't realize, however, is that the narcissist's lack of appreciation and reciprocity is based upon a childhood involving overindulgence and feelings of abandonment and neglect when the overindulgence ceased.

But, it's in the codependent's best interest to get over this and either get good food from someone else or learn how to "cook" for themselves. Their quality of life won't be good unless they do. Otherwise, they're going to resemble the motherless monkey who's bonded with a blanket and shrivel up. Part of the codependent's aversion to doing so is rooted in their own childhood upbringing when they were conditioned to equate "low-maintenance" with being "good."

As they go through life, such a codependent may be fortunate enough to come across others who genuinely care about the monkey's "starvation" and try to "feed" it. If they don't due to the reason given in the previous paragraph - that is, "eat" the "food" out of believing "low-maintenance" is "good" - they'll continue to perish slowly.

If a malignant narcissist comes across the monkey, the wilted state of the animal will remind them of the depression behind the periodic episodes of neglect and abandonment of *their* "cook" and - instead of having compassion - will resent the monkey, if not mistreat it.

Empathy for the Grandiose Self (NPD, M-Based ASPD)

What do I mean by this? I'll share a personal story. When I was a freshman in college, I had to make some changes to my curriculum which caused me to enter into an elective writing seminar course about a week or two late. I was given the assignment - which was a bit vague - but managed to complete it by the time the rest of the class did.

When I received my first draft back, I was astonished with the results. Not only was there not a single negative comment on my work, but the professor wrote - verbatim - that it belonged in an anthology!

Really! And it went on: copious amounts praise ensued without an iota of constructive feedback. Naturally, I didn't think there was much - if anything - to do in order to improve upon it. I was reluctant to, actually, since I feared it might ruin it. As far as my personal value, my confidence as a writer increased, especially since I was a science major.

You can imaging my surprise and let down when, upon receiving the second and final draft back, the grade I received was mediocre. This was hardly the expectation I was given based on the feedback I received. Needless to say, I was rather let down by the result. Narcissistic personalities will face this kind of scenario in life but, for them, it hits closer to home since their self-concept is based on it.

At some point, if they perceived themselves as "special," "superior," or "better than others" (usually because they were given that impression), reality is going to serve them a bitter piece of humble pie (or a whole humble pie in the face, in some cases.) And this happens to most of us to some degree. But when this expectation is based on the environment one was raised in, possibly since birth - our *identity* - this can be a huge blow. To me, this is deserving of some compassion.

For the some malignant narcissists, it's probable that they were placed on a pedestal by a codependent parent who, standing at the pedestal's base, acted as the child's cheering squad. That is, they were inappropriately ego-spoiled, just like I was in the writing seminar. Provided the child was young at the time (and they most likely were), doing so is actually a form of disservice, especially likely were), doing so is actually a form of disservice, especially if the hero worship was excessive. Because the bar was raised so high with respect to their sense of self as at such an early age, the child will be bound to experience great distress when they're not able to maintain the bar at that level as they grow older. This will certainly be a crippling factor as they age into adulthood when the beauty, intelligence, or other aptitude starts to fade.

Otherwise, on a subconscious level, the narcissist may know that their grandiose self is false, or at least a role they relentlessly try to inhabit, depending on their level of self awareness. Coming to terms with this isn't a cake walk, and it may be akin to a hamster on a wheel - it keeps running but never gets anywhere. The effort to maintain this illusion will, at some point, grow tiresome - perhaps even impossible: the hamster either stops running or it suffers a heart attack. The realization that "the party's over and not coming back" is a gruesome realization: it's more like a mid-life catastrophe than a crisis. But, the understanding that the true self is eternal - and unconditionally lovable - will hopefully replace this rude awakening.

Cult of Personality (NPD)

Especially if the bar that was their self-concept was raised at an extreme level while growing up - thanks to "ego-spoiling" - malignant narcissist adult will likely gravitate toward positions of gravitas as they get older. I'm sure many of you can think of certain politicians or CEOs who have a god-like image or self-concept. Overindulging the child's ego at such a young age is bound to cause the later-in life narcissists to perceive prestigious positions as "prizes" when get older. It's typical for narcissists to gravitate to powerful and prestigious positions within academia, politics, law, etc. Not only does it boost their ego, but it can satiate their power and control proclivities as well.

Hypersensitivity to Cognitive Dissonance (NPD, M-based ASPD)

Someone with a grandiose sense of self will assuredly have an adverse reaction if/when life reflects back any feedback contrary to their grandiose sense of self. A mother may ask, "How's the cake I made?" (believing it to be the cake of all cakes.) "It's good!" responds her child. The feedback, not being something akin to "This is the best goddamn cake in the country and those neighboring it, Mother!" this sends the mother into a snit. This is a stupid, hypothetical example, but you get the point.

COPING STRATEGIES FOR DEALING WITH THE NARCISSISTIC GRANDIOSE SENSE OF SELF:
- *"Observe, don't absorb"*: With any "coping strategy," whether is grandiose sense of self or another trait, "non-judgement observation" is going to be my first suggested method. "Observe, don't absorb" not only prevents us from taking on any negative energy, it can actually allow you to see the pain behind the behavior. They may even recognize it and, in some cases, share it with you. By observing "the grandiose sense of self," examining it with a fresh pair of eyes will likely reveal causes behind it to you as well as the person exhibiting the behavior.
- *"Take the Center Lane"*: As much as I hate to admit it (or do I? Yeah, I guess I do… Hell, who am I kidding? No, I don't), when I historically came across a personality type who had a propensity to broadcast a grandiose sense of self - to put themselves on a pedestal - I usually found a way to kick the pedestal out from under them. Without the

help of a finishing school, I'm proud to say I've changed my tune (a bit.) It is not the fault of the Cluster B that they were raised to view themselves as "special" or "superior." My recommendation here is not to inflate or denigrate the false self of the Cluster B: *simply **take the middle road** by treating the Cluster B as normally as you would anyone else without indulging or (like me) whittling down the Grandiose Self. In order words,* **"With Narcissistic Supply, don't give, but don't deprive."** In doing so, they may respect you more (than those who provide narcissistic supply) and you won't regret hurting them if you kick their pedestal away. By taking the middle road, it may actually become evident to the Cluster B that they're "self" is grandiose and they may tone it down on their own without any pedestal-kicking.

- *"Kick them off the pedestal":* I don't suggest this from the start, but if they consistently take center stage with everything, drop a sandbag on their head. If they're always putting themselves on a pedestal, shorten the pedestal or take it away completely. Thisis best accomplished through *ridicule.* By *making fun of them,* this helps to deflate their inflated ego.
- *Use these interactions to build your own self-value:* If you're dealing with a "have," this tends to mean "you deserve." The narcissist needs to lower their pedestal (on their own) and you deserve to have yours raised (by yourself.) If they have more money, that means you deserve more. If they have a better career, you deserve one just as good. If they talk about themselves a lot, you deserve to be listened to more, and so on. If it isn't equal, make it that way. If the narcissist doesn't comply, simply go away, but take your self-value with you.
- *Empathy:* For God's sake, if a narcissistic Cluster B personality ever opens up to you about the problems they faced during childhood, please express your support. Whether unrealistic expectations were made of them or they were required to perform duties either atypical or burdensome for a child of their age, you don't have to carry their cross but please express your empathy. I'm big on the Golden Rule and, deep down, all of us want to be valued and understood. Doing so will lessen their symptoms as well as your plight if you have no other choice but to share a space with them.
- *Set Boundaries:* Hopefully you won't need to do this after "Observe, Don't Absorb" and "I'm Okay, You're Okay." But, if the self-promotion is excessive, set a boundary. My recommendation is using "truth mechanisms." In this case, simply say: "You seem to think quite highly of yourself." Or, "Are you going to keep talking about yourself?"
- *"Go No-Contact":* If possible, and if excessive and unrelenting after "smiling and nodding" and treating them with "I'm okay, you're

okay," you may wish to consider going "no contact." This is a commonly suggested approach to Cluster B's, but not always an option. More about this option will be discussed later.

RED FLAGS:
- You get the consistent sensation that "it's their world, and you're living in it."
- It's all about them and never about you.
- High personal pronoun density on their end: "I," "me," "mine," "my," "myself."
- They put you down to prop themselves up: or "light you on fire to keep themselves warm."
- They talk "at you" rather than "to you."
- There's evidence of hypersensitivity to cognitive dissonance with respect to inflated/grandiose sense of self.
- They superimpose their shortcomings/issues that the Grandiose/False Self (fragile ego) shields themselves from: aka "Offense Mechanisms."
- Lack of sexual attraction/activity within relationships.

CHILDHOOD CONDITIONS CREATING A GRANDIOSE SENSE OF SELF:
- Parented with over-amplified self-concept or "ego-spoiled."
- Being overindulged with self-worth and praise by parent(s) or family.
- Tapped as a source of psychological support they were incapable of/too young to/too inexperienced to accommodate.
- Raised in an environment where they were given preferential status.
- Inhabited "Golden Child" role within dysfunctional family.

UNDERLYING ISSUES BEHIND THE GRANDIOSE SENSE OF SELF:
- Extraneous need for narcissistic supply
- Feelings of inadequacy/ineffectualness
- Low self-worth
- Entitlement issues
- Abandonment issues
- Unlovability Issues
- Addictions to reliance on narcissistic supply

- Being objectified
- Animosity toward depressive personalities

4

<u>*Lack of Empathy and Emotional Support*</u>

Q: "Do you think these pants make my butt look big?"
A: "I think your butt makes those pants look big."

"Lack of Empathy" vs. "Antipathy" (NPD, M-Based ASPD, BPD)

Before proceeding with any material regarding this chapter's subject, it must be said that the NPD and potential ASPD "Lack of empathy" is actually ironic: they *are* able to employ empathy, but it's usually used for the wrong reasons. This characteristic suggests that these types are *incapable* of empathizing with someone else. They *can, but prefer to dispense whatever empathy they're capable of employing onto themselves.* That is, they empathize primarily with *themselves* and expect or demand others to do the same. What's usually behind the limited or absent observational empathy and emotional support from such individuals is *not* a neurological or genetic impairment: these types *absolutely* have the ability to empathize with others. They're just not in the habit of doing so.

In the case of NPD, *the culprit behind this is childhood "empathy-spoiling." Here, the child is not only dosed with high-octane empathy from their caretaker(s) way too much and way too long, the child is trained not to return it or empathize with someone else.* In short, it truly is "all about them" since they were raised that way. In truth, they are literally stuck in the Adult-toddler phase. It's fine - and appropriate - to *exclusively* care about a child's feelings and emotions when they are little. At this stage in their life, they're young, vulnerable, and not strong enough to care for someone else or themselves on their own. But, *if they grow into adulthood* (notice I didn't write "mature into adulthood") *and it's still "all about them" in which others need to tend to them **while they** not only don't care about others **but find it as burdensome as a toddler would** (and should) - **that is an adult toddler.** They are literally expecting the same treatment which is age-appropriate for a toddler: "Care about ME,* *it's all about ME, I can't take care of YOU."*

The only other possibility for the above motto would stem from someone who gave so much of themselves already, it's reached the critical stage where self-focus, attention, and a *requirement* to say "no" to others became mandatory for self-preservation. Such would be the case for a codependent or BPD.

Another basis for the lack of empathy and emotional support is a victim mentality rooted in abandonment or neglect (M-Based ASPD), and/ or the withdrawal of narcissistic supply from a reliable source (NPD.) The latter of which is oftentimes due to another party's attempts at gaining attention or deriving support from the malignant narcissist. If moral support is sought from the narcissist, this will most likely conjure disdain - again, due to a victim mentality which exploits Abandonment issues (whether real or imagined) to make it "all about them" or they've been spoiled and conditioned to act this way due to a sense of Entitlement.

The psychological mechanism behind the above is this: the empathic capabilities of narcissistic individuals *are active*, but they're redirected onto *themselves*. Again, this is due to a long-lasting history of being *empathized with* and never *empathizing toward* - in short, empathy-spoiled. They "hurt so bad" that *all* of their empathy "*must*" be focused upon themselves: it's the "poor me" on steroids. The narcissist's victim mentality - whether justifiable or not - not only usurps and absorbs their own emotional awareness onto themselves, but *demands* the empathy and emotional attention of others *to such an extent* that the narcissist feel justified in robbing other parties of theirs through whatever psychological violence they deem "appropriate." This "appropriation" is *completely* proportional to the volume to which the narcissist's victim mentality is dialed to. This "psychological violence" takes the form of what is known as "narcissistic injury" or "narcissistic rage" (or the adult-version of temper tantrums.) In short, the victim card is played to such a degree, not only is it exploited to *demand* empathy from others, it absolves them from providing any empathy toward others since it's regarded as a "self-righteous nuisance." "*My* cup is empty; I don't need to care about *yours*. *You* need to fill *mine!*" - but this is even *after* theirs has been filled.

If it sounds like a selfish, immature, self-involved, self-pitying, attention-demanding, tantrum-throwing adult-version of a toddler, that's because it is. The only thing is, a toddler who is vulnerable and dependent *requires* this to a certain extent. The behavior of a self-infantilized adult who behaves this way is outdated.

For example, say Sarah and Mike are a couple. Sarah is

accustomed to talking about herself substantially more than Mike, who's usually more quiet and supportive. Mike listens to Sarah's likes, dislikes, opinions, and problems quite often. He also supports her wishes and desires and provides an attentive ear when things aren't going her way. With her trials and tribulations, Mike offers Sarah his support. One day, Mike experiences a nasty interaction with one of his coworkers who simultaneously took credit for his work and blame-shifted her incompetence and mistakes onto him. When he gets home and vents to Sarah about his experience, Sarah, who expects Mike to listen to her, not only finds this disdainful, but wonders why Mike is talking about himself and not her as per usual. Irritated by this, Sarah tells Mike that he should see a therapist.

Another example is an employee who goes to work a bit unhappy. The night before, she found out her boyfriend was cheating on her and broke up with him. Because she seems out of focus, her boss asks her if anything is wrong. When she confides in her about her boyfriend's infidelity, the reaction she receives is cold, refuting, and dismissive.

What's happening in both the case of Sarah and the employer is a hyper-sensitivity to anything either resembling the drain they experienced as children from a parent who was overly depressive or consistent childhood exposure to empathy- or attention-spoiling.

For a Maternal-based ASPD, withholding empathy and emotional support stems from a long-withstanding grudge against the neglectful or abandoning parent who relied on the child for excess sympathy or was ineffectual. Even if this "abandonment" took more of a form of deprivation, the narcissist will - with some degree of consciousness - withhold empathy or emotional support because, to them, they've been "gypped" in some way or another - usually in the form of attention, material, physical, and/or financial provisions. Since they know their target was deprived of empathy and emotional support growing up (and this usually was a depressive mother), depriving their targets of such support serves as a form of subconscious retaliation or resentment.

Otherwise, the aversion to providing empathy and support to others stems from "empathy-spoiling" or "ego-spoiling." Most often associated with NPD, such persons will feel disdain for and irritation toward the person who seeks support from them.

If the childhood abandonment was acute enough, this would propel the narcissist to react adversely and may result in mistreatment or abuse - thus falling under the "Lack of Remorse" category.

But this childhood neglect or abandonment may not have even

been logistic: it could very well be the case that the narcissist-to-be did in fact have a parent who was overly reliant on the child to provide emotional support and empathy to the point where the child's needs were eclipsed (this would be Maternal-based ASPD as described in Chapter 2.) The youngster may have even felt "drained" by the parent if the "poor-me parades" were excessive. However, as an adult, the narcissist is likely to be hypersensitive to anyone in distress since it triggers their early childhood experience and they subsequently have an adverse reaction. Even if the other party is simply "having a bad day" without tapping the narcissist for any sort of support, the adult version of this child will find it extremely irritating. Such persons present a demeanor that it's only okay if *they're* going through something and anyone else who might be is a pain in the ass. Heaven help the person who is actually experiencing some sort of crisis, catastrophe, trauma, or life-changing circumstances, because the narcissist is liable to make matters substantially worse.

The "covert narcissist" (we'll get into this "diagnosis" later in greater detail, especially since it's a recently coined term and *not* a condition listed in the DSM) - with their propensity to excessively play the victim far past any realistic needs for support - may very well be someone starved for empathy and emotional support while growing up. Here (and perhaps with the Grandiose Narcissist as well), the love, care, and respect goes only in one direction - theirs - and any attempts the other party makes to establish reciprocity will conjure irritability. At the very least, they will be confused because *they* were victimized when they didn't receive love, care, and respect so, because they were deprived, they *deserve*. And *they deserve* not to give it as well since *they* didn't receive it in the past. A good litmus test or psychological diagnostic to perform if you are suspecting that you're dealing with a narcissist is to deliberately go to them for empathy and emotional support. The covert narcissist will not provide it; instead, it will trigger them to vent about their own problems without an iota of recognition of yours. It's almost as if they're saying, "Well, no one was there for me either!" (And they're probably right!) The grandiose (and sometimes the covert as well) will find it incredibly irritating, in which case their feelings of disdain will be evident. In this case - and especially if the person has been spoiled or relies upon others to boost their self-esteem/ego - they may even seem taken aback since it's supposed to be about them, dammit!

Regardless, it needs to be emphasized that narcissists *absolutely* have the ability to provide empathy and emotional support; they just choose not to because of their victim mentality. If they did not have the ability to empathize, they would have no idea what "buttons to push" or have laser-like precision when it comes to emotionally hitting their targets "where it hurts" - which is usually below the belt and without any reservation. And, *if they did not have the ability to empathize and provide emotional support, they wouldn't have appeared this way during the early stages when you met them during the "mirroring stage."* It may even be the case that they *want* to treat you this way going forward with consistency, but their early-childhood issues of neglect and abandonment or withdrawals from excessive doses of narcissistic supply (or narcissistic injury from past encounters) prevent them from doing so. In all fairness, they may not be conscious of the "issues" behind their lack of empathy and emotional support. They may have a vendetta against "mommy," but it's in their subconsciousness.

"That's YOUR problem!" (NPD, ASPD, BPD)

The previous chapter touched upon the origin of the narcissistic trait of Lack of Empathy by examining how the codependent parent's excessive reliance on their young child as a source love in the form of attentiveness, nurturing, and/or support with respect to self-worth fostered a sense of resentment.

I know many readers have experienced something similar to the following: when met with a unfortunate situation, be it a relationship breakup, a layoff from a job, dealing with a highly toxic boss or coworker, or even a death of a friend or loved one, going to a narcissist for support not only backfires, it makes things worse. Instead of presenting a supportive, caring, or even acknowledging demeanor, it's one of irritation, dismissiveness, or disinterest. You may even feel like you've caused *them* to experience a loss in doing so.

This sort of reaction can even take on a passive-aggressive flavor. When I was little (ages five through nine), I had next to none of this kind of support when I was down, something was bothering me, or I was having a hard time with something. Knowing such support was not available, I tried to keep it to myself, if for any other reason, to spare myself any accompanying disappointment to that which was already bothering me. With respect to my mother, the repeat scenario went like this: If something was bothering me, my mother would ask me what was wrong. Knowing how she would react, I told her not to worry about it. She would then proceed with pressing me for the reason I was down and, eventually, I would cave in and tell her. "Well that's *your* problem!" was her canned response. My internal reply was, "Then why ask me?"

The causality behind this is described in the first paragraph of this chapter: as a child, the "Cluster B" had at least one parent (or family member or members) who was overly needy in this regard. Because the young child was drained by a "poor me" mother or father, he or she will grow up being hypersensitive to anything resembling it. Coupled with this is the "Cluster B's" sense that they are, in fact, being overly tapped since they're already providing support in other ways. In my mother's defense, she most certainly was - too much, in fact.

I Don't Get It (NPD)

The other factor to consider with such a parent/child relationship is the likelihood that the child was bestowed with copious amounts of attentiveness, nurturing, and/or support with respect to self-worth to the point where they don't understand the need for others to receive this sort of attention. Metaphorically speaking, a "rich kid" can't sympathize with what it's like to be poor let alone be charitable. This exacerbates the lack of empathy already
present.

But I'm Giving Already! (M-Based ASPD)

Recall back in Chapter 2 (subheading "Messiah Complex"), it was described how the inability of the depressive (or codependent) parent to adequately care for the child's physical, material, and financial necessities was supplemented by the child's requirement to assist, since this inflation of the child's ego and confidence by said parent fueled the child's efficacy and ability to perform. Since the child is already making this sort of contribution, taxing the child with additional requests (or demands, in some cases) to provide psychological, spiritual, or empathetic support to the parent(s) and/or others is bound to frustrate them.

This is akin to a family, say, back in the 1950s that has a father figure working an overly demanding job to "bring home the bacon" (the material support.) He gets home; "Hi, honey! How was your day?" asks the doting wife (nurturing support.) "Fine," he replies - and he's lying: he hates his job and wishes his wife would either pitch in or spend less. "How was yours?" (translation: "blabbity-blah-blah.")

If the wife even thinks about telling him about her personal problems, forget it. He's tired and, after a day of spending his energy trying to provide for his family, the last thing he wants to do is play therapist. If so, he's getting a drink or an affair on the side out of spite. Genuine empathy is the last thing that's coming out of him unless the wife thanks him for or at least acknowledges the contribution he's already making. Actually, empathy is almost guaranteed to come from him if the wife asks something like, "Is there anything I can do to help out?"

Now, by asking "How was your day?" the wife most likely will be under the impression that she's providing that support. However, this is probably not the kind of support the husband is looking for in this example - and this is based on his upbringing as it is with respect to hers.

Admittedly, this example is anachronistic, but I'm sure readers will be familiar with relevant cases in their own life.

What The Hell? (M-Based ASPD)

Please pick a number from six to eight. Now, imagine a little boy who's age is the number you picked. He's stranded at home, alone, hungry - starving, actually - because his single parent mother was out all night long bar-hopping. He's scared, angry, screaming, and breaking things out of protest. When he hits his mother when she finally gets home the next morning, she scolds him for being a "bad boy."

Now, pick one of the two numbers you didn't pick. That's the age of the little girl who wants her father to play with her, but he's passed out cold after downing a bottle of whiskey. She's alone and thinks her father doesn't love her. She's scared, panicked, and smacking her father, fearing that he may not wake up, and smacking him into lucidity isn't helping.

The last number is the age of a little boy who is trying to process his thoughts and emotions on his own, but her smothering nurturing is getting in the way, interrupting and frustrating him. He gets the feeling her "attentiveness" is more about herself and getting *her* needs met rather than his and he has a subsequent tantrum. Perhaps if she's "attentive" to him, he'll feel sorry for her. This is a repeat occurrence in his childhood.

As adults, the first child is likely to grow up and become a domestic abuser, seeking out irresponsible or negligent women and lash out at them as a result. The second will grow up attracting emotionally unavailable men - probably addicts - who catalyze panic and rage when they are emotionally cold, conjuring a disdain for men in general. The third adult-version of the child is likely to form relationships with women posing as "caretakers" when, in actuality, these women "wear their heart on their sleeve" and are looking to him to "carry their cross."

In all cases, a lack of empathy for those dealing with depression or addiction is likely to manifest when they mature into adulthood.

Ghosting (NPD, M-Based ASPD)

Severing ties with someone with whom we're in a failing relationship isn't easy or fun, especially if the other party had their heart invested to some degree. In my experience, I've learned the importance of ensuring that the other party feels both cared about and loved while ties are being severed. In calling a romantic relationship or marriage off, this sort of practice of presence and love is mandatory if there's a slightest chance that both parties can be civilized or friendly toward each other after the breakup. The party who's breaking things off would need to allow the emotions of the other party to release while setting boundaries if the other party gets offensive or out of line. Tears, anger, disbelief, and pleading tend to cycle from this party when they're told that things are coming to an end. Breaking up with someone who loved you can be one of the most difficult things to do, but offering them respect, patience, and care allows the other party to know that you in fact *do love them, but deep down inside, you know it needs to end.* If you treat the other party with love during the entire process, this can make the process much easier for everyone. The pain of feeling unloved can be difficult, especially if the other party did have genuine feelings for you. By knowing that you did - and still do - love them until the very end (and even past it) can allow the other party to remember you and your relationship with great appreciation and view it as a valuable experience.

This is, of course, provided the other party did not engage in abuse, maltreatment, or some form of infidelity, which some narcissistic personalities are and known and prone to engage in (and will be prone to engage in even if treated with love, care, and respect during the breakup process.) In such cases, they're liable to blame *you* for *their* transgressions. In these cases, cutting things off "quick and clean" is probably the best way to go about this. I'd suggest going "no contact" afterward and not allowing second chances.

However, the circumstances which many people experience are the opposite: here, the Cluster B personality is the one who's breaking things off and none of the above happens. Instead, the "dumped" party is subjected to the final stage of the "Idealize, Devalue, Discard" cycle and ruthlessly discarded without any sort of closure or compassion. Especially if the other party had their heart involved, this sort of acute abandonment can be devastating, not to mention heartless and cruel on the narcissist's part.

What's happening here is a reenactment of an abandonment episode the narcissist experienced during their own childhood when their parent was too depressed or lacking in self-love to care for the child who developed into a narcissist as an adult. This sudden and abrupt severance is the adult narcissist retaliating against their mother or father way back when during the time their parent did not take care of them, fostering a sense of abandonment in the narcissist child. Again, recall that narcissistic personalities tend to arise from parents' excessive adulation, love, and praise (pedestal pushing) of their child while simultaneously neglecting or abandoning their child's needs. This leads to the Grandiose Self qualities of the adult-child. The Grandiose Self along with Abandonment issues produce the lack of empathy, conscience, and remorse qualities the adult subsequently exhibits.

That being said, a narcissistic personality who performs such an abrupt, heart-stomping, and sometimes traumatizing end to a relationship is essentially revealing their own traumatic and unhealed experience with abandonment when they were a child. It's almost like a forced method of gaining empathy: the other party actually *feels* the anguish, helplessness, strandedness, anger, and betrayal the child-version of the narcissist went through during their early years. It *is* a projection of the narcissist's inner hell - remember: the childhood-origin thought process is, "It's *your* fault I feel bad. *Take it.*"

If the other party is an "empath," this can rupture their world and take a very long time to recover from. The advantage a child has over an adult is that they're more resilient; the disadvantage is the child has this narrative imprinted on their psyche and subconsciousness, causing them to treat others with a lack of empathy and emotional support. The adult-version is liable to go through life subjecting others to the same trauma they experienced as a child much like a "burn 'em and turn 'em" man-whore.

Oftentimes what the narcissist is doing (albeit subconsciously) is creating the circumstances which lead to neglect or distancing from the other party. That is, their unhealed Abandonment schema - having roots in being spoiled and/or neglected during childhood - causes their fear to manifest. Then, we have an escalation: after excessive control of the other party, the narcissist subsequently "discards" or "ghosts" their partner. The "discard" or "ghosting" is actually a rebuke of the other party for not tending to their Abandonment issue sufficiently (in the narcissist's mind, in most cases.) The narcissist subsequently "moves on" to another party where the drama cycle is repeated; the other party is put in the back of the "rolodex."

After "mommy" or "daddy" does "their time" alone for not taking care of the Adult-toddler sufficiently (while the narcissist cycles though other parties reenacting the same drama with the same ending), the Adult-toddler eventually cycles back and seeks to grant them access back into their life.

Infidelity (NPD, M-Based ASPD)

I'm sure many readers can identify with the sense of disbelief, anger, betrayal, and even shock they felt upon learning about their narcissist's cheating within a relationship, especially after they've given so much to both the narcissist and the relationship. The non-narcissistic partner is likely to be utterly baffled over the fact their demonstrative dedication was not only in vain but painfully unappreciated. Looking back in hindsight, they may realize they were in a complete no-win situation: catering to the narcissist's demands wasn't good enough and any boundaries they may have set weren't honored either. If they gave everything, it wasn't good enough. If they tried to be fair and balanced, that wasn't acceptable either. Basically, they're right: *nothing* they could have done differently or better would have prevented the narcissist from engaging in infidelity. Nothing *anyone* the narcissist is going to be involved with in the future is going to change this either, even if it's with another narcissist (they're liable to cheat more, actually.)

The only chance the narcissist *may* stay faithful would be the case where the other party was so balanced, so self-aware, and so self-loving to the point where they were an Ascended Master or something akin to one but even this probably wouldn't ensure monogamy. Their character would have probably made the narcissist envious which would have resulted in betrayal. In truth, such a person would have broke it off with the narcissist within a very short period of time.

If the other party gets the feeling that the tight rope is to thin to walk across to keep their narcissist's fidelity, they're absolutely correct. So why is this? There are a few reasons.

First, the narcissist needs a constant source of excitement, adoration, adulation, or some other form of narcissistic supply to maintain their interest. This is due to the spoiling one or both of their parents provided as a child - at the *very least* this was either ego-spoiling or empathy-spoiling. The adult version sees their potential partner as a drug and expects the drug to elicit these sorts of feelings in them. They want the

Mommy 2.0 drug where "mommy" never stops the narcissistic supply and the sense of excitement and novelty. If the drug fails, it's a bad drug and needs a replacement. If the partner is also a narcissist, the excitement may continue (along with childish selfishness), but the fact that both parties are selfish and expect to be catered *to*, this is going to end up with both parties cheating on each other - *a lot*. Otherwise, any time the drug falls short of stimulating the narcissist, the alternate solution is an exciting affair, cocaine, or both. (I wish I were joking.)

Second, the fact that they were ego-spoiled actually causes an addiction as well as commitment-phobia: they can't commit to anything monogamous because, basically, their inflated ego starts to drop. They'll start to get antsy, irritable, and frustrated regardless of how functional and fit their partner may be since their ego is used to getting a "novelty boost." They actually feel a rush over something *new,* and this is something they've grown accustomed to - the novelty of the new tryst itself provides the rush that they're looking for. So even if *one* partner provided a consistent stream or even a crescendo of narcissistic supply, it most likely would have never been enough.

Third, if the narcissist was parented by an excessively needy parent or one who relied on their child too heavily for emotional support, any inkling of such behavior from a future partner is going to be received by the narcissist as a turn off. Their hyper-sensitivity to the parent's neediness (which is a "downer" instead of a reason for concern) as a child gives the adult narcissist reason to retaliate with a third party (or more) as an adult. Their parent may not have been "needy" either; the parent could have "empathy-spoiled" them and/or never required the child to empathize with others let alone their parent(s.)

Because their partner (read: surrogate parent) fell short of being a constant "upper" by periodic "down" times, this is unacceptable. Being "down" and not providing the narcissist with excessive, persistent, and constant attention when, how, and to the extent narcissist wants it is equivalent to being defunct. The drug is not only bunk, it's producing the opposite effect it was intended to create.

Fourth, if the "drug" is not available, the narcissist goes elsewhere for the drug. It's really as simple as that. This is rooted,
again, in any residual animosity the narcissist feels towards the parent who abandoned them, whether that abandonment was logistical, psychological, or perceived as betrayal. And this depends on whether or not the narcissist was actually abandoned or neglected; they may have just stopped being spoiled.

Fifth is a lack of performance persistence - and it's completely unrealistic. Since narcissism usually involves objectifying others, the narcissist's partner, to them, is basically a robot: an entity who caters to their every whim and does whatever it needs to do and however it needs to get done without undergoing any sort of wear or deterioration. If the partner shows signs of weariness, tiredness, necessity to recharge, or aging, it's the partner who is flawed, not the narcissist's unrealistic expectations. The trophy partner is not only supposed to evade tarnish, it's supposed to make breakfast, lunch, dinner, shopping trips, clean, praise, provide undivided attention, fold laundry and more while all the while looking like a model and behaving like a cheerleader. But, again, this "robot" status is simply an updated version of the codependent, self-sacrificing parent - a person who allowed themselves to become a human doing instead of a human being. Otherwise, "Mommy" *deserves* to be punished for her inattentiveness, lack of proximity, lack of self-care, and more.

Sixth, if the narcissist has any early-onset experiences of parental abandonment - whether that involved being neglected, being required to adopt age inappropriate responsibilities, episodes of betrayal, or abandonment itself - the infidelity acts as a childish means of retaliation. Here, the "hurt people hurt people" meme is apparent.

For all the above reasons, the causes behind the perspective that promiscuous men are viewed as "studs" or "playboys" while promiscuous women are seen as "sluts" becomes more apparent. Since it's usually a mother placing her son on a pedestal or with whom he has a "special" relationship with, "her" lack of fidelity and self-worth (due to no one loving her) earn her "tramp status." But, again, I cannot stress enough: it needs to be taken into consideration that this sort of bond/dynamic extends to the child's infancy. Thus, the infantile behavior dates back to distress experienced while an infant.

In all cases, the narcissist has yet to empathize with the fact that their parent(s) and their future partner are human and have physical and psychological needs. It's guaranteed that the narcissist perceives the other party as an object, thing, or resource (think "Human Resources" of many corporate cultures) as opposed to a human like themselves (if that is in fact true.) This subtopic could easily be included in the chapter entitled "Lack of Remorse" that follows, but I've decided to include it here since it's basis is due to a lack of empathy.

So, when infidelity occurs, it's typically representative of the childhood-origin mindset where the child "gets back" at the parent for behaving or not behaving in a certain way and thus retaliates in the form of cheating. Since their partner is "Mommy 2.0," the narcissist's child self is the one reacting. Despite being an adult, the narcissist still has a "wounded child" psychology which is used to justify any instances of infidelity which, unfortunately, involves the petulance and rebelliousness their inner-child still feels.

COPING STRATEGIES FOR DEALING WITH THE MALIGNANT NARCISSIST'S LACK OF EMPATHY AND EMOTIONAL SUPPORT:

• *Childhood Origin Empathy:* "I bet it was hard growing up in a household where you were expected to take care of others' needs." A more generic version would be, "

• *Stop Giving:* If they're not going to provide you with the same emotional, mental, or psychological support you give them, stop giving it. Only start again if/when you start receiving it from them. Don't expect it to happen; it may never and it's not your problem.

• *Treat the Malignant Narcissist the Same Way They Treated You:* I only recommend this strategy in situations where you cannot go "no contact" with them and setting boundaries hasn't worked. If you are mistreated by a malignant narcissist and say your peace or set a boundary, their reaction is likely to be one of irritated dismissal. They may say you're "over-reacting" or "being too sensitive." *If they can't empathize, make them sympathize*. Treat them the same way and, when they have the same adverse reaction as you, tell them they're "over-reacting" or "being too sensitive." Trust me: they won't like it, but they'll get the point.

• *Vocalize Your Inner Critic:* In order to prevent any entanglements with malignant narcissists, it's helpful to deactivate conditions which may provide the fodder. It's been discussed already how depressed personality types who neglected or abandoned them helped shaped "the monster." Therefore, it's crucial that we address our own "issues" which create this depression. Usually, this is due to a negative monologue criticizing the self. By speaking this monologue out loud, "I'm stupid," "I'm ugly," "I'm fat,""Nobody loves me, " etc., we see not only how absurd these mantras are, but sometimes where they came from! If we keep telling ourselves that we're "ugly," this is usually due to someone in our early years - a parent, sibling, "friend," - implanting this upon us when we were vulnerable and impressionable.

RED FLAGS:

- Apathy and/or disdain when seeking emotional, psychological, or mental support.
- Support hypocrisy: Your hand is giving, but your other hand isn't receiving.
- Inability or unwillingness to relate to your circumstances.
- They have a "do as I say, not as I do" philosophy.
- They treat you in a way in which they would not want to be treated.
- Their definition of the Golden Rule is "They're Golden, they Rule."
- Belittling, deprecating, and humiliating treatment of others.
- Hypersensitivity to perceived slights, lack of attentiveness, or lack of indulging the "false self."
- Sporadic and unprovoked outbursts of anger or rage.
- Displays of inexplicable irritation, frustration, and agitation.

CHILDHOOD CONDITIONS CREATING A LACK OF EMPATHY AND EMOTIONAL SUPPORT:

- Being raised in an environment of neglect and abandonment, sometimes severe
  enough to induce trauma.
- Being required to take on excessive responsibilities.
- Being "empathy-spoiled" as a child.
- Not being required to empathize with others while being raised, especially parents.
- Parental physical and emotional abuse coupled with
  parental enabling.

UNDERLYING ISSUES BEHIND A LACK OF EMPATHY AND EMOTIONAL SUPPORT IN THE CLUSTER B:

- A feeling of being uncared for.
- A feeling of being inferior.
- Feelings of contempt and retaliation for being inferior and not being cared about.

5

Demeaning, Bullying, and Belittling Behavior

"If you want a picture of the future, imagine a boot stamping on a human face—forever."

- George Orwell

Black Mirror (NPD, M-Based ASPD)

I'm sure many readers can relate to a situation where, when they needed empathy and emotional support, they received the exact opposite. They may have even "vented out loud" - not even looking to anyone for support - and received an adverse reaction.

In other cases, they may just be going through some "stuff" and trying to keep this to themselves, yet even *this* conjures berating, belittling, or deprecating comments from a narcissistic personality type.

An example of this is the bully-target dynamic, where one kid, perhaps shy, reserved, or keeps to themselves, catalyzes the bully's physically and psychologically torturing behavior. In adult versions, the "bully" may somehow "know" the target's "weakness" and use the respective "issue" as a springboard for psychological assault.

Why is this? More specially, *how* is this? How does this particular personality type seem to "know" which buttons to push or vulnerabilities to exploit?

The answer is quite simple: years and years and years of conditioning, particularly with a parent who had similar "issues" to the target. Such malignant narcissists are not "smart" nor do they possess a "sixth sense" or anything of that nature. The reason behind their adverse reactions is rooted in the childhood-origin circumstances they faced as a result of any neglect and abandonment they received from their parent while they were in a depressive state. If the conditions were extreme, the malignant narcissist's response to other people's "issues" If the conditions were extreme, the malignant narcissist's response to other people's "issues" may be wildly disproportionate because, as a child, the resulting conditions were extreme. This is also the causality behind their hypersensitivity to others' "issues" as well: as children, this hypersensitivity developed as a survival mechanism. If they don't lash out at mommy for being so "bummed out" as to forget to make them dinner, they'll starve.

Also, another reason for malignant narcissist's reactiveness to others' issues is, deep down inside, they take it personally. This, too, is most likely something they were unable to avoid developing due to their upbringing. Harkening back to the Messiah Complex concept, as children, many malignant narcissists were made out to be mommy's (or daddy's) "hero," "apple of their eye," "special," "mini-me," etc. This child may also see themselves as the "cure" for their parent's "woes" (or "issues.") This sort of perception of the child by the parent strengthens the bond. So, when "mommy" is down because she feels unlovable, the child feels she being made to feel unlovable. When daddy's own abandonment issues arise, his son feels abandoned but holds his father accountable.

Regardless of the "issue" at hand, *because of the lack of distinction between the child's sense of self from their parent's, the child has next to no choice in inheriting the parent's "issues" - it's almost by osmosis that the child does so. This child does not know, "That is you, this is me." The younger the child, the more reliant they are going to be on others' behaviors toward them to develop their sense of self. But it is because of this, as mentioned earlier, that these children are prone to adopt **offense mechanisms** as a result, which are bound to continue into adulthood,* especially in close relationships. This is the reason so many of us who do not have malignant narcissistic personalities have faced the "I'm rubber, you're glue" game when interacting with them. This is because the malignant narcissist was geared from a very, very early age that *their parent* is the causality of their "issues" since their parents disposition is what they identified as their persona. They'll continue this entangled self-conceptualization based on others' dispositions until they sever this "cord."

This is precisely the **Projection** mechanism described back in Chapter 3 under the subtitle "Offense Mechanisms." *"It's YOUR fault I feel 'bad.'"*

But this extremely close proximity between self and non-self

(parent) is the reason many of us heard others who have been in relationships with malignant narcissists say, "It began to feel like I didn't know where I ended and the other person began." Again, this
is because this is a relic-dynamic from childhood which has not yet been healed. The child - whether a malignant narcissist or not - faced extreme conditions with respect to their parent's behavior. The trauma-based response, therefore, is indelible to the human psyche. For malignant narcissists whom experienced traumatic neglect or abandonment, this may take on the appearance of "lashing out" but it's more like a reflex - it's the kid screaming from the crib when they were in desperate need of something. For an adult codependent who, say, "freezes" and goes into "fight or flight" mode bearing the brunt of unprovoked and acute "narcissistic rage" (and this is common), this is due to the adult codependent's childhood-self experiencing such rage while growing up. Like the malignant narcissist child, the codependent child will have weak distinction between their "self" and that of their parent. Such parental "flares ups" shock the child as a result and, unless the adult version of the child "goes back" to these episodes of parental volatility and perceives their parent in a different light, they will continue to be hypersensitive to similar behavior as an adult.

How to Make a Bully (ASPD, M-Based ASPD, P-Based ASPD)

Since this subject was touched upon in the preceding subheading, I figured I'd go into this in a bit more detail. In truth, I wish I could make both this subject as well as the previous one under a chapter pertaining to both "lack of empathy" as well as "lack of remorse" (which will be the next chapter) in addition to "belittling behavior" since they apply to all three.

Bullies, I can tell you right now, are most often the product of a psychopathic or malignantly narcissistic father and a codependent mother. The reason behind the bully's aggression is being the recipient of the father's abuse (which is usually physical and psychological) and the mother's fecklessness in preventing it. The reason behind the bully's animosity toward weak-willed individuals is his mother's unwillingness or aversion to protect the child (though it is likely that she consistently caters to the "false-self" she created in her child and her narcissistic supply is all she's really good for.) Thanks to her propensity to divorce reality - even at the cost of her child's welfare - her kid not only suffers physically and psychologically, but the kids of other parents as well.

Unable to target stronger individuals as a release (such as his father) and coupled with a hatred for the weak (thanks to his mother), those who are "weak" are easy targets. Such targets, unfortunately, were likely to be raised in narcissistic-leaning households, with their "weak" disposition due to repeated cases of being "shell-shocked" by an abusive or unloving household. (If you've seen the movie *Moonlight*, think of the main subject as a boy.)

Despite being obvious, it's worth highlighting that the bully is the "baby" of an extremely divergent Malignant Narcissist/Codependent relationship. Regardless, an upbringing resembling this one to whatever extent is highly likely to procure a child who is, at best, demeaning and belittling.

"I'd Like a Side Order of Bitch"

I know many readers can personally relate to the following scene: You're out on a date for the first time and, before you get to the restaurant, your suitor seems over-the-top wonderful. He or she is showering you with praise and seems to have a great, engaging, ebullient personality. His/her personality may seem even a bit contrived and manufactured, but you might write it off to nerves. When the maitre'd asks how many are in your party, your date's response is dismissive and curt. After the two of you are seated, your date returns to the ingratiating rapport he or she established with you earlier. Then, the waiter comes. Your date's attitude toward the waiter is condescending, snide, curt, demeaning, dismissive, even rude or deprecating, and it stays that way during every interaction your date has with the waiter throughout the night. You begin to feel both sorry for the waiter as well as embarrassed to be associated with such a jackass who apparently has a Jekyll and Hyde personality.

Why did your date behave this way?

In short, your date - either consciously or subconsciously - carries a vendetta against the care-taking, subservient parent who neglected his or her needs, failed to provide consistent and ample narcissistic supply or material support, and/or was overly depressive while growing up. The waitstaff are, in the malignant narcissist's conscious or subconscious mind, being subjected to guilt by association and it is the catering nature of their jobs which causes this association.

Many of us would perceive such a personality type as an asshole. In all fairness, we don't know what happened in the malignant narcissist's early years which caused the inner-resentment toward their care-taking, codependent parent and the subsequent conscious or subconscious disdain toward those resembling this parent. It could be that the malignant narcissist was simply psychologically spoiled by such a parent and never thought about being grateful for what they were given. Or, it could be that despite the parent's attentiveness, they earned little, causing the young malignant narcissist to be resentful and embarrassed because they appeared "poor" as a child growing up (or didn't have the things their peers had and therefore didn't fit in.) The malignant narcissist's parent may have been so "giving" and attentive toward others, she gave little to herself and was so "spread thin" there was barely anything left.

Whatever the case might be, a possible cause for the malignant narcissist's demonstration of belittling or deprecating behavior would be unresolved resentment toward a codependent parent.

When You Go Low, I Feel High (NPD, M-Based ASPD)

The projecting quality of the malignant narcissist's offense mechanisms is often the reason behind belittling, demeaning, or deprecating comments. Their self-esteem is low because the ego-bar that is the Grandiose self has been lowered or unsupported by narcissistic supply, so someone else is responsible. (Again, *"It's YOUR fault I feel 'bad.'"*)

Whether or not the target is aware that they are being demeaned and belittled (that is, it's done behind their back), the malignant narcissist resorts to putting others down to make themselves feel better. Often referred to as "lighting others on fire to keep themselves warm," this behavior is both parasitic and toxic - but the pun is that it is completely ineffective in healing their issues in the long run. Actually, it doesn't end up healing anything; in truth, it just makes things worse.

They will label others as "stupid" so they can feel smart. They'll relish in others' failures so they don't feel so much like one. They'll take pride in feeling superior to others' appearances so that they feel attractive. They'll humiliate others so they don't feel ashamed. You get the point, as dull as it is.

Recall that there's nothing "self" generated in terms of self-worth on part of the malignant narcissist personality type. This was something that was dispensed heavily upon them during their upbringing and continue far past the time when it should. As they get older, they will rely on others' accolades, approval, esteem, and narcissistic supply to maintain their sense of "self-worth." Again, and in short and in reality, it's not self-worth: it's "worth provided to them by others." Like the metaphor provided earlier, they need other people to "feed" them rather than being capable of "feeding" themselves.

When the malignant narcissist's self-worth is low (and it will be unless someone or something else is fueling it) and no one is available to boost it, the other option is to resort to deprecating others. That is, if they push others' pedestals down, their pedestal doesn't look so short. This is the next best option for them to maintain their "self-worth" if no narcissistic supply is available to them. Whether or not they vocalize or exhibit their deprecating, belittling, or humiliating remarks, this sort of behavior gives the narcissist a short-term sense of having self-worth. The problem is, there's nothing self-sufficient (or genuine) about the fleeting sense of self-worth or superiority they feel when they act like this. Because their "worth" is based on compare and contrast, their true feelings of low self-worth are always going to be both present and apparent when they're alone. (And this is part of the importance of going "no contact" or employing the "grey rock" method. Eventually, they'll run out of sources of "kindling" and freeze. Enough of this "no contact" will eventually put the malignant narcissist into a "deep freeze." Maybe then they'll learn to love - or "warm" - themselves and, eventually, others.)

Especially if the person behaving in this manner is a grown adult, I'd recommend cutting off all contact and keeping it that way. For a grown individual, the fact that this behavior is so immature, I find it remarkable that they don't feel embarrassed and ashamed. Even if it is the case that the malignant narcissist belittles or demeans someone else showing signs of low self-worth while they themselves have no "issues," this is indicative of a lack of empathy which most likely has it roots in childhood where the were parented by a parent of similar psychology. Instead of the adult offering support and empathy or at least non-reactiveness, the malignant narcissist instead engages in the same behavior as their child-self and proceeds to belittle, demean, and humiliate.

Also, I mentioned earlier that projecting will makes things worse for the malignant narcissist who does this. Not only will this cause their issues to go unhealed and coagulate but, because of all the mistreatment of others' sense of self-worth, these episodes will coagulate in their subconsciousness. Because they violate their conscience when they do this, they're likely to grow increasingly paranoid as they "progress." Not only will they need a larger "fire" to keep themselves "warm," but a big jug of water to wash down the medication. Moreover, if others get the sense that the malignant narcissist is pulling this crap with them, they're much more likely to develop their own self-worth and have nothing to do with the

malignant narcissist in the future. They're liable to discover what a magnificent piece of shit this person is and want nothing to do with them, even in their own minds. And nor should they.

I'm well aware that the objective of this book was to present an unbiased examination of the early childhood conditions which cultivate the malignant narcissist personality type but with regard to this subtopic, this sort of behavior is so pathetic and parasitic, I truly could not care less if my words come across as judgmental or offensive.

When you go High, I'll Feel Low (NPD, M-Based ASPD)

Uh oh. What's *this* about? What happens to the malignant narcissist when someone else who isn't a malignant narcissist starts to "outshine" them in some way? Their inner monologue goes something like this: "Oh no…oh no no no…this can't be… I can't have someone who actually has healthy self-worth, self-confidence, *and* consideration for others *and* who is more talented than I steal my thunder. No no…this needs to stop."

But, rather than the malignant narcissist developing his or her own empathy, consideration, or talent, *sabotage* is the answer. In fact, this is their *only answer*. And this is because cultivating healthy *self*-worth would mean they would have to admit that they don't have it. Having genuine empathy and consideration would mean having to resolve the resentment behind their Abandonment issues *and to understand why* their abandoning parent was abandoning, not to mention to acknowledge that, up until now, *they really haven't empathized with anyone.* Increasing their talent would involve having to develop intrinsic self-worth as opposed to relying on the narcissistic supply from others - and why squeeze a cow when you can get the milk for free? This would also require the malignant narcissist to admit they're flawed and not as great as they had thought. My stars! Talk about cognitive dissonance.

Look out: the Grandiose Self is about to have a grandiose baby. In the most innocuous case scenario, they'll logistically sabotage the other party who actually has self-worth. This will come in the form of shortchanging the person who threatens their "greatness" in terms of resources, time, attention, or some other commodity with the hopes that it will dim the "spotlight" that the malignant narcissist so desperately craves to be on them - at all times.

If this doesn't work (and it may not especially if the other party is adept to handling such challenges), the belittling, demeaning, and degrading behavior seeps in. Here, the malignant narcissist will decide which path to take, whether that's to try to dish out this sort of bullshit directly on their "competition" or to do it passively and denigrate them behind their back. Whatever the case, *something* must be done in order to lower the other person's "pedestal" so that the malignant narcissist doesn't continue to feel "less than." God forbid they should try to feel comfortable in their own skin on their own. No, a king should *never* have to do that kind of work.

What's likely to happen if the malignant narcissist senses that the other party has a good sense of self and is genuinely liked by others is that they'll sabotage the other party *directly with no witnesses. This places the other party in "checkmate" because if the other party goes to others for help,* the malignant narcissist *can simply deny it.* Here, there's at least the chance that they get away with it: if there's no proof or eyewitnesses, they can't be convicted. If a third party brought in to adjudicate (such as in the case of a workplace fallout scenario), justice will depend on this party's own personal mental health and wisdom. It's kind of like the synopsis of the 1993 Macaulay Culkin/Elijah Wood movie *The Good Son* where a mother faces the gruesome decision to choose between the life of her own biological but diabolical ("diabiological?") son or a different, innocent child. If the third party doesn't have a keen eye for crazy-making, crazy's going to win. However, if the innocent party "loses" and has to leave the situation for any reason, they still win: they now are awarded the opportunity to sever ties with both crazy *and* stupid. Hopefully, they'll realize that the longevity of their inclusion would have been short regardless because, if this scenario plays out within an organization of any type, it's a House of Cards. Start looking for a new job or another situation unless you feel like some time off while collecting unemployment.

This sort of immaturity, unfortunately, also plays out in some relationships because, God forbid, sometimes the non-narcissistic partner shines brighter. This is sad because the mutual support and encouragement seen in healthy relationships is not only absent, it's absolutely one-sided. Worse, any success the malignant narcissist realized during the course of this relationship was predicated on their pedestal being higher than their partner's, and the height of this pedestal is due to, in part, the partner's moral support. Now, and without having any reciprocal moral support (and perhaps just the opposite: humiliation and ridicule), the partner on the sidelines starts to shine instead. And now that they're shining, they receive psychological sabotage from their malignant narcissist partner instead of the very positive reinforcement they had given to their partner in the past. In such a case, this "Angel In Disguise" is more like a "Rung On a Ladder." Most likely, it's a launchpad. Like Tina Turner with her rise to greatness after her stint with Ike, the partner in the above scenario is the human version of a phoenix.

Nanny Issues (M-Based ASPD)

Although less common, a child raised by someone other than a parent is likely to grow into an adult who harbors inner resentment toward said parent if that parent is "still in the picture" somehow. The adult may act out not only through demeaning and belittling speech, but other characteristics of M-Based ASPD may emerge as well.

RED FLAGS:
- Frequent potshots, insults, and other degrading comments.
- "Lighting others on fire to keep themselves warm."
- Noticeable pleasure when witnessing others' misfortunes.

CHILDHOOD CONDITIONS CREATING DEMEANING, BULLYING, AND BELITTLING BEHAVIOR:
- Being raised by a narcissistic/codependent parental couple.
- Being raised by an emotionally, psychologically, or physically abusive parent.
- Being "ego-spoiled" as a child with expectations falling short throughout life.
- Not being protected from abuse during childhood.

UNDERLYING ISSUES BEHIND DEMEANING, BULLYING, AND BELITTLING BEHAVIOR:
- Abandonment/neglect issues.
- Feelings of contempt and retaliation for being inferior and not being cared about.

6

<u>*Lack of Remorse*</u>

"You never want a serious crisis to go to waste."

- Rahm Emanuel [1]

High Parental Ethical Boundaries (M-Based ASPD, P-Based ASPD, BPD, HPD)

Oftentimes, the reason some malignant narcissist's resent what some codependents regard as "goodness," "ethical behavior," or "proper character" such as attentiveness, kindness, humility, complicity, low-maintenance, meekness, integrity, and an unwavering conscience is due to the "guilt by association" character such individuals have with the narcissist's codependent, depressive parent. With others, it's due to draconian restrictions placed upon them as a child for being unable to measure up before they were developmentally ready. It's very possible that this conditioning even took place during the "terrible two's."

Otherwise, part of the moral learning curve involves making mistakes and doing things wrong. Severely reprimanding such behavior before the child was genuinely able to know better is certainly going to have a backlash. Plus, anytime any of us are placed in a situation where the expectations placed upon us are unreasonable or even impossible, we're likely to grow resentful and rebel.

While pigeonholing *any* kid to adopt these qualities without erring is an unreasonable expectation, those who are best able to inhabit this "little angel" role will not only be resented by those who are unable but also targeted. Who can blame them? To such kids, these "little angels" are "goody-goodies" or more appropriately, "ethical narcissists." Through "compare and contrast," their "goodness" - usually contrived -

makes them feel "bad."

I'll give an example: when I was growing up, I was placed in a Roman Catholic Grade school up until sixth grade. My first grade nun *loved* me and thought I was a little angel, so it was easy for me to inhabit that role. Thank God in a way, because this nun was ferocious. Personally, I don't think it had to do with anything about me as a person except that I was looking to do what I needed to do to get by. Honestly, I think it had to do more with my haircut, which was fairly conservative. Her targets were the "bowl cuts": the boys with this sort of haircut had very little to do aside from act like a little boy to ignite her wrath. And I do mean *wrath*. She would grab them by the hair and swing them around - *lifting* them off the ground - before locking them in the closet for an indefinite period of time.

Once, our class was attending a children's mass and I was standing in a pew next to a "bowl" named Ryan. The congregation was singing, "Hosanna! Hosanna! Hosanna in the Highest!" Ryan, wanting to have fun, began singing "Lasagna in the Highest!" Hearing this, the nun went ballistic. But you can see how a disproportionate degree of discipline with respect to "bad" behavior can cause some kids to resent and rebel against being "good" as an adult - especially on a routine basis. It's possible that Ryan, if after so many episodes of being the recipient of such punitive measures, grew up to be an adult who rebelled against social mores and norms.

It's also the case that, since many codependents did not receive love in the form of nurturing, attentiveness, and care with respect to self-worth, they may treat their kids with such punitive measures similar to my first grade teacher. If their kid playfully teases them or takes something that doesn't belong to them, the parent may "fly off the handle" and discipline them too much. If met with repeat occurrences, the kid may grow into an adult with a lack of conscience or remorse. They may (and probably should) feel resentment over being made to feel guilty over something of which they just didn't know better about at the time.

With respect to myself, for a long time I was resentful toward "narcissists" and "psychopaths." Considering what they're capable of doing, it's understandable. But, I have to admit, it had become so acute, my attitude became close to the "morality policewoman" that was my first grade teacher.

Regardless, it is precisely this hyper-punitive or overly reprimanding discipline of a child's amoral character which can lead to a lack of remorse as an adult. Overly blaming, guilting, or shaming a child for behavior for which they did not know better is highly likely to lead to this.

"You Can't Handle the Truth!" (NPD, ASPD, BPD, HPD)

Pathological lying is a trend common in narcissistic personality disorders which has a similar childhood origin recipe as the preceding subheading. Here, instead of the household making it okay to tell the truth or "come clean" after lying, there are severe consequences for doing so. Specifically, the punishment outweighs the crime significantly enough, the child feels that they're better off lying about their behavior and that justice will be honored more so if they do so. (And they're probably right.)

Going back to Catholic School, this happened in my 5th Grade Class when the nun left the classroom. Before leaving, she instructed the class that they were not to talk to each other. Several minutes after she left the class, a few of us exchanged a few words to each other, but we quickly went back to being silent. Upon the teacher's return, a "little angel" decided to narc on the class and the teacher subsequently asked who among us was talking in her absence. Another kid and I confessed, believing it was best to tell the truth. For doing so, we received a month's worth of detention. Needless to say, we never told truth to this woman again because she was unequipped to handle it appropriately.

The characteristic of pathological lying common to some Cluster B's *may have similar roots in their childhood, where a parent, guardian, or some other influence was severely reprimanding even when the child confessed.* Whereas I received a litany of detention, some kids may get the crap beaten out of them for doing something just as innocuous.

Such punitive treatment may also cause some adult versions of these kids to lie and cheat out of rebellion to the abusive treatment and deliberately scam, cheat, or engage in some other form of illegitimate behavior or betrayal. Until they revisit and heal the childhood conditions which led to this, they're going to have more difficulty in modifying or ending this behavior.

Another factor which may have contributed to the malignant narcissist's penchant for pathological lying is *being raised in a household where there were little boundaries or repercussions for lying.* In other words, the pathologically lying adult "got away" with lying as a child and never matured out of it. If they were spoiled or placed on the proverbial "pedestal" as well, they may carry a sense of entitlement into their adulthood. If the codependent or depressive parent also had a weak sense of reality, the child's lies may have "slipped through the radar." This could also be the reason we see the typical "gas lighting" behavior exhibited by many malignant narcissists: the fibs which worked in the past are tried in the present.

Yet another condition lies with children who are raised by two Cluster B parents - both of whom are manipulative and pathologically lying. If a child is raised in such conditions, they may become liable to believe that lying is "okay" since it was a part of their family culture. They may even be encouraged to do so or witness their parents "getting off" on pulling the wool over others' eyes. If the family lineage has a history of malignantly narcissistic members (and many wealthy families do), this characteristic is guaranteed and solidified.

Personally, I was at the receiving end of such behavior in the workplace. I had worked as a manager for a store owned by a malignant narcissist couple. After I left (due to the malignantly narcissistic antics), the wife tried to shortchange me on my earnings. I won't go into detail but, after I filed a wage claim, I was informed by the clerk of an over-the-top slanderous (and wildly bogus) smear campaign brought forth by the wife. Regardless, their young son - who I believe was in third grade at the time - was reprimanded by his school for displaying pathologically lying behavior. His mother thought it was funny/cute.

Shame and Guilt (M-Based ASPD, P-Based ASPD)

A common method of punishment for violating moral and ethical codes which causes malignant narcissistic traits is dispensing excessive shame and guilt.

This can be seen in the prototypical "bad boy." Mommy's out of sorts, the little boy does something wrong or impish to poke her back into functionality or sobriety, then mommy discovers the transgression and subjects him to a tirade of shame or guilt on account of it. Now he's a "bad boy."

Regardless, if the shame and/or guilt disposed upon the child is excessive or disproportionate to the behavior, the backlash is going to develop lack of remorse in the child.

Just as with the son who needed words of encouragement during his homework but instead was barraged with comments about "how stupid" he is and follows up believing it and resents his mother later in life in the form of being unsuccessful, the "bad boy" needed some attention but instead received the shame-based message that he is "bad." His resentful revenge is liable to take the form of being remorseless as he grows older until he learns to forgive his mother. He's also prone to "poke" others in a similar fashion when he gets older.

Extrapolated Victimhood (M-Based ASPD, P-Based ASPD)

Sometimes a child *may* actually do something wrong, unethical, or harmful to the parent or someone else. Like shaming or "guilting" the child, the parent over-amplifies the extent of the transgression and plays the victim far beyond appropriate which, in turn, not only drains the child but conjures residual resentment toward the parent who behaved this way.

As an adult, such a child who holds lingering resentment toward the repeated circumstances involving being made to feel more remorse than appropriate is liable to exact vengeance on others without remorse. The lack of remorse compensates for the excess of remorse they were unjustifiably made to feel during previous episodes from their childhood.

What's highly probable is that, after the first episode of being made out to be a "demon" when he was really just an imp, the child retaliated against "Mommy" for making him feel worse than he deserved. This is understandable since children do not always have sufficient ability in articulating their feelings. He acts out in defiance setting "Mommy" off again, who overly-reprimands his bad behavior by laying on the victimization too much and a vicious, escalated cycle ensues.

This situation is most likely exclusive to M-Based ASPD which, again, is often co-morbid with NPD. Again, the former's pathology is rooted in issues of abandonment (usually neglect) whereas the latter involved being over-indulged, spoiled, or enabled.

In the case of P-Based ASPD, the child was subjected to psychological or physical abuse and may have done little to nothing to catalyze it. Or, the parent's own neglect/abandonment issues were stimulated by the child's uncooperative behavior and the parent flew off the handle. Here, the child will grow up resentful of the parent's disproportionate discipline and lash out at others, self-inflict, or develop addictions. Thus, the likelihood that they will violate their conscience and experience a lack of remorse is less than that of M-Based ASPD.

Excessive Neglect and Abandonment (ASPD, BPD, HPD)

Referring back to the early childhood experience of my former employee who spent time in a correctional facility for spousal abuse, severe neglect and abandonment can serve as the foundation for violent behavior in an adult. While my employee was noble and accepted accountability for his behavior, not all adults will. In some cases, they will truly exonerate themselves of all accountability or even justify their behavior. It wouldn't be a surprise if, in a smaller percentage of cases, the perpetrator made the claim that the abuse "just happened." If the unresolved childhood trauma such a person faced was, say, life-threatening for them as a child, I would say I would have to believe them. In the latter cases, the likelihood of there being remorse is slim to none.

Excessive neglect and abandonment is also a potential culprit behind relationship infidelity. If the child-version of the adult felt betrayed by the parent when neglected or abandoned, the unhealed adult may act out on this sense of betrayal by retaliating.

Childhood neglect can also lead to adult malignant narcissist remorseless behavior such as theft and white-collar crime (if the trauma-based neglect came in the form of material deprivation) and ruthless and cut-throat career advancement (if the neglect came in causing the feelings of failure or "preferential betrayal"; see below.)

Preferential Betrayal (NPD, M-Based ASPD)

This is similar to neglect and abandonment, but here it is wounds involving the early childhood bond of parent/child that the child senses is betrayed. Especially if the child has a Messiah Complex, if such a parent demonstrates preference for the behavior, aptitude, presence, looks, personality or some other attribute of another child, this can also lead to both remorseless child and adult behavior being rooted in the unhealed episodes of betrayal experienced by the child. (The fact that the child was *over-indulged* prior to this, the parental preference for another child triggers not only the Abandonment schema but also the Entitlement - which makes things substantially worse.)

An example of this can be seen in the 2007 film *Margot at the Wedding*. The films two leads, played by Nicole Kidman and Jennifer Jason Leigh, are a pair of sisters and the title character (played by Kidman) is attending the wedding of her estranged sister Pauline (Leigh) in Connecticut. In one scene, Pauline recounts to her nephew how, when they were little, his mother used to place her on a baking sheet and sprinkle her with paprika before putting her in the over. In another scene where the two sisters are having a feud, Pauline assaults Margot with the charge that their other sister (also estranged from Margot) has diagnosed her with Borderline Personality Disorder (Margot most likely had NPD or M-Based ASPD.)

Such preferential betrayal is sometimes experienced by the older children in dysfunctional families and is often felt by the Hero when additional children are born. If such children feel a sense of neglect or betrayal because of the attention or preference given to the newborn, they're prone to engage in remorseless (though usually unintentionally harmful) behavior to their younger siblings, like putting them in the oven.

Or sitting on their head - which is what my thirteen-month older twin sisters did to me. Luckily for me, I was born with twin middle fingers: one dedicated to each of them.

Such childhood episodes of parental betrayal could also serve as the psychological foundation behind the malignant narcissist's tendency to engage in relationship or marital infidelity as an adult. Depending on the scenario, the malignant narcissist sense of betrayal could be triggered when they witness their partner showing interest - whether real or perceived - or providing attention to another party. The malignant narcissist is not only likely to *not* feel any remorse in cheating on their partner, they will feel justified in doing so - and subsequently blaming their partner for their behavior.

One Side of the Story (P-Based ASPD, BPD, HPD)

Something that is liable to strengthen a lack of remorse (or at least the chance of resentment) is only hearing one side of the story. Imagine being placed on trial for allegations which weren't true and only the plaintiff's side was heard. Or, the allegations were true but certain evidence was not seen or heard that would have shed a different light on the situation, such as committing murder but out of self-defense.

I'm sure all of us can identify with this to some degree or another. For this reason, it is so important not to judge or jump to conclusions when you aren't completely sure you have heard all sides of the story or have all your ducks in a row.

This is liable to be a condition behind the behavior of some Cluster B individuals. During their early years, they may have had judgement passed on them or experienced some sort of "sentencing" when some details of the "case" were missing. If this is the case, and especially if they were young, the residual resentment would likely take on a lack of remorse as they got older.

Sometimes, additional information puts things in context. Say a woman's boyfriend at some point cheats on her several months into the relationship. While he may be guilty of infidelity, it's due in part to unhealed wounds of being cheated on in his past relationship. While this doesn't exonerate his behavior or the residual hurt and betrayal his girlfriend feels, but knowing this would alleviate her burden if she has taken this personally.

Regardless, being judged unfairly can foster a sense of resentment - which is understandable. If being judged and sentenced unfairly has gone on too many times for too long, the "convict" rightfully sees no sense in being law-abiding, but instead rebels. There's no sense in being good or innocent - punishment comes anyway - so the spoils of crime are sought to accommodate for the unfairness. Who can blame someone who's been repeatedly innocent but branded guilty for throwing in the towel after a while?

This is precisely the upbringing of those raised in abusive households and Paternal-based ASPD develops as a result. It's awful, because jails and prisons are filled with individuals with this sort of upbringing. Thanks to many prisons being privatized, their fate is actually *capitalized on.*

Who-who-who Gonna Love Me? (M-Based ASPD, P-Based ASPD, BPD, HPD)

The title of this subheading comes from a line from the 2009 movie *Precious* during a scene in which the abusive and sadistic mother of the title character meets with her estranged daughter in the office of a social worker in an attempt to regain custody. When the social worker brings up the early childhood sexual abuse Precious endured at the hands of her father, her mother claims she allowed it in order to keep her husband, blaming her infant child for her own abuse and alleges that Precious, as a child, was trying to steal her husband. In an attempt to inspire both sympathy and clemency, the mother asks, "Who-who-who gonna love me?"

This is an example of a "victim mentality gone awry" where the perpetrator (or accessory to abuse) plays the "victim card" as an excuse to inflict (or enable) the abuse they're committing (or permitting.) Because they weren't loved, it's okay that their child was abused. Because they were cheated on, it's okay for them to cheat on their partner.

This is a common reason Cluster B's and other perpetrators commit violations of others' personal well-being. Because they were never healed, cared about, or sympathized with, it's okay for them to subject others to the same treatment. The use of this philosophy is what compromises the conscience, and *this is oftentimes the culprit behind the lack of remorse.*

Recall back from Chapter 1 (subheading "*Parents Tend To Give That Which They Didn't Receive*"), it was described how certain families play a game of "leap-frog" with their children: that is, they provide to them that which they didn't receive. One generation will provide the material support (but not the emotional) to their children while such children are liable to provide emotional support (but not material) to *their* children.

Because of the lack - whether it is material or emotional - of support the child received growing up, the child may not only hang onto such a grudge, but use this grudge as leverage to justify retaliation. Usually this act of rebellious retaliation is against the very form of love they *were* given. An example of this is a child who received a good deal of financial support growing up but none when it came to emotional. If the child proceeds into adulthood with this grudge still intact, it is likely to inhibit their ability to manifest the very financial support as an adult on their own (let alone for others.) Out of retaliation, the adult version of the child may seek out ways to financially drain their parents as a vendetta.

Conversely, a child who was endowed with an overindulgence of emotional nurturance but next to nothing in terms of financial support and carries a subsequent grudge into their adulthood will lash out at their parents emotionally or psychologically. Instead of subjecting them to financial loss, they will - like the previous child - "hit them where it hurts": in this case, their parents' hearts. This is because this child knows *directly* that their parents perceive emotional nurturance as "love" because they gave it due to not receiving it as children. What such parents can expect is not an emotional loss, but a toll taken upon their psychological and emotional wellbeing. These parents can expect their child to degrade, devalue, insult, and engage in other forms of psychological and emotional abuse as well as play "mind games." As the child "matures," the material depravity during childhood and the resulting grudge they carry on account of it will inhibit their ability manifest emotional support (for themselves and others.)

Whatever form of retaliation either child engages in, the adult versions of both children are likely to justify their behavior and develop a lack of remorse on account. Since it is the "child" version who is unhealed, this justification may seem valid to the perpetrator.

Note that, like the example from *Precious* given earlier, it could be the next generation's children who receive the brunt of the grudge. That is, a grudge against the parents for material deprivation may result in the child inflicting emotional and psychological distress upon their children. (*"I'm going to make you feel stupid because mom wasn't there for me growing up."* Now, *"It's YOUR fault she wasn't there for me growing up."*) And, a grudge against the parents for emotional deprivation may result in the adult version of the child taking this out on their children in he form of material deprivation. (*"I'm still mad at my dad for not loving me, so I can't feed you right now."*)

If not directed at parents or children, romantic partners often bear the brunt of such unresolved resentment *since it is likely that the partner resembles the parent in some way.* If their partner is lacking in material or financial performance, the adult-child who born the brunt of this lack will inflict emotional and psychological abuse on their partner. If their partner is lacking in emotionally supporting performance, the adult-child is likely to neglect, abandon, "let the ball drop" when it comes to financial and material wellbeing, or worse: deliberately jeopardize the physical wellbeing of their partner.

It should be mentioned that if such unresolved resentment has *no outlet*, be it due to circumstances or by choice, the adult-child does not (or refuses to) inflict their hell onto their parents, children, or partners, the adult-child is likely to self-inflict. A version of this is someone who sabotages their physical and financial health due to unhealed wounds created by a non-nurturing or abusive parent. The flip-side of this is someone who sabotages their mental, psychological, or spiritual health due to unhealed wounds from a neglecting, abandoning, or materially/financially depriving parent.

Now, if *a traumatic event* is behind the adult-child's "grudge," this can almost guarantee what will seem like extremely remorseless behavior toward parents, children, partners, or even self. If a child, say, is beaten with a baseball bat by his father (I know of one such person), such a drastic form of abuse involves violations of emotional/psychological *as well as* physical/material safety. This is a pronounced example of the conditions someone who may develop Paternal-based ASPD may face while growing up. This abuse against emotional/psychological and physical/material safety reflects the core issues the Paternal-based ASPD is bound to adopt mentioned back in Chapter 2: *Unlovability* and *Vulnerability*, respectively. The adult version of this child may be prone to seemingly uncontrollable assaults on others' emotional and psychological health as well as their physical, if not their own. (The real-life example I know, miraculously, *does not* subject others to this sort of mistreatment. If anything and, despite claiming he has Narcissistic Personality Disorder per a professional diagnosis I find both unacceptable and inappropriate, he self-inflicts or self-sabotages.)

If such parents are recipients of retaliation from their unhealed yet abused children, they can expect this to happen if they never apologized or tried to make up for the trauma they inflicted.

Frat Boy Psychology = Monkey see, Monkey do (NPD, P-Based ASPD)

This subtopic is similar to the one preceding it - very similar, actually, since it involves the "it was done to me, so now it's okay for me to do to someone else" philosophy. Like fraternity boys who inflict the same humiliating and demeaning treatment on their pledges they received while pledging, some adults do this as well. It's more than a "rite of passage," though. It's just as juvenile when an adult does it albeit more dishonorable and the consequences can be more substantially more severe.

Sure, this can be seen in some families when a father abuses his son because he was abused as a child and no one loved *him,* but this can also be seen in many hierarchal organizational structures as well. This trend was explored in greater detail in *TSOA* but it's worth reiterating in this chapter since it is a mindset of many Cluster B personalities to justify mistreatment, neglect, deprivation - basically the superimposition of any "issue" listed previously. I think it's safe to say that this pervasive mentality is the reason many of us have developed a disdain for corporate culture. "Higher ups" may subject lower-level personnel to scarce resources, longer work days, draconian mandates, etc. to the point where it makes the ability to perform job duties next to impossible. Otherwise, it causes post-traumatic stress disorder in employees or some other stress-based illness or on-the-job injury (which is in itself a negative feedback mechanism, considering the drain it places on healthcare premiums and workman's compensation.) It's become so severe in some cases that the "burn 'em and turn 'em" culture is the company's quintessential "revolving door" since apparently no one is capable of performing the job functions under such conditions. Subsequent high-turnover of employees is indicative of this. Such malignant narcissistic "leadership" is unlikely to accept responsibility (since it, like the NPD or M-Based ASPD personality itself, has a victim mentality rooted in abandonment and neglect.)

The "frat boys" within such organizations are likely to rise up the chain in command, since their propensity to inflict the "hazing" they've endured onto their subordinates is substantially higher than those who have a conscience and/or empathy. Acting as "secondary psychopaths," they'll have little to no compunction performing mass layoffs, invading employees' personal privacy, scapegoating organizational dysfunction, providing pittances for raises, and cooking the books in addition to creating hellish working conditions for their employees (since it was done to them.) *Honorable behavior would mimic the father who was beaten as a child and refuses to beat his own children for that very reason,* but that's not the case here.

The stupidity of this trend lies in the fact that supervisors who are mindful of the conditions in which their employees are working will not only achieve better results (because employees can actually get the job done) and motivates through positive reinforcement rather than whip-cracking, the fact that they have a conscience and empathy serves as a deterrent for promotion since - oddly enough - such qualities are perceived as a "weakness" or a "liability." Moreover, supervisors who express more loyalty to their conscience than they do to toxic directives will be expunged or will leave the organization on their own.

I've seen it happen time and time again.

It needs to be emphasized that *there is no use in setting boundaries with such "bosses" or "leadership" against workplace mistreatment unless you plan to expedite your own dismissal.* A mature mentality would involve: "I was treated in a way in which I didn't like, therefore I'm *not* going to treat others the same way."

These types *are not mature.* Again, since they "went through it, you need to as well." It's a pouty adult-baby saying "I was treated in a way I didn't like, therefore it's okay for me to treat others the same way."

The concept that we are all "victims of victims" is actually *exploited* by these types: "I was victimized, therefore it's okay for me to victimize." Ironically, they perceive themselves as "strong." No, they are not "strong" by any stretch of the imagination: in fact, they are extremely *weak.* Again, a "strong," honorable person would think "I was victimized, therefore I won't victimize others since I know what it was like." The former creates an environment where the fear factor is high and creates dysfunction whereas the latter creates a climate of productivity *because a fear factor doesn't inhibit it.*

While we're here, it's worth noting that the meme "We're all victims of victims" is not always true, unless you consider being spoiled a form of victimization. Again, this is what happens with narcissists or those who were diagnosed with NPD: again, the "Abandonment" issue is actually an "Entitlement" issue. When they stop being *spoiled,* they *think* they've been abandoned. It's the subsequent *perceived* abandonment which they use as a excuse to inflict suffering on others for "abandoning" (read: spoiling) them. Thus, we are, in fact, *not* all victims of victims because narcissistic victimizers *were never victimized - just unspoiled.* In the workplace, the Adult-toddler boss/supervisor will scream, yell, throw tantrums, blame shift, scapegoat, sabotage, set people up for failure - basically create a hostile environment where fear reigns, workplace politics rule, and productivity is impossible. Note
that if *any* of this *ever* happened to them, they would also have a tantrum. Thus, they sure as hell are not "victims of victims" - just victims of not being spoiled, or "Victims in Disguise."

Parental Abuse (NPD, M-Based ASPD)

In addition to the content presented in the subheading *"Who-who-who Gonna Love Me?"* above, another causation of parental abuse is narcissistic injury. In short, having to share the love, care, respect, and attention they receive from their spouse with their child causes the narcissistic parent to resent the child. This resentment can cause said parent to psychologically sabotage and abuse the child
since the child is seen as a drain on the source of narcissistic supply the parent was not used to sharing until the child was born.

This is a similar dynamic to that described above under the heading *"Preferential Betrayal"* but instead of the third party being another child, it is the narcissistic parent's son or daughter. *When the malignant narcissist parent sees that his or her spouse is dispensing love, adulation, praise, attention, adulation, comfort, etc. upon their child, the narcissistic parent will regard this as a sort of betrayal, but instead of the spouse being blamed (unjustifiably), it is the child (also unjustifiably.)* As is the case in the movie *Precious,* the child bears the brunt of the spousal betrayal and is subsequently abused by the mother. Only in this storyline the situation is more warped: the "care" the child is receiving which catalyzes narcissistic injury and a sense of betrayal in the mother is actually sexual abuse committed by the father.

This is actually quite easy to comprehend: While growing up, the narcissist-to-be who is placed on a pedestal by one or both parents seeks to mimic that "bond" with a life partner as an adult (again, "we marry our parents.") That "cord" connecting the narcissist is therefore transferred from their parent to their spouse; that is, the spouse becomes the new source of narcissistic supply instead of the parent. If the spouse has a child (and especially if the child is the same gender as the narcissist), the narcissist will consider the child a threat to that "bond" and, since the bond needs to remain intact for the narcissist, the target then becomes the child whom the narcissist considers to be a threat to that "bond."

It's worth noting that this sense of spousal betrayal and narcissistic injury is the part of the psychology of the bully's father described back in Chapter 5. Prior to the child's birth, things *may* have been somewhat fine in the marriage. (Well, not really since the father is a malignant narcissist and the mother is a codependent enabler.) When the doting narcissistic supply the wife bestowed upon her husband no longer belongs *exclusively* to the husband once the son is born, the husband takes this personally. And this is because endowments to his self-worth and ego were consistently provided by *his mother* while growing up (again, we marry our parents) and the husband never learned to self-sooth or self-love on his own. The husband, disdainful toward his son for "robbing his stash" of narcissistic supply, abuses or psychologically sabotages his son - and this is usually performed while the mother isn't around.

This domestic set-up makes sense when you think about it: the codependent mother can't grasp the concept that "poopy-kins" could ever be a bully because he's just the sweetest (piece of shit) when he's in her care - as he should be since he's infused with adoration, praise, warmth, etc. (And this, by the way, is where the malignant narcissist picks up the ability to manipulate others and appear as a "little angel (in disguise).") If the husband is covert in abusing his own son, this would make the mother's disbelief of her son's bullying behavior all the more rigid. This is because her limited or impervious perception of the abuse prevents her from considering any conditioning which would cause her son to bully other kids. Her son is unlikely to inform her about it since doing so would likely invoke the behind-the-scenes abuse from the father. Since the father is a malignant narcissist and likely to be an excellent manipulator, the son may not think the mother would believe him anyway. More likely, the son will probably not say anything since he knows nothing different.

The father is unlikely to feel remorse for such abuse because, to him, it's his wife's duty to provide him with narcissistic supply. Again, this is due to the father marrying his "mother" - the "cord" has just been reattached from his mother to his wife. **Now, with the offense mechanism of *projection,* it's not only his wife's "*fault for not making*" *him feel better,* his son is the reason he "feels bad."** The son is seen as a threat because the father sees the "cord" which attached him to his wife being severed and reattached to his son.

Notice how the attention the mother gives her son triggers the Abandonment schema in the narcissistic father. The only difference is, not only does the father feel Abandoned, but since the cause of "Abandonment" is attention being redirected to someone else (the son), the father also experiences *Unlovability* as well. Combining these two - Abandonment and Unlovability - we have *Betrayal. It is because of this Betrayal that the target of the father's projection is his son and not his wife.*

Narcissistic parental abuse need not be based on a sense of spousal betrayal either. If the child progresses and begins to develop aptitudes, talents, or traits which the narcissistic parent feels is surpassing their own, this too will cause narcissistic injury in the parent. This injury is likely to result in physical, psychological, or emotional child abuse as well.

However, *since we're on this topic,* it's worth speculating that the feelings of betrayal which emerge from this scenario may also inspire the father to engage in infidelity. This is provided he also holds his wife accountable for his feelings of betrayal. If it's also "her fault he feels bad," he may take this out on her by cheating on her.

So, it the end, both his son gets abused and his wife gets betrayed all because *he feels insecure.* Again, *nothing actually happened to the father here.*

Baby Out With the Bathwater (NPD, M-Based ASPD)

A final reason for a malignant narcissist's lack of remorse is guilt by association; that is, since qualities like empathy, care, compassion, humility, and altruism are linked to the same parent(s) who didn't maintain the over-indulging or neglected the child in some capacity, the narcissist rejects such traits in himself, often seeing them as weaknesses.

COPING STRATEGIES FOR DEALING WITH THE CLUSTER B LACK OF REMORSE:

• *Childhood Origin Empathy:* "I bet the conditions for you to be good when you were little were excessive." "I bet you weren't treated with fairness growing up."

• *"Them, not you":* It's important to understand that oftentimes the reason for remorseless behavior is due to the perpetrator repeating mental "finger-pointing," blaming, or an "internal victim monologue" or letting a past event "rent space in their heads." If, say, a person harbors resentment toward their mother for being neglectful because she was depressed, they will either have adverse reactions to depressive types (regardless if their depression is reasonable or not) ranging from disdain to violence. I sincerely hope it's not the latter. Regardless, it's important not to take any deprecating comments, emotional outbursts, tirades, personal digs, cheating, etc. personally because oftentimes it is their pathology speaking.

• *Heal, let it go, and do your best to forgive:* For the reason behind this, see *"Who-who-who Gonna Love Me?"* above. If we ourselves start a repetitive mental cycle rehashing what the perpetrator has done, we're liable to set ourselves up to inflict our suffering onto others or start harming ourselves with addictions or other behaviors since we've set up a victim mentality. End it and be glad it's over.

RED FLAGS:

• Inability or unwillingness to accept accountability for their behavior
• "Bad Boy" or "Bad Girl" image.
• Displays of enjoyment when subjecting others to emotional, mental, or physical distress.
• Irritability when they are not the center of (your) attention.
• "Gas lighting" or pathologically lying behavior. (Specifically, promoting self as being a "horrible liar.")
• Possessiveness or jealousy.
• Making *you* feel bad for how badly *they* behaved.
• Being a part of a "shit rolls downhill" campaign.

<u>**CHILDHOOD CONDITIONS CREATING A LACK OF REMORSE:**</u>

* Being raised in an overly reprimanding environment with respect to moral or ethical behavior.
* Being raised in an early environment where "coming clean"had severe and inappropriate consequences.
* Being shamed or guilted for behaviors that were intended to illicit a different response such as attention.
* Being raised in an environment with extreme neglect or abandonment.
* Being subjected to sexual, emotional, physical, or psychological abuse or trauma.
* Being spoiled as a child.

<u>**UNDERLYING ISSUES BEHIND OF A LACK OF REMORSE IN THE CLUSTER B:**</u>

* A feeling of being uncared for.
* A feeling of being inferior.
* Abandonment issues.
* Feelings of contempt and retaliation for feeling inferior and not being cared about.
* Deep feelings or a sense of betrayal (Unlovability due to Abandonment.)
* A repetitive "victim mentality"; letting past events rule mindsets.

7

<u>*Need to Control*</u>

"Who controls the past controls the future."
- from George Orwell's 1984

Control Freak Out (NPD, M-Based ASPD)

As would be expected from the material presented in previous chapters, a likely causation for the Cluster B's (NPD, M-Based ASPD) need to control is rooted in childhood episodes of neglect, abandonment, or incompetence at the hands of a codependent or depressive parent. Such unresolved issues are prone to cause the adult version of such a child to "fly off the handle" and become volatile over situations where expectations and duties are not fulfilled by another party, even when such expectations and duties are menial or inconsequential. A modest example of this is an employee who arrives to work five minutes late (which is within the confines of the law for most states as not being "tardy"), setting off a tantrum from her manager. Such a situation could be triggering the narcissist's imprint of enduring severe abandonment as a child.

A more common experience occurs within relationships, particularly with a possessive partner. Here, the malignant narcissist is obsessively involved with the whereabouts of their partner, even when they're in close proximity in some cases. This is most likely due to the panic and fear the child version experienced when their parent was not available, imprinting "issues" of unlovability, abandonment, vulnerability, etc. onto the child's psyche if not self-concept. Again, this is due to customarily being spoiled or actual abandonment or neglect. If the child's abandonment or neglect was due to attention being given to someone else, this most likely caused a coupling emotion of betrayal.

Many of us can relate to being involved with the adult version of such a child: the "grown up," consistently wary and controlling of his partner's whereabouts, often accuses the partner of infidelity (even though the allegation is false and not based on any evidence.) The result is ironic since it's usually the narcissist who is the one being unfaithful while their partner is overly attentive and monogamous.

The need to control as means to mitigate "issues" or childhood-origin trauma can be seen with all the schemas. When the malignant narcissist feels unlovable, they default on the Grandiose Self by *Overcompensating*. When they're facing deprivation, they hoard, become miserly, or short-change. When they feel abandoned, they control and monitor whereabouts. With exclusion, they're the "life of the party" or "center of attention." When they feel like a failure, they'll backstab, take credit for others' accomplishments, distort or concoct results of their performance, or self-promote. When they feel vulnerable, they'll sabotage or harm the other party, blame-shift, or "dig up dirt." If mistrust is present, they'll beef up security. When they feel fear of not being perceived as perfect, they monitor and silence dissenters. If they feel subjugated, they dominate. With entitlement, they remove or circumvent any rules, safeguards, firewalls, or red tape within respect to themselves but keep them intact for others.

If this sounds like a corrupt United States politician, CEO, or mafia don, you are correct. If the "receiving end" sounds like the typical "corporate culture" (or American, for that matter) or children within a dysfunctional family, that's some "extra credit" right there!

"Manipulators on Ice!" (NPD, M-Based ASPD)

Piggybacking on the previous subtopic, the resulting behaviors from the malignant narcissist's associated "issues" may not be so overt. Depending on the Cluster B - and especially in the case of "covert narcissists" - the control mechanisms may be subversive and manipulative. Instead of relying on the Grandiose Self when feeling unlovable, they'll sabotage the self-worth of others or "play the victim" to extract compliments, accolades, narcissistic supply, attention, empathy, or care. They'll "bug" the place or rely on "moles" instead of ostensible security cameras when they feel mistrusting. They'll psychologically sabotage those they perceive as successful when they feel like a failure and so on.

The causality behind the passive form of the control freak out is likely the same: being raised in an environment where neglect and/or abandonment was present.

The narcissist's manipulative behavior can also serve as a passive-aggressive form of retaliation for not receiving the lop-sided excess their used to and want to manifest (whether that's narcissistic supply, material support, getting others to indulge the ego, which itself is a control mechanism - controlling that the scales always tip in their favor. Again, their "self-worth" isn't rooted in the "self" whatsoever: often, it's based on placing their pedestal higher than others or whittling down the pedestals others are standing on.

Since we're on the topic of manipulative behavior (and this should probably fall under the "Lack of Remorse" chapter), I'm sure any reader who is familiar with malignant narcissists is highly aware of their manipulative character. The manipulation could be anything from exonerating their hyper-controlling behavior (it *is* their inner child, after all), covering up their misdeeds, or trying to get back into the "good graces" of the party who either set boundaries, cut them loose, or was discarded by them. With respect to the last, the malignant narcissist typically presents a demeanor of being reformed, repentant, or remorseful in order to open the curtain for Act II because they've cycled through their rolodex of narcissistic supply and now it's your turn again. *They're back!*

"Lord Jesus! They finally get it. It's been healed! An early Christmas Miracle!" you say. And now it's *you! You* who they finally appreciate! Sweet holy angels and Glory to God in the Highest!

Nope. Not at all. It's more like "Lasagna in the Highest." (Thanks, Ryan.) "The Lord" can't help them and neither can you. It's just act…a monologue they've prepared for such "second auditions." Personally, I'd rather see *CATS*.

Overindulgence With Respect to Care (NPD, M-Based ASPD)

As most of you already know, it is oftentimes the case where a codependent gives *too* much. Whether it is due to providing excessive care, attention, or even performance, if the expectation is given to he child that he or she will be excessively catered to because such care and effort was given for a sustained period of time, the child will get used to it. In short, the kid will anticipate 110% one-hundred percent of the time. Again, this is called "empathy-spoiling" and "attention-spoiling."

Even if it's 100% one-hundred percent of the time from cradle to "leaving the nest," the adult-version of such a child is spoiled, expecting others to cater to their every need and poo-poo any "issue" they might have. Because they were raised as such, any person they come across who does not meet their "expectations" will be seen as a dissident, enemy, or "someone who does not love them."

For instance, if a malignant narcissist is accustomed to another person being at their "beck and call" over a sustained period of time, the malignant narcissist will freak out if the other party is delayed in their response. Such a freak out is likely to involve measures to control or at least coerce the response they're looking for, which is usually attention, care, or narcissistic supply. In relationships - whatever kind it may be - the codependent will have to take some ownership if they "gave" too much and overindulged the Cluster B.

Love Bombing (NPD, M-Based ASPD)

As many readers are probably familiar, malignant narcissists have a tendency to "love bomb" potential romantic partners during the initial stages of acquaintance. This occurs during the "idealize" phase where the malignant narcissist inundates their potential partner with a litany of messages expressing interest, whether it is loving, sexual, or both in nature. Many believe that the purpose of this activity is to hook the target into "bonding" with the Cluster B.

This may seem like a sort of control mechanism used to lure "prey" in but, in truth, this *is* an attempt made by the Cluster B to bond with a prospective partner. However, what the malignant narcissist is doing is a reenactment of their early childhood experience when they bonded with one of their parents, most likely their mother. Just like the intensity of the love-bombing itself, the initial bond between parent and child was also intense - the love, adulation, and attention bestowed upon the child was probably immense - but it went on for too long. But, unlike an adult, this influx of love and adoration is liable to fuel the child's ego. The child has no choice in this: the younger the child, the more impressionable they will be. The earliest years is when a child forms their self-concept - their ego - and this formation is completely based on the feedback they receive from others in their environment. If saturated in adoration and adulation, the child will have no choice but to believe that he or she is "special" as a result.

But, because this very parent was likely relying on this bond to fulfill a void within herself, she was liable to expect this close bond of love, affection, and adoration to be mutual. That is, she *gave* love *in order to receive it*. Also, because she is an adult, she's liable to expect (or need) this bond to last longer than the child is comfortable with because this child has other developmental needs such as exercise, food, exploration, waste release, self-discovery, etc. Naturally, the child is going to become fidgety and irritable if "bonded with" for too long: it puts the "mother" in "smother." This is why we see the irritation in the malignant narcissist after the love bombing phase is over - it's reminiscent of an early life experience: they feel *cramped, stifled*. Now that they've got their fix, their stone needs to get rollin'.

In light of this, it's easy to understand why a codependent would become so confused by this sort of "hot and cold" treatment. During the love bombing phase, the codependent is under the impression that the malignant narcissist is highly interested in them. In truth, the malignant narcissist may very well may be - it's just that their attention is directed elsewhere, but their "disinterest" is really the childhood-origin remnant described in the previous paragraph. Nevertheless, the codependent will still be confused because, to them, the goal of their relationship-seeking endeavors is to solidify a lasting, consistent bond of love…for once! At last! And this is because they had the opposite experience with one of their parents: whereas the malignant narcissist was overindulged with love and attention by their parent to the point where it was burdensome and frustrating, the codependent went *completely* without when it came to bonding with one of *their* parents, and it's usually the father. And this makes sense when you consider that it's historically been the father who's been the "breadwinner" for generations and was not emotionally available on account of such. It's also been the case that, for many generations, the father's role was to be more of a disciplinarian than a loving figure.

The case for the codependent may actually be worse. The parent whom with they did not bond may have offered the opposite of love and attention: *abuse*. If this is the case, the stakes are even higher when it comes to being the recipient of love bombing. When the "idealize" phase ends and progresses into "devalue" and "discard," this can be utterly devastating to such a person. Since I'm on the topic, I'd like to mention that this is a dynamic I've seen in many gay men. Usually wanting verification that they're loved and cared about by their father, many homosexual male children often receive the opposite. At best, they feel rejected or frowned upon by their father figure - which will deplete their confidence and sense of self-worth while simultaneously skyrocket their need to be loved to the point where it feels detrimental. At worst, they are abused or disowned by such a parent and probably will have a very difficult life as an adult, not to mention one that's beyond codependent. Instead of a relationship, their love life is liable to be haphazard and sporadic.

Whatever the case may be, the previous material should provide insight as to why the "devalue" and "discard" phases occur after the "idealize" phase: the "devalue" represents the frustration and irritation the

Cluster B's inner child experienced while growing up whereas the "discard" represents the subsequent tantrum the child would throw if the parent persisted with "the bonding." One reason is that the partner was being too clingy. Another reason for the "devalue" and "discard" stages is due to being with a partner who didn't spoil them to the degree the narcissistic Cluster B was expecting, or that things didn't revolve around the way the malignant narcissist wanted things to go. (As you probably figured out by now, "thinking for two" is impossible for Adult-toddlers.)

The maturation process with respect to relationship initiation will involve greater equanimity for both malignant narcissists as well as codependents. For the malignant narcissist personality type, they will need to realize that the "rush" of approval and validation they feel when love bombing is based upon utilizing others for self-worth and attention. They also need to understand that pretending to love someone in order to feel worthy is unfair to the other party, that they do have to consider and have genuine feelings of love for them. For the codependent, they need to abandon the concept of a "soul-mate," or someone who will "complete them." They need to lessen the expectation that their "soul" needs to be "bonded" with another's in order to be at peace; that there needs to be room or breathe unless you plan on becoming something akin to Siamese Twins. Both parties need to equilibrate realistic expectations of "togetherness" and "separateness," that is, all relationships involve union and distinction between the parties. Reparenting practices would benefit both parties as well.

Although the topic of love bombing has been included within a chapter discussing "a need to control," I'd like to reiterate that it's not necessarily my belief that the malignant narcissistic personality type engages in this behavior so much out of conscious control than to revivify something which is familiar to them.

Abandonment-Based Trauma (M-Based ASPD)

Under this subheading, we'll start with the M-Based ASPD trauma-based controlling behavior first since it has already been discussed in previous sections. Here, the childhood-origin Abandonment issues behind this disorder, unlike NPD, are *genuine:* that is, the episodes which caused fears of abandonment *were due to* being abandoned and neglected, *not* due to a break in spoiling the child like NPD. Unlike the NPD, who cries when they're not catered to, put on a pedestal, made the center of attention, agreed with, given what they want where, when, and how, etc.,

etc., and more etc., the M-Based ASPD *did* face episodes where their psychological, physical, and emotional wellbeing was neglected or jeopardized due to Abandonment. Keep in mind, however: the chances of NPD and Maternal-based ASPD being co-morbid are high. That's not to say that one tends to outshine the other or that one is predominantly apparent over the other.

The range of severity behind the episodes of childhood abandonment or neglect is vast: it could be something akin to leaving the child alone for a bit too long than the child was ready to handle to leaving a child of the same age alone for days. The abandonment could have took the form of neglect, requiring the child to be "more grown up" than age appropriate, whether that involved taking care of other children, earning an income, or being a caretaker themselves.

In the case of controlling behavior, however, this is most likely due to some acute trauma the child had faced. As "bad" as things like physical duress and abuse, enslavement, torture, confinement, or other extreme forms of control seem on the surface, provided the person inflicting has Maternal-based ASPD and *not* NPD, the traumatic episodes of Abandonment the "perpetrator" endured were equally pronounced. A person with HPD might engage in controlling behavior, but it's usually manipulative instead or forceful or abusive.

With BPD and *especially* Paternal-based ASPD, the trauma was different. Instead of trauma based in experiences of Abandonment, those suffering from these disorders were the recipients of abuse - similar to those methods described in the previous paragraph. Being the recipient of extreme forms of abuse is more likely to happen with those who develop Paternal-based ASPD than BPD. Whereas the BPD is likely to develop addictions and self inflict (remember, men diagnosed with BPD are four-times more likely to commit suicide), P-Based ASPD individuals are prone to addictions, self-inflict, and/or inflict harm onto animals or property. Suicide or over-dosing is likely among these types as well. Unless the P-Based ASPD is co-morbid with Maternal-based ASPD (the equivalent of an adult bully), they will most likely *not* harm other people or even control them.

COPING STRATEGIES FOR DEALING WITH THE NEED TO CONTROL:
- If possible, *Observe, don't absorb.*
- If the controlling behavior is verbally, psychologically, or physically abusive, ask: "Why are you so angry?" Try to get them to start

a dialogue. Use "truth mechanisms" in the form of questions.
•	Do not indulge "love-bombing": take it as a red flag.
•	Set boundaries: do not "give in" to excessive demands/ unreasonable expectations.
•	Do not accept anyone back who has discarded you for not acquiescing to their controlling demands.
•	Discard anyone who expects you to succumb to their controlling demands.
•	*Gradually Ween Them Off:* If "no contact" is not an option, set boundaries and stick to them. Mentally prepare yourself for adverse reactions and tantrums.
•	Be conscious about how much you are giving and the effect it has on you and what you're receiving in return. Also, understand that "giving" out of obligation or *for the purpose* of receiving *is not* the same as doing things out of love.
•	Is what you're giving being acknowledged/appreciated? "Giving" is a gift and (exempting the necessary "giving" within a healthy relationship or the bullet-points in your job description for which you are getting paid), if the "gift" isn't appreciated, then it isn't deserved. If it isn't deserved, then it needs to stop being given. This goes for *any* relationship: family, romantic, marriage, friendship, professional, etc. Giving into the malignant narcissist's controlling demands or unrealistic and unreciprocated expectations is not "giving" nor is it being "received": it's being *stolen*. Whether or not they were raised in a neglectful or abandoning environment or spoiled, if they are adults and do not at least *acknowledge* the times when you are giving and *what* you're giving - let alone not reciprocating - cut them off and cut the cord.
•	*No J.A.D.E: Justify, Argue, Defend, or Explain:* If you find yourself being put on the defensive because the other party seeks to dominate you or control you, whether it is respect to your behavior, opinions, preferences, likes, dislikes, etc., do not justify, argue, defend, or explain. Simply ask, "Why are you putting me on the defensive?" This is different from someone asking for clarity, further embellishment, additional information, or reasons you feel the way you do. There's a difference between controlling and dominating and trying to understand and keep an open mind. Learn to make a distinction between an un-winnable debate and a discussion. The first stokes conflict until the other party relents, the other seeks to *resolve* conflict and the objective to seek the truth (not "win") and/or cooperate. Narcissists always create conflict until they get what they want due to an Entitlement issue that gives rise to a sense of Abandonment or an Abandonment issue which gives rise to a

sense Entitlement.

RED FLAGS:
- You're innocent but being treated as if you were guilty.
- Love-bombing.
- Playing the victim.
- Excessive demands/Unreasonable expectations.
- Expectations to be over-indulged/spoiled.
- Your hands are giving but not receiving.
- It's "Their way or the highway."
- Disproportionate, volatile, and seemingly unprovoked reactions.
- Conflict is created by them but never resolved by them; it's only resolved by your capitulation and agreement (which isn't "resolution"; it's tyranny.)
- No co-operation on their part.
- Close-mindedness.
- Conversations and discussions are turned into debates.
- Being placed on the defensive.
- Overly-reprimanding behavior.

CHILDHOOD CONDITIONS CREATING A NEED TO CONTROL:
- Raised in a neglectful or abandoning household.
- History of parental betrayal.
- Over-indulged as children and/or adults with respect to ego, empathy, attention,freedom, or material goods (including finances.)
- Traumatic episodes of abandonment or neglect.

UNDERLYING ISSUES BEHIND OF A NEED TO CONTROL IN A CLUSTER B:
- Fear of Abandonment/Neglect.
- A sense of Entitlement.
- Fear of Unlovability/Inadequacy.
- Fears of betrayal.

[1] https://www.youtube.com/watch?v=Pb-YuhFWCr4

8

Karma Chameleons

The Adulation-Seeking/Shame Cycle

If the excessive care or emotional incest were present in the child's life, this would also account for the "Idealize, Devalue, and Discard" cycle being present if not pronounced. The adult version of this child will later seek out narcissistic supply and find that the cost of doing so involves being excessively nurtured and/or being required to nurture to the point of having personal boundaries violated, compromised, or infringed upon. The uncomfortable, irritating sense of being smothered in too much love or being required to give it causes the cycle to spin faster, more so if the reminder of emotional incest were present.

Before going forward, it needs to be stressed that the reason the Cluster B seeks out narcissistic supply as opposed to genuine attentiveness to their "issues" is due to the very "false/grandiose self" their parent created by over-amplifying their self concept. Here, the child fears that the "issues" or insecurities of the true self won't be acceptable since their parent seems to love the child because they're "perfect." Thus, any "flaw" or "defect" revealed about the child will cause him to feel that he will be rejected. This is because the idealized perception his parent(s) subjected him to requires him to measure up to an ideal in order to be loved.

But this sort of adulation-seeking at the cost of compromising personal boundaries can produce shame and resentment toward the other party in such individuals as well as toward themselves, which requires an ego-boost to "fix" the false self which involves the need for more narcissistic supply, which leads to resent the narcissistic supply which leads to adulation-seeking, which leads to shame, and so the cycle continues until the individual truly loves themselves.

The potential history of being subjected to emotional incest and/or bartering excessive care for narcissistic supply would also create an aversion to becoming vulnerable or open in romantic relationships, a resistance to or receiving affection, or a hot-and-cold temperament: all of which often seen in Cluster B personality disorders. More so, if shame is present, this would increase the likelihood of such behavior.

The following figure depicts the Cluster B's psychological stages during the "Idealize, Devalue, and Discard" Cycle fueled by shame and low self-worth:

Figure 1: Cluster B's Idealize, Devalue, Discard "Shame Cycle"

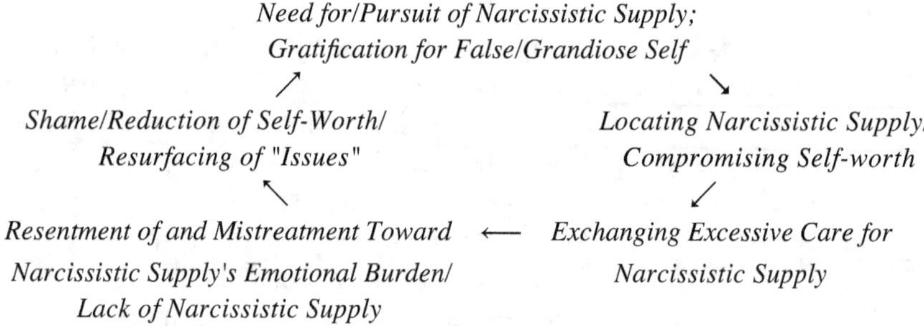

A real-life example would look like the following: Kevin, a handsome, athletic, and charismatic young man enjoys the attention (or narcissistic supply) his appearance and personality inspires from women. The praise, ogling, hero-worship, and attention from such women makes him feel good. In truth, he has been relying on such supply to feel good about himself for so long, he's essentially unable to rely upon himself to provide such supply let alone be aware of the "issues" he has.

While Kevin is alone for some time, feelings of inadequacy (or some other "issue") begin to arise. He starts to feel his self-worth or self-confidence fade. Being unable or unconditioned to tend to this issue on his own, he seeks out approval and admiration from others as a surrogate.

To accommodate this, Kevin decides to go to a nightclub and meets Cindy, a nice, attractive girl who takes a liking to Kevin rather quickly due to his charms and good looks. Kevin likes Cindy as well because of her good-natured demeanor and attentiveness. Plus, she's attractive herself. Her attraction to him is evident, which causes Kevin to feel better about himself. After a night of chatting, usually involving Kevin talking about himself while Cindy attentively listens, the two decide to exchange numbers.

Kevin capitalizes on subsequent interactions with Cindy (albeit unconsciously) to illicit more narcissistic supply. As he does so, Cindy is increasingly becoming more vulnerable, seemingly "wearing her heart on her sleeve" more and more, which causes Kevin to feel increasingly agitated, although he can't place his finger on why he feels this way.

As the interactions progress, it seems to Kevin that Cindy is becoming less accommodating when it comes to being attentive toward him. Rather, she seems increasingly pouty whenever Kevin talks about himself, and he finds this irritating as well.

As time goes on, when Cindy's emotional needs require more attention, Kevin's frustration builds to the point where he lashes out at her. He berates her with belittling remarks and "dumps" her without any care or closure, devastating Cindy.

Kevin then isolates for a bit (provided he doesn't already have someone on the side) and when the same negative feelings resurface that were present before he went out to the nightclub previously, he goes out again, resetting the cycle.

Kevin is going to continue this cycle until he addresses and attends to the root causes of the lack of self-worth which propelled him to go out seeking narcissistic supply at night clubs. Moreover, he will not be in a healthy relationship unless he is willing to be vulnerable with himself and his partner about his lack of self-worth (as well as its childhood origins.) Otherwise, if he continues to use "narcissistic supply" as a drug to anesthetize these issues - to have others "be his self-worth" for him - "the wheel" will keep spinning unless life throws a stick in its spokes.

What Kevin *needs to convert* in order to develop a healthy relationship is *his reliance upon narcissistic supply as an anesthetic to his issues to a willingness to practice vulnerability and disclosure of these very issues directly to his partner*. This gives his partner a chance to truly love him (and his *true* self) as opposed to enabling his false one. What scares Kevin about doing this is what might happen if he's open and honest.

But it is only when he does so that will Kevin be able to break this cycle on his own.

Wicked Pisser

Expanding on the previous example, there is a reason why people codependents like Cindy find themselves repeating these kinds of scenarios in their own lives. As many of you probably suspect by now, this is due to the childhood-origin conditions people like Cindy faced while growing up, namely a parental source who was unable or unwilling to assist them with and attend to the feelings of low self-worth and self-value the child might have or loving the child to begin with. Usually, the child in this case was looking for reassurance or affection from the parent.

Say that, as a very young child, Cindy was keenly aware of a quality about herself and was afraid that others would not like her on account of having this quality. Not only may they not have liked her on account of it, but possibly harm her in some way if they learned about it. Say that she feels extremely vulnerable, especially if members of the opposite sex were to learn about it. If this is the case, then it is likely that a child like Cindy may develop a demeanor of shyness or withdrawal around others.

In addition, Cindy learns early on that the environment she's growing up in does not welcome "problems": she learns quickly that if she's sad, insecure, ashamed, or self-loathing, receiving parental support is not welcomed.

It may also be the case that Cindy never received love in the form of attentiveness or affection from one or both of her parents, particularly her father.

Feeling ashamed, vulnerable, isolated, and low in self-worth, she deeply hopes that her father in particular will still love her if he were to find out her "secret." Her sensitivity toward his potential disapproval causes her to be sensitive around him, taking on a demeanor of being sweet, demure, insecure, and innocuous. Part of the reason such a demeanor exists is because of her fears regarding her father's potential adverse reaction to learning about her "issues." To win over favor with him in order to safeguard her own security, she may even provide a kind of childlike source of narcissistic supply to the father, trying to "butter him up."

The sentimental, vulnerable, and needy quality Cindy adopts

around her father is an attempt to gain reassurance and affection from him. This is due to wanting to create an environment that's safe and warm enough where Cindy *can* open up. (Now that I think about it, this is probably the reason a Cluster B will appear overly-confident and grandiose; *the objective to create a safe environment is the same.*)

But it is this precisely this element of feeling unlovable and trying to gain affection, reassurance, validation, or approval from a parental figure at a very young age which sets the **shame/resentment cycle** *in life.* Especially if met with irritation, disdain, or contempt, *the resulting emotional condition the child* (and subsequent adult) *will feel is shame toward self* (because the emotional support they reluctantly seek conjures humiliation when the parent rejects or refutes it) *and resentment toward the parent* (or other adult because they, in essence, not only neglected her needs but reinforced her lack of worth.) For a child, *this sort of treatment or expectation to be self-reliant with respect to self-worth and subsequent rejection of the child for expressing such needs is abuse.* Imagine a child who's hungry and approaches her parent in order to be fed only to be treated like a burden whether or not she is subsequently fed.

Moreover, since the child was not assisted with identifying and resolving her be unlikely that she will develop one as an adult. Also, because the developing child's sense of self is completely shaped and determined by the feedback from others, the child will not apply the "this is me, that is you" mentality which healthy adults have in their interactions with others. If this sort of weak or missing "ego boundaries" transpire while in adulthood, this can cause a child like Cindy to be an "empath" - or one who "takes on" other people's energy and emotions and the tendency to let others "shape" her self-concept. A child like Cindy is also liable to have poor boundaries as an adult, especially if they were disregarded as a child.

Regardless, the sentimental, needy demeanor carried by a child who seeks comfort, validation, and approval may catalyze an adverse reaction in the *father* since his daughter's passive advances resemble the neediness or (emotional) incest that was present in *his* upbringing with his mother. Instead of having care and concern for his daughter, he thus experiences irritation and frustration.

Whether or not (emotional) incest was present in the father's upbringing, the child's passive but persistent attempts to forge a warm, loving connection to receive support for her low self-worth will only be seen by the Cluster B father as his child's insecurity and neediness. Instead of attending to her issues (because she's not open with them), he is prone to become frustrated and angry with his daughter's behavior, perceiving her as weak and insecure. Because of this, Cindy is likely to receive retaliation or disdain for her concealed and unhealed "issues" rather than the comfort and reassurance she's looking for. Worse, she may feel - and actually receive - rejection from her father which, again, is the precise fate she was looking to avoid in the first place.

To reiterate, if her behavior is met with rebukes from her father, Cindy's issues and insecurities not only go unresolved, but she'll begin to feel a growing resentment toward her father because of his insensitivity, lack of love, and rejection. As she grows older, Cindy may even develop a rebellious nature with respect to her father, which is out of protest to what she perceives as her father's hatred toward her. Her father is likely to respond to both the insecurity and rebellion with punitive responses, blame, and shame.

If this carries over into adult relationships, Cindy may harbor an underlying vengeance against or animosity toward men. "You didn't love me growing up, so I won't love you back!" or "You hurt me when I needed you, so I'm going to do the same thing to you."

If Cindy does not directly retaliate against such men, her compensatory behavior would be to self-inflict: "You didn't love me so I'm going to [fill in the blank with any sort of self-destructive behavior] myself!" Or, "If somebody doesn't love me, I'm going to kill myself!" This sort of psychology is most likely the culprit behind the self-harm and suicidal tendencies behind Borderline Personality Disorder.

Like Kevin, Cindy is likely to become stuck in her own cycle when she pursues relationships as an adult. And, like Kevin's cycle, Cindy's starts with "issues" of some sort which caused her insecurities - which may be, at the very least, a lack of attention and affection. To soothe these insecurities, albeit reluctantly, she seeks comfort in the form care and attentiveness from men, but bears an internal fear that - if this insecurity is disclosed to or discovered by these men - she will be rejected, unloved, abandoned, mistreated, or even abused.

Because of this fear, Cindy (like her child self) presents a demeanor which is sentimental, esoteric, and needy while being overly-attentive herself. It's likely that she regards - or at least has the hopes that - such men she's attempting to get involved with as "savior" figures, "soul-mates," or those who will finally provide the nourishing attention to the very issues she's held in private for so long. (Just like she did with her father.) The problem is, the more she "milks" these men for such nurturing without disclosing the source of fear that is her "secret issue," the more these men are going to resent her. What first seemed to these men to be a confident woman now takes the appearance of being needy and draining, when the prolonged or escalating need to be coddled could have been avoided had she the courage to disclosure her "issues" as opposed to anesthetizing them with the men's "care."

Before proceeding, just as Cindy is described as "soul-mate" seeking above - someone who will finally "love" her - Kevin has his own version. Because he was raised at a very early age to be a "Messiah" or an ideal (because that is how he was seen in the eyes of his mother and made him feel super-human), he will seek out a "soul-mate" who sees him in a similar way, but on a consistent basis. In light of this, you can see how the "Idealize, Devalue, Discard" cycle is a projection of his own experience. His mother "idealized" him at birth, at some point "devalued" him for things probably beyond his control or awareness, thus making his grand sense of self feel "discarded." He subsequently subjects his "dance partners" to the same treatment.

Back to Cindy: what some men may not realize is that Cindy may be deathly afraid of disclosing her fears, just like Kevin (or some of these men, for that matter.) Regardless, her fear of rejection or unlovability is going to manifest itself in some way shape or form unless she, like Kevin, can resolve the "issues" which started this cycle on her own or at least be willing to have the courage to be open with her issues in relationships when she feels comfortable doing so. Both Kevin and Cindy are also going to have to contend with the fact that, even if they have resolved their "issues" on their own and/or have the courage to be open and vulnerable in relationships without "playing games," they may still face the rejection or unlovability they were so afraid of.

Cindy's version of Kevin's cycle would look like this:

Figure 2: Codependent's Idealized, Devalued, Discarded "Shame Cycle"

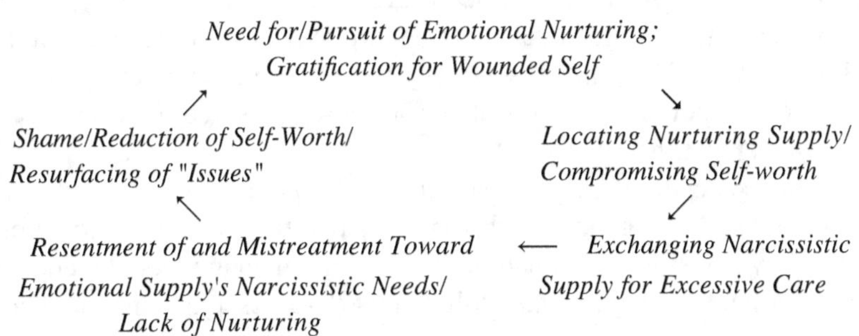

Like Kevin's pursuit of narcissistic supply, Cindy's pursuit of comfort and nurturance could involve shame-inducting degradation: with Kevin, it could be as extreme as partnering with a prostitute; for Cindy, a jerk or a sleaze bag. It could also mean they may "lead people on" and engage interested others without being genuinely interested in them. As displayed in both cycles, there is a chance that self-worth will be compromised if this occurs. If so, Kevin is liable to default back onto the "Grandiose Self" whereas Cindy takes on "the suffering in silence victim."

What's sad, though, is that with the Kevin/Cindy couple, neither realize that it is *highly* probable that the "issues" one of them has, the other also has: they're basically two-sides of the same coin. With respect to anesthetization, one seeks out narcissistic supply whereas the other seeks out nurturing. This is the premise behind what's often referred to as "Karmic Relationships" or "Twin-Flame Couples."

And here's the irony of this scenario: If one ends up hating the other, it's likely they hate themselves for the same reasons. What results in this case is a game of psychological Chinese Finger Cuffs which gets futile after about two minutes.

The bigger shame is that neither may appreciate the fact that the other *also* was required to authentically "love themselves" at a very early age without outside support and expected to do this in a conditionally loving environment. The early childhood sense of fear and isolation they felt growing up, the other felt as well. So, Hell started early for both of them.

If it sounds like a penultimate pisser, that's because it is…

But, neither Nick or Cindy should be hard on themselves because of the fact that this condition was imprinted on both at such an early age and went through stages as time progressed. Who knows: this "Idealize, Devalue , and Discard" cycle both endure may have started close to birth. But both would benefit to know they were deprived at a very young age of a very important need. It's okay for both to be loved for who they are as they are at all times.

Especially if being subjected to a "discard" causes her extreme grief and sadness, Cindy needs to realize that this is only due to being raised by a dysfunctional parent who was not mentally healthy enough to care for her properly. As an adult, Cindy *does* deserve someone who is caring about her insecurities. Thus, she needs to disconnect the "cord" that her insecurities or needing support and validation is never burdensome. Karma Chameleons ◇ 157She also needs to understand that adults who resemble the parent in the picture are also not healthy.

Locus of Liability

In a way, Cindy's upbringing is like a "photo-negative" of Kevin's: both present the same image, but the light colors in one image are dark in the other. For Kevin, he was brought into the world with his self-worth overindulged by one (or both) of his parents. Because of this, he finds his *parent* liable for any "issues" he encounters since life is not reflecting the expectation his parent(s) imprinted upon him.

Cindy is the opposite: her self-worth/sense of self was either disregarded or worse - diminished - since she was a little child. When she falls short of gaining the very reassurance and care she needs to counteract the negative sense of self her parent(s) shaped from the very same parents, she finds *herself* liable for having these "issues." If the parent induced these "issues," Cindy may have resentment toward them as well.

Because of this, Kevin and Cindy are prone to adopt *offense* and *defense* mechanisms respectively as they grow into adulthood, precisely because one parent was passive in inducing these "issues" while the other was aggressive, respectfully. Or, "It's *your* fault I feel bad about myself" versus "It's *my* fault I feel bad about myself." Future partners will be the scapegoat for Kevin's issues whereas Cindy will blame herself for having issues that her partners find undesirable. Kevin is therefore likely to make Cindy feel responsible for the very transgressions he committed while Cindy accepts responsibility for Kevin's. (If escalated enough, Kevin will blame himself for not being "good enough" whereas Cindy will target her partners for not loving her.)

It's also worth mentioning that Kevin's "issues" were founded on the abandonment of his parent whereas Cindy's was founded on betrayal due to being unloved:

Because Kevin's early upbringing involved a close bond with his parent which involved an elevated self-concept (or with a parent who catered to him), it will be *his parent's fault* that he's not being made to feel lovable, provided for, attended to, safe, etc. Again, *offense mechanisms* will be used by Kevin when he feels unlovable, deprived, abandoned, vulnerable, his trust has been violated, etc. That is, it's someone else's fault he has a schema, and this is due to Kevin's feelings of being ***abandoned*** by such a parent.

Because Cindy, on the other hand, not only *did not* have this sort of bond with her respective parent but tried to forge it by *extracting* such reassurance against feeling unlovable, deprived, abandoned, vulnerable, etc., from said parent only to go without, she *blames herself* and subsequently uses *defense mechanisms* to manage her issues. Unlike Kevin, her "issues" are founded on parental **betrayal**. A worse case scenario would involve Cindy, as a child, receiving the opposite from her parent: being made to feel unlovable, deprived, abandoned, vulnerable, mistrusting, etc. whether or not she went to the parent for love.

With this in mind, it's easy to see why couples like Kevin and Cindy often involve infidelity and loyalty, respectively. Because, to him, Kevin's "issues" are his partner's fault, he will seek someone else who doesn't "cause him to feel" unlovable, deprived, abandoned, etc. Because he feels abandoned, he feels no compunction against abandoning his partner (thus *betraying* them) by cheating on them (as childish and immature as it might seem.)

Because Cindy is seeking love, comfort, appraisal, and approval her partner (who resembles the one who fell short of doing so during her childhood, thus betraying her), she's under the false belief that her loyalty and persistence to such a person will eventually provide her with the love, comfort, appraisal, and approval she's been hoping for. Unfortunately, what plays out as a result is an unending spree of chasing a dangling carrot, if not a rotten one. Because of her accrued feelings of betrayal, Cindy may retaliate herself and cheat on her partner, if not worse.

In both Kevin and Cindy's cases, the result of not deriving what they are looking for - narcissistic supply and emotional nurturing, respectively - results in shame and low self-worth since they've been "rejected."

Part II:

In The
"Real World"

9

"Did He Ever Love Me?"

A common question those who have experienced a relationship severance with a malignant narcissist is, "Did this person love me?" This tends to be asked usually by those who were the recipient of the idealize and devalue treatment and subsequently discarded.

The short answer is: "How much love to you think an Adult-toddler with a life-long history of being over-indulged, abandoned (real or imagined), and therefore expectant to *take* and *inflict* is going to be able to *provide?*"

Now, of course this is a curt answer but, if the question that is the title of this chapter has had any bearing on your post-breakup mind, the likelihood that you were not only involved with a "narcissist" but someone who genuinely had elements of NPD if not the disorder entirely. Please go back and read the description of this disorder from Chapter 2.

So, "did he ever love me?" Exactly how much love can you expect an adult-version of a toddler to give? How much love do you think they're going to be able to give you or *anyone* else they get involved with?

If they *did* "love" you, it's the exact kind of love a spoiled toddler would be able to give. This sort of "love" would look like the following: the narc ex "loved' you for making him feel good; "loved" you for making him the center of your world; "loved" you for overlooking his shortcomings and bad behavior; "loved" you for looking the way he wanted you to; "loved" you for providing him your undivided attention while giving you little to none in return; "loved" you for being there for him when he wanted and for how long he wanted; "loved" you for doing what he wanted to do when he wanted to do it; "loved" you for behaving and responding to ways he found favorable; "loved" you for giving him what he wanted and when he wanted it; "loved" you for being available when he wanted you to be available; "loved" you for indulging his adult-tantrums and epithets; "loved" you for making *his* "issues" *your* problem;

"loved" you for taking the blame for his bad behavior; "loved" you for buying into his fantasy world of make-believe and lies; "loved" you for making his opinions and beliefs your own without question; "loved" you for never needing anything from *him*; "loved" you only when you were the human version of a robot; "loved" you for allowing a grown adult to behave like a brat... The list goes on and I think you get the point.

If the narcissist is the one who discarded you, it's usually because they sensed you weren't willing to capitulate to the above. The "toy" didn't make him happy. Believe it or not, it's likely that they see *you* as the perpetrator and *themselves* as the victim. If you left the relationship, clearly you sensed the above was going on to some extent.

Or, the narcissist, because of their own abandonment/neglect issues, perceived you as defunct in some capacity - maybe not earning enough money, taking good enough care of yourself, or whatever physical parameter they deemed as deficient. Whether this is pertinent or not depends of course on the situation.

So, what's this *really* about? Why did this happen and why did this go on for as long as it did?

Let's drill down on this a bit...

For many of you this question is rhetorical (especially since it was brought up earlier in this book), but why do you think this interaction occurred?

If you guessed parental issues, you're correct. If you've guessed that it was an opportunity to break the chains of deeply ingrained codependency, you're ahead of the game. But let's get more specific...

Those of us who've had a relationship experience as described above most likely had a parent who was very similar. For most of us - and since NPD is more common in men - the ex-partner was male and their psychology was most likely that of our parent while growing up, but not in all cases.

Since both men grew up being catered *to, while simultaneously being neglected,* their expectation of you was to follow suit. What you did, how you appeared, how you behaved, your beliefs, your talents, your aptitudes, your opinions were all to be *extensions of him and governed by his will. If he "approved," they were "good." If he did not "approve," they were "bad."*

Moreover, it is almost impossible for a narcissistic parent to instill a sense of rebelliousness in any child they subjugate. Since narcissists err on the side of control, this sort of imprint is a guarantee. Thus, in ways which range from being passive and seemingly innocuous to overt and aggressive, the child retaliates against such subjugation. For this reason, codependents may be consciously or unconsciously antagonistic to the narcissist.

Keep in mind, however, the issues behind the narcissistic personality. The early episodes of entitlement produced a child with raised bar of expectation or standards to adhere to. Factor in abandonment and neglect - especially if they were acute - and this is guaranteed to produce a controlling personality. If they've threatened the child's safety, the later in life adult is likely to become an abuser.

So, "Did the Narcissist love me?" The answer's probably "yes": they loved you as much as they were capable at the time.

10

Dogville

"In our world, there will be no emotions except fear, rage, triumph, and self-abasement.
The sex instinct will be eradicated. We shall abolish the orgasm.
There will be no loyalty except loyalty to the Party. But always there will be the intoxication of power.
Always, at every moment, there will be the thrill of victory, the sensation of trampling on an enemy who's helpless."
- George Orwell [1]

The Dysfunctional Family: The Quintessential "Patriarchy"

As mentioned before, when a malignant narcissist is at the head of a household, the family turns out dysfunctional. Children born into the family inhabit the following dysfunctional roles, usually in the following order: The Hero or Golden Child, The Rebel or Scapegoat, The Lost Child, and the Mascot or Jester.

Also mentioned before, malignant narcissists tend to view people as "things" or objects. This is due to Entitlement and/or Abandonment issues being at the core of their self-concept - which others are to be the source of their narcissistic supply and cater to their whims, respectively.

Right here, I ask that the reader to regard the following with sensitivity and compassion. Because, as crass as it sounds, parents who are malignant narcissists will raise their children akin to how some owners will raise dogs: the dogs are "adopted" in order to "make" the owner "happy," behave in ways the owner finds appropriate, and do what the owner would like them to do. The adopted "dogs" cater to the "Owner's" unhealed abandonment and entitlement issues.

Take note as well that the "raising" of the dogs is usually assisted by someone who is codependent to some degree.

For now, the dysfunctional roles of The Hero, The Rebel, The Lost Child, and The Mascot will be correlated respectively to the following "dog roles" within the dysfunctional family: "Good Dog," "Bad Dog," "Kick Dog," and "Trick Dog." To expand on the dysfunctional family roles, we'll add two more: "Guard Dog" and "Stray Dog."

[1] htttps://www.youtube.com/watch?v=PGuKyBimFvM

The "Owner"
Since heads of households who program the dysfunctional roles within the family's children have malignant, narcissistic traits, they will anticipate receiving love, care, and respect but not feel compelled to *give it*. For those having NPD in part or in full, this is again rooted in an *Entitlement* issue born out of being overindulged as a child. For those having what's described in this book as M-Based ASPD, this is due to an *Abandonment issue* arising from abandonment, neglect, and/or taking on additional responsibilities. *Take note that this can be psychological abandonment as well where the child had to give up their true self. And take note that the same child could have been both overindulged AND abandoned which would make them co-morbid for NPD and M-Based ASPD or at least having some resulting characteristics.*
Whether it's a core "issue" of Abandonment or Entitlement or both, feelings of abandonment lead to entitlement and when entitlement isn't catered to, feelings of abandonment and withdrawal arise. It's due to this abandonment that *others* are held accountable when negative thoughts and feelings arise in such individuals - it's *their* fault. To mitigate these "issues," *projection* is employed: "You're bad," "You're no good," "You're [fill in the blank.]" Conversely, others are often held responsible for making this personality type *feel good*. Again, this is typically the reason a malignant narcissist will seek to have children in the first place - in order to make them feel good, much like a child would want to adopt a puppy: *not* to have to take care of it, but for their own enjoyment which would, at times, be better presented in quotes as "enjoyment" since this "enjoyment" can be quite sadistic.
Just for clarity, let's look at a simple example of what the Abandonment-to-Entitlement or Entitlement-to-Abandonment-to-Entitlement looks like: A man enters his favorite restaurant where he always gets great service: whenever he orders his food, it arrives to his table within five minutes. One day, he goes in places his order, and five minutes go by. No food. Another five minutes go by; still no food. It takes another five minutes until the food comes to his table. During the extra ten minutes, the man is restless, anxious, and getting a bit upset. When the food comes to his table, he asks why it took so long? The waiter apologizes and mentions that a couple of their kitchen staff called out due

to an illness and, referring to a party of twenty-five across the dining room, the establishment met an unforeseen and unprecedented spike in traffic volume prior to his arrival. The man, "used" to getting his food within five minutes and upset for "having to wait three times as long," demands that his next meal be free of charge due to both feelings of abandonment and neglect as well as his grandiose self (ego.)

Because of this, children born to a malignant narcissist are often raised much as an owner might regard his dogs or servants: do what I expect of you, or else you'll pay. Because his expectation of *loyalty* is betrayed or abandoned (at least in his mind), the dog who is *supposed* to be loyal or his "loyal servant" but falls short is seen as "bad." The malignant narcissist thus feels *entitled* to compensation or *entitled* to inflict punishment - but this can happen *even when* the "dog" or "servant" is unable to fulfill the malignant narcissist's expectations despite valiant efforts.

And, much like a child seeks to have a dog or the latest toy, a malignant narcissist seeks to have a "son" or a "daughter." Especially with the case of M-Based ASPD, this is actually heartbreaking to observe since their inner child feels abandoned and it's their abandonment which has gone unhealed. However, when the "dog" is brought in and *doesn't* satisfy or cater to the narcissistic parent's Abandonment or Entitlement issues (as well as its grandiose self), problems arise. Also, love, care, and respect usually go in one direction - to the narcissist - save for times when the "dog" *does* appease the narcissist's Abandonment and Entitlement issues.

Consider this with respect to the material presented back in Chapter 3: Grandiose Self under the *"Messiah Complex"* topic. With the codependent parent's imperative for having a child in order to have "someone to love me," it's the same for the narcissist: it's just different in terms of what "love" means. In the case of the narcissist, it's a type of loyalty: "someone to make me happy" - again, much like an owner would regard his dog.

Because of this, others are also objectified in the sense that they are "good" or "bad" depending on how they make the malignant narcissist *feel*. This is why *their feelings become "facts" to them*. The "fact" that they feel "bad" or "good," to them, is essentially **the other person** and *not just what they're doing or not doing* since the person is seen as an *object*. This trend will be readily apparent starting with the first born - The Golden Child - since they will readily based their **self-concept** - *and not just their behavior* - as "good" or "bad" depending on whether their actions are perceived as "good" or "bad" by the parent - *much like a dog would his owner.*

This is different from raising a child to exhibit good behavior and character in that the child is always seen as "good" but the behaviors are separate from the child herself - that is, just because she does something "bad" doesn't make *her* "bad." Calling a little boy "bad" because he almost stuck his finger in an electrical socket is different from preventing him from doing so and explaining *why* it is "bad" for him to do so. Otherwise, the child's self-concept is based on his behavior, not who he is as a person.

But, it goes beyond that: as a child gets older, he or she will be considered "good" or "bad" whether or not he accepts the same beliefs, has the same opinions, obliges to never question the logic or "authority" of the parent, grooms themselves a certain way, obeys or disobeys without being told the "why" behind it, and more. In essence, the child becomes stripped of their autonomy, critical thinking ability, their separate sense of identity, and bases their self-value on others' approval or disapproval, most often those in positions of power, leadership, or authority.

And this is not to suggest that the child not display love, care, and respect to their parent: *hardly.* But branding the child as "good" or "bad" to an excessive extent *will* cause them to be hypersensitive to others wants, needs, feelings, wishes, opinions, and belief systems of others while abdicating their own as they proceed through life, not just the narcissistic parent. Not only are they liable to become overly empathic, but since their behavior is so dictated and conditioned, the "cord" is so tight they probably won't be able to "fly solo" once the leave the nest - if they do actually do so. The more a child is "raised" by a parent in such a manner, the more this is likely to happen.

Note how this trend conditions the child to develop low or absent boundaries as well as codependency throughout childhood and well into adulthood. Since the child abnegates his/her own wants, needs, opinions, etc. to derive "love" which is really "approval" from the narcissistic parent (which is *selfish)* the child is being "raised" to believe that such self-abnegation is necessary in order to realize even the possibility of being "loved." The child is "taught" to be low-conflict and *obedient,* usually since "going with the program" may reap in "rewards" of acceptance and approval whereas "going against it" leads to over-the-top punishment of some sort. *And they're liable to get involved with similar personality types in relationships as an adult.*

So, with narcissistic parenting, three elements are focal: 1) Love, care, and respect go in one direction - toward the parent (the opposite is often returned); 2) The child is conditioned to "black and white" thinking, that they're "good" or "bad" depending on their behaviors and not their behaviors having a "good" or "bad" outcome; and 3) The children are held responsible for the parent's happiness or unhappiness.

With those three things in mind, the "Owner" of such "dogs" will base the approval he has for his dogs on **what they do for him, their loyalty, and the way they "make him feel." Again, there's nothing wrong with** *any* **of this: it's when it goes in** *one direction - toward the Owner - that the dysfunction kicks in. In functional families, love, care, and respect go in all directions - between parent and child and amongst siblings. It is THIS objective which all good parents should be mindful of and the "culture" they try to uphold and personify.*

Also, keep in mind that we're only observing the effects of one parent who is narcissistic. The other parent could be similar or not. And then there's gender differences as well as sons tend to be treated differently by their fathers than their sisters as well as by their mothers. It's much more likely for a mother to inflict abuse on her daughter (usually emotional or psychological) than her son whereas it's much more likely for a father to inflict abuse on his son (emotional, psychological, and physical) than his daughter - which is probably why the differences between BPD and P-Based ASPD (which, again, is actually Factor 2 of the PCL-R) are seemingly cosmetic (and why BPD is often referred to as "Female Psychopathy) - but this is a generalization, of course.

Good Dog

I want to stress that just because a person was the first-born, an only child, or even a "Golden Child" does not mean they have developed NPD or have become a "malignant narcissist." The "Hero/Golden Child" *might* shows signs of being *narcissistic,* but may *not* be diagnosable as having NPD specifically. I would think that, more often than not, they would *not* develop NPD if raised in a dysfunctional family, unless the child was also over-indulged, spoiled, or preferred. And this is not to say that such a child won't develop malignant narcissistic traits, either. But the Hero and the Messiah roles born out of dysfunctional families are shaped by other conditions as well.

However, with the Hero/Golden Child, the "spoiling" they receive that fuels their narcissism comes in the form of "approval." This approval *absolutely* can lead to narcissism especially if this child is placed on a pedestal taller than those of other children in the family. Since they've bartered their authentic self to meet the criteria to suit the parent(s) ideals, they receive "preferential treatment" in the form of *approval* in return. Thus, they're the "good kid" - in their eyes, their parent(s) eyes, and the outside world's - who gives the dysfunctional parent(s) the false impression that they're capable of raising a healthy child. Like the NPD/ M-Based ASPD co-morbid, **when the "preferential treatment" in the form of approval stopped, they felt abandoned and if/when actual abandonment *did* occur, they felt *entitled* to "preferential treatment" and approval: the parent needed to "make up" for abandoning them and/or ceasing to approving of them.** The "approval-spoiling" is similar the *ego-spoiling* described in Chapter 2 under Narcissistic Personality Disorder, just more sporadic.

As such, the "self-worth" (which is really a piece of the The Owner's "Grandiose-Self pie") the Hero/Golden child possesses is and will be *contingent on the approval of authority figures as adults*. If the "authority figure" is a malignant narcissistic themselves (just like their parent), the Hero/Golden child is prone to do whatever the "authority figure" wants them to do so long as they're approved of or seen as "good" by such an "authority figure." The adult child version may become a "people pleaser," but the pleasing not only gives them a surrogate sense of value since they appear "good" in the eyes of others, but it can be used to boost their own narcissism. Basically, in life, such a Hero/Golden Child becomes the human equivalent to a well-trained dog: "Perform the preferred behavior, and I'll give you a treat" *and the "treat" is approval.*

The Hero/Golden Child is the "Good Dog" because they're well trained - *trained* to give the "owner" love, care, and respect and meet his expectations, regardless of how unrealistic or self-directed they might be. After this, and because of the narcissistic parent's self-focus (grandiose self) along with Abandonment issues and the subsequent expectation to be catered *to,* "training" other "dogs" becomes a problem. Thanks to the narcissistic parent's Abandonment-based victim mentality (or sense of Entitlement), it goes against the "owner's" grain to give the very attention he or she feels *entitled* to receive. In truth, the "owner" thinks it's all about *him.* Even with the "Good Dog," it's all about him. The "Good Dog" was just first in line and easier to train.

Because of the "treats" the Hero is given, they're both dependent on the "owner" as well as loyal to the "owner," seeing the "owner" as good - again, much like a dog. After all, their self-worth exists because of the "owner" despite it being contingent on the approval of said owner. Based on the "tricks" the Hero performs and their frequency, the more he is told he's a "Good Dog" and perceives himself as such (which is narcissistic.)

So, it's not only possible that the Hero/Golden child will gravitate to career positions in life which their parent finds "acceptable," but also ones which resemble a sycophant, toady, or some sort of "yes man." This doesn't have to be within an hierarchal organization. Any prominent politician who is a psychopath in real life will likely have "Heroes" as constituent bases or campaign teams. If it *is* an organization which resembles a large-scale version of a dysfunctional family, they will rise in the ranks due to their "self-worth" being contingent on carrying out directives, regardless of how toxic they might be or whom they're supporting or protecting. A fictional example would be the dogs tending to the pigs in George Orwell's *Animal Farm*.

But this poses a problem for the human species. First, the likelihood of malignant, megalomaniacal, narcissistic, tyrannical psychopaths gravitating to positions of power and control is huge: it's built right into their pathology. Such positions serve as bait for those with a grandiose sense of self, with glib and superficial charm, who demean and bully others, who exploit others for personal gain, with a lack of empathy, with a penchant for pathological lying, with a fixation of power and success, with a superior sense of self, with a need for continual admiration, with a sense of entitlement and obedience from others, and who envy others or believe others are envious of them. In other words, those with a escalated condition of Narcissistic Personality Disorder. Whether the regime was ostensibly tyrannical or not, human history has proven this to be the case.

Since the Hero/Golden Child of a dysfunctional family has been raised to placate this sort of personality type, they will assist such tyrannical personalities in realizing their objectives of obtaining ego-based power and control over others. Again, this is all because the tyrant was over-indulged and/or neglected as a child and the Hero was trained to kowtow to that over-indulging and neglect. At the very least, they will be loyal and/or not prone to question the mental health of malignant narcissists.

Now, if conditions within a population *promote* the prevalence of dysfunctional families, this *guarantees* the production of Heroes/Golden Children within a population. This is something I made the case for in my pervious book *The Toxic States of America*. Since they are *usually* the first born, the Hero/Golden Child prototype is bound to outnumber other dysfunctional roles such as the Scapegoat and the Lost Child. Since this *is* the case, the probability that a narcissistic psychopath (or group of them) will assume control *and receive support in doing so thanks to Heroes/ Golden Children who still inhabit their dysfunctional role and subsequently endorse, promote, and support such "leadership"* is **extremely high. *In other words, the majority will support tyranny in large-scale dysfunctional populations.***

This is *precisely* the mass-psychological dynamics behind the rise of dictators such as Adolf Hitler. In the case of Nazi Germany, the Hero's/ Golden Children's dependency on an authority figure's stamp of approval for self-value was accomplished by appealing to their supposed ethnic background: the Aryan Race being *superior. (If that's not ego-spoiling, I don't know what is.)* Since "Daddy's approval treats" were given, his supporters and benefactors within the German population subsequently endorsed and capitulated to any belief, ideology, wars of aggression, or mass madness "Daddy" (in this case, Hitler) promoted and embarked on.

If these "Heroes/Golden Children" (take note of the whopping irony here) had any*true* self-worth or value, Hitler would have gotten *nowhere* in Germany.

But they didn't and look where the *Hell* that got them.

In addition to enabling malignant personalities while being "rewarded," the Hero/Golden Child will also be highly susceptible to any propaganda placed in front of them in the guise of "news media" - just like with Nazi Germany. They will regard it as "the gospel" without any use of critical thinking skills or scrutiny. ***Or research.*** Despite most published articles - whether in print or online - **not having any references or citations to purported facts, figures, statistics, *or data,* the Golden Cult-member sops it up like a thirsty sponge - *without question.***

"If Daddy says it's true, I won't be 'good' if I question it or don't believe it. And *you're* bad if you question or don't believe it either."

Bullshit. And you're "Daddy" is as bogus as your "self"-worth. There's no need to research *that.*

Is the above the same as a first-born loving their father? Of course not. Is it the same as being respectful? No. Is it the same as being responsive to boundaries? No. It's when "Daddy" has a sense of Entitlement with respect to his Ego and needs for attention, empathy, freedom, and material goods. It's when "Daddy" trains his "dogs" to equate "obedience" with "goodness" that we have a problem. And not that obedience is "bad," but it's when the Owner exploits that obedience to realize his objectives of despotic control, generating narcissistic supply, and entitlement which many "Good Dogs" in the population readily enable with their "loyalty."

Note also that the political opinions, viewpoints, ideologies, and candidates which "Good Dogs" are likely to endorse *and defend* are primarily based on two things: 1) Whether or not they feel like a "Good Dog" (ie., social justice warrior) for doing so; and 2) Their Narcissism. These two factors are likely to be simultaneously effectual, but the latter will usually determine who or which candidate they gravitate toward and endorse as a result of their narcissism.

I hate to use the word "narcissism" with respect to the Good Dog because narcissism, as described earlier in Chapter 2 of this book under the Narcissistic Personality Disorder Section, involves being over-indulged, spoiled, or being enabled - again with respect to at one of the following: Ego, Empathy, Attention, Freedom, and Material Goods. Narcissism also implies *dependency* on being spoiled - or having an issue of Entitlement.

We all do *need* those five things to an extent, regardless of what age we are. Especially for those who have *given* their energy in the form of empathy and attention and allowing others to have freedoms (which involves staving off tyranny at a national level), providing for their material goods, and making contributions to their ego, they need to replenish somehow. When we can provide those five things *on* our own *to ourselves* makes an adult mature and self-sufficient, but also asocial (notice I didn't write "antisocial." They *would* become antisocial eventually if they were always "giving" and never "receiving" - which is *absolutely understandable*. They'd also become antisocial if they were able to provide themselves those five things on their own yet other adults tapped them for contributions on a routine basis.)

Before proceeding, notice how Adult-toddlers will *hoard, be selfish, and expect an excess with respect to those five things:* They'll expect *others* to consistently boost their ego, empathize with them, give them attention, provide them with boundary-less liberties, and endow them with a surplus of material goods and wealth - *without giving back in return.*

Getting back to the Good Dog: Whereas the "Owner's" narcissism revolves around *receiving* love, care, and respect due to a core issue of Entitlement, Abandonment, or both, the Good Dog receives "treats" in the form of love, care, and respect when he behaves or acts the way the

Owner wants. However, these "treats" really aren't "love" - they're "approval."

So, if a Good Dog supports the same candidate and causes as the Owner, they're "good." (Ego-treat.) They're also "good" if they subscribe to the same ideologies as the owner, whether that is Liberal, Conservative, Left, Right, Democrat, Republican, etc. The same applies to political views. Or cultural ideologies. Or religious ideologies. If the Good Dog were to "disobey" their narcissistic Owner at any time, he would be seen as "disobedient" and may run the risk of becoming a Bad Dog (the role which follows.)

Actually, they're not good; they're actually useless - that is, except to the owner *whom they enable*. Much like the pigs in George Orwell's *Animal Farm* train *their* dogs to protect them, the Owner does with the Good Dog within the dysfunctional family. *The protection, however, is for the Owner's narcissism - rooted in a sense of Entitlement because they were Abandoned, Spoiled, or both.* Again, part of the role of the Hero/Golden child is to give the parent the impression that they're capable of raising a healthy, well-rounded child when this is hardly the case. The Hero/Golden child is used for *appearances: to give the public the impression that things are fine in the household or at least with the parent as well as protection; their loyalty serves as a fortress defending the narcissistic Owner from any scrutiny.*

So, if the Good Dog takes on a career path palatable to the owner (usually because it appears nicely to the outside world), lives a "normal and convention lifestyle," and has grandkids to "make" the Owner happy - the Good Dog continues to be a Good Dog and continues to have "self-worth" thanks to the "treats" he or she receives.

Due to the "ego-treats," the Good Dog acquiesces to the Owner's wants, ideas, feelings, opinions, beliefs, etc. and abdicates himself in the process. This will effect him later in life, not only with respect to living a hollow life that is unfulfilling, but with respect to the culture at large. Since the "ego-treats" are conditional, the Good Dog is conditioned to perceive certain behaviors, beliefs, concepts, ideas, etc. as "Good" or "Bad." Whether he adopts these beliefs or goes against them makes *him* "Good" or "Bad," respectively - they are "*ego-treats*" after all. The Good Dog is also trained *not to question* beliefs, concepts, doctrines, etc.; that would make him "Bad." Thus, the Good Dog is *trained not to think critically - only whether something is "good" or "bad" based on someone else's approval.*

As such, *not only is* the Good Dog is trained *not to think critically, but that "questioning" makes them bad.* This conditioning may be so ingrained - the propensity to perceive oneself as "Good" or "Bad" based on the *approval of an authority figure* - that the very thought of questioning whatever reward-based behavior or capitulation being imposed on them is soul-crushing. He's also conditioned *not to question the character of his owner since his very self-worth and esteem - his ego - is dependent on it.*

This makes the Good Dog highly susceptible to brainwashing, manipulation, and fortifying those with tendencies to resemble (or become) Cult Leaders. By challenging the Good Dog's acceptance of the Owner's "word" or the "word" itself, whether that is in the form of doctrine, "news," or other unsubstantiated "claims" made by the Owner, the Good Dog will regard this as a challenge to their own "goodness" or sense of "self-worth" since both are continent on *loyalty.* This is due to the Good Dog perceiving himself as "good" based on the extent to which he is obedient to his Owner regardless of whether or not such obedience in the best interest of the dog or caters to the selfish/egotistical/devious objectives of the Owner. Thus, challenging this "dog's" loyalty is, to him, an affront to what he perceives as his "self-worth." But, this "self-worth" is anything but since the "worth" is based on someone else's <u>approval.</u>

This is precisely why a Good Dog will "go on the attack" when presented with evidence countering that which they were brainwashed to believe. Because it disrupts the dogma they unquestioningly adopted out of "good behavior," disproving their dogma is, quite sadly, regarded as them being told that they "are bad" even though they truly believed themselves as "good."

It's worth mentioning that anything the Good Dog is "Good" for believing or accepting as "truth" which *isn't* the truth or *cannot be substantiated* is usually indicative of the Owner's deviancy.

The Good Dog will not question the character of a "leader," especially ones who provide ego-treats, "solutions" which are actually scapegoats for problems, and positions and ideologies with ulterior motives, manipulating the Good Dog with false validation: that is, the Good Dog is easily swayed by means of *approval* of the Cult Leader (or Owner.) The Good Dog will believe news stories - whether on TV, online, or in print *regardless if the "outlet" is Conservative, Liberal, Left, or Right* - without question despite there being no source referencing whatsoever; they're "bad" if they don't. Despite no evidence being provided *whatsoever,* the Good Dog accepts whatever is being presented as *facts.*

This false sense of self-worth conditions Narcissism within the Good Dog. The more they capitulate, the "better" they are.

But remember: Narcissists manipulate and gaslight - a lot. If narcissistic personality types are behind the news story's content, then the story is most likely a lie to some degree. Also remember that, to a narcissist, their feelings are facts as well. So the "facts" presented may actually be the way the narcissist feels the "facts" ought to be. Narcissists reinvent history all the time, even in everyday conversation. But accepting a news story as true without any *evidence* is like a teacher grading a term paper chock-full of "facts," "quotes," "dates," and descriptions *without having a bibliography* and giving it an A+.

But this is *precisely* was a Good Dog does: he accepts anything an "Owner" says; he'd be a "Bad Dog" if he didn't. But just because something is *said* doesn't make it *true*. Just because something is *written* doesn't make it true. What makes something written or said *true* is *evidence* supporting what is being written or said.

However, again, most news stories *do not* provide source material. By all means: go online, watch the news, and see if *any* journalism today provides a "bibliography." Again, the Good Dog runs the risk of being "bad" if he were to research or fact-check anything being said in an article or story in order to verify whether or not it is in fact *true*. Since he's also trained to be *loyal,* it would be *blasphemous* to cross-reference anything particular to the ideology set he subscribes to - whether that's Left or Right.

Since the Good Dog's conditioning is based on being a "good" dog or "bad" dog, "Us" versus "Them" comes naturally. If their "Left" is "good," then "Right" is "bad." If their "Right" is "good," then "Left" is "bad" - by *default*. Since they're "right" and others are "wrong," the treat the other side like the following: with grandiosity and expectations of superior treatment from other people (It's their way or the highway); continually demeaning, bullying and belittling others (examples: "Libtard," "Republithug"); with a sense of entitlement to special treatment and to obedience from others ("I'm right, you're wrong. Agree with me or pay.") They'll actually bark and growl if you have an opposing viewpoint.

However, the beliefs which the Good Dog hold are *themselves* predicated on whether or not they've been trained to perceive them as "good" or "bad." They don't question *why* the beliefs they hold make them "good" or if contrary beliefs may have value. In short, there's no critical thinking or analysis: since an "authority figure" gave the dog their stamp of approval for accepting such beliefs. They'll subsequently jump on cultural movement band-wagons (consisting of other Good Dogs) precisely because *dogs run in packs*. In order to receive *more approval* (to compensate for authentic self-worth), it's very likely that such Good Dogs will promote their beliefs on social media, such as Facebook or Twitter. Plus, being a "social justice warrior" and championing their "cause" makes them feel *dutiful - and this dutifulness which makes them feel like a "Good Dog" comes straight from being trained to appease their Owner - whether that is "God" or someone or something else.* Really, it's based in their upbringing.

All the while, most of them have been brainwashed into accepting their respective beliefs and are subsequently manipulated for doing so…

…just like a dog is trained to perform tricks, protect, and behave the way his narcissistic Owner feels he should.

This dynamic is clearly seen in cults and organized religions (which are the same thing; the difference is size), especially with those which is why they have missionaries in the first place. The ego loves *size.)*

Once in a while, a Good Dog will come to the fantastic realization that - not only have they been exploited - but their Owner needs them more than they need their Owner.

They also come to the sad but liberating conclusion that their owner never really loved them because their owner was acting out of self-interest. But they come to the amazing conclusion that - without the Good Dog - the owner is *nothing*. When this happens, the Good Dog understands *their clout and their undeniable power to exert control not only over their Owner, but to their limitless freedom and that of others.*

And this is a sight to behold when it *does* happen because, then, we finally see the birth of a soul. In dysfunctional families, when the Good Dog comes to the painful yet overwhelmingly freeing understanding that their entire lifestyle, ideological system, religious beliefs, behaviors, career "choices," and personality exist *solely* to cater to their Owner's narcissism, whims, selfishness, and bogus public persona and was *never* about them, is when they *finally* come into their power. Here, the Good Dog discovers they have *leverage*. And not only *leverage, but real authentic power.*

This may even take place while the Good Dog is still in the house. They may find they have the ability to "nip" at their Owner and train their Owner *not* to engage in the malignantly narcissistic manner described earlier in the book.

Whether or not the Good Dog realizes this while they're living at home or not is when they achieve real independence and true-self love. Never again will they reliant on "treats" from others. They'll be able to see reality more clearly and that their mind, body, and spirit which was help captive by their owner now belongs to *them*. Now, *they have independence - from their Owner and any other Despot and Cult Leader which may cross their path again.*

The opposite of this case scenario is the Good Dog is either reared or becomes so narcissistically enmeshed with it's owner, *it does anything it wants.*

Guard Dog

If the Hero/Golden child is completely contingent on their narcissistic parent's approval for their "self-worth," their "Good Dog" becomes a Guard Dog. This is the ultimate henchman: doing whatever and becoming whomever the Owner wants them to be. There is no autonomy here whatsoever. The Guard dog looks to the owner for everything, incorporating every message of approval in the form of ego-treats, and abdicating all sense of self to be molded into the very Dog the owner wants the dog to be.

This usually happens with the first born of a highly narcissistic parent whose core issue is Entitlement as opposed to Abandonment and it's often (but not always) coupled with having the other parent being extremely ineffectual to the point of severely neglecting the "dog."

Here, the narcissistic extension from parent to child may be so strong, the child may actually look like a miniature version of the parent.

The only saving grace about this situation is that the "relationship" between Owner and Dog is…."tight?" I don't know how to describe it. There's no contention between the two since it would be like the narcissist arguing with himself about topics or beliefs, but that would **never** happen. There's next to no dichotomy, so there really can't be any conflict.

The Guard Dog is the metaphorical dog who never leaves his Owner's side; his Owner's side is actually the only "treat" he needs. It's like the "treat" is a continuous stream of approval delivered psychically from parent to child: no other communication is needed. It's like the Owner's personal Secret Service.

The Guard Dog is just as narcissistic as the Owner. Lord help any other dogs that come into the picture because any narcissistic abuse they receive at the hands of the owner is literally going to be duplicated by the Guard Dog. Lord also help the spouse of the owner who is going to wish he or she never procreated since they literally became the "odd man out" once the Guard Dog was "adopted." Now, he or she unwittingly helped their spouse produce their clone, as if their partner was a covert alien or something. He or she may actually have had thoughts about packing up their bags and leaving quietly in the night, which may not be such a bad idea.

Leave it for the X-files, that's my advice.

Otherwise, the Guard Dog may be the quintessential "Chip off the Old Block," "Daddy's Little Girl," or "Mini-Me." Because the ego is spoiled to such a high extent from the start, the grandiosity in the child's sense of self is huge. So is their subsequent Entitlement, and so is their subsequent "Abandonment" when things don't go their way.

If additional children are born, the Guard Dog will seem like an Alpha Dog and even more bossy than the Hero/Golden Child.

Because of the dog's high degree of narcissism, they will engage manipulation and intimidation in order to get their way. They'll also resort to projection as a means of mitigating their "issues" for the same reasons provided in Chapter 3 under the *Offense Mechanisms* section.

Because of the severely tight bond the Guard Dog has with their Master, any allegations against their character - despite it being grandiose, manipulative, pathologically lying, abusing, corrupt, whatever - will not only be defended by the Guard dog, but they're prone to attack.

As a citizen, the Guard Dog will grow into a henchman if not a narcissistic psychopath themselves, provided that is what their Master is. They will unflinchingly adopt and defend to the death any propaganda, criminal activity, religious dogma, or vernacular which comes out of a corrupt outlet whether that is an organization or a individual. These are the mega-zealots, the fanatics, the fundamentalists, the balls-out dogmaticians. Carrying out orders of narcissistic psychopaths comes as easily as breathing. Personally, I can't stand them and their narcissistic "holier than thou" attitude.

Siblings born to this child can expect to be second-class citizens within the family. That's the best case scenario. Otherwise, not only will they be the recipients of narcissistic abuse from the Master, the Guard Dog will join right in. And, the Guard Dog will inflict their own suffering on their own when given the chance. After all, projection is their coping mechanism.

The likelihood of the Guard Dog breaking free from their dysfunctional role is slim to none as is their reading this material. My advice to the reader is to be mindful of the Guard Dog/Master relationship and - if noticeable in a potential partner with respect to one of their parents - avoid this individual at all costs. If the Guard Dog is a sibling, *fight back, and fight back **hard.***

Bad Dog

Since the second-born into a dysfunctional family is coming into a situation where their older sibling has been placed on a pedestal and/or conditioned to succumb to rewards-based behavior, the standard is already set and they're coming into this world at a disadvantage. Here, the child has to compete with the performance of an older child with more experience and success in capitulating to their narcissistic parent's demand. In order to go through their childhood unscathed, the Bad Dog will need to "out-appease" the Good Dog.

Good Luck.

Because the age-difference alone starts them off at a disadvantage, the younger child struggles to meet the performance of their older sibling who is more advanced in their development. Despite this being a highly improbable task for the young child, the narcissistic parent - already devoid of empathy and compassion and impervious to employing objectivity upon the new child's disadvantages - still holds this against the second-born. Remember also that the narcissistic parent perceives their children as objects, not developmental beings requiring a good amount of love, care, and respect from an early age. The second-born will continue for a while to try to measure up to the expectations and performance of the first born and it will be completely in vain. Through constant compare and contrast, the child will routinely feel like a failure. Instead of giving words of encouragement or support - let alone treating the child with his or her own learning curve irrespective of their older sibling - the child's poor performance is used as negative feedback thanks to unfair compare and contrast.

Yet negative feedback is all the second-born is liable to receive. Whether or not the narcissistic parent's core issue is Abandonment (even in the form of neglect) or Entitlement, the impossible expectation that this child will measure up will trigger negative feelings in the narcissistic parent - which, as we know from Chapter 2 - are other people's responsibility: in this case, the second born will bear this brunt as well.

So now, this young child not only faces an uphill, insurmountable battle in trying to please their narcissistic parent, failure to do so brands them "Bad" by such a parent.

The new dog is now a "Bad Dog."

Thanks to being set up for failure from the start and receiving no words or love, support, or encouragement - actually just the opposite: the child is liable to be told they're stupid and "bad" - the child understandably starts to rebel: just like a dog would act out.

And thus begets the escalation which causes a lifelong rebellion against the uncaring, unfair world they were born into: earning them the dysfunctional label, "The Rebel."

Provided the narcissistic parent(s) is overt in their negative feedback, the child - the Bad Dog - will start acting out in passive ways. This is akin to a real dogs tearing through shoes or peeing on beds. The passive ways of rebellion are (bogus) verification to the dysfunctional parent(s) that the dog is "Bad" when, in truth, they're cries for love the dysfunctional parent is too feckless to see.

This escalation continues throughout the childhood, leading to poor scholastic performance, drug use, and other forms of self-sabotage. Despite this, the Bad Dog still wishes to be seen as good by the Owner, but gets few if any treats.

Making this worse is co-inhabiting the home with the Good Dog who *does* get treats. Now, the Bad Dog not only feels *Unlovable* and a *Failure* (the two hallmark schemas behind *this* tragic role), these two schemas are reinforced by the presence of the Good Dog itself.

Now that the Bad Dog has adopted the belief that they're both Unlovable and a Failure, and because they're seen as such by the narcissistic parent, and because they can't measure up on account, they're Scapegoated for this as well. It's now *their fault* (here comes the projection again) that they can't do anything right. Because of this, and along with the narcissism ingrained in them by the Owner as described previously, the Good Dog now exploits the Bad Dog's "incompetence" to boost his narcissism. In doing so, the Good Dog issues messaging to the Bad Dog that they're Bad as well. After all, the Good Dog had to go through this sort of treat-based hazing; whatever frustrations they harbored for having to do so now has an outlet which is smaller and weaker.

Once the Bad Dog comes into the picture, the "shit rolling downhill" character of dysfunctional family becomes apparent.

But because the Bad Dog is now *blamed* and *exploited,* the issue of *Vulnerability* is now introduced into their self-concept. The Bad Dog receives additional negative feedback that they're "no good," "bad," and "a failure" from the parent(s) who never should have reproduced in the first place as well as an older sibling.

The escalation continues, with the "shit rolling downhill" catalyzing the rebellion. The rebellion and failure catalyze more scapegoating, and the Bad Dog becomes worse and worse. Soon, they internalize self-concept that they are Unlovable, a Failure, and Vulnerable (susceptible to abuse) when all they needed and wanted was love, care, and respect. (Notice how these schemas correspond to Borderline Personality Disorder.)

As adults, the self-fulfilling incompetence will manifest in a failing career path, possible drug use, possible crime, and other unfortunate circumstances.

As citizens, they will not be "productive members of society" (through no fault of their own) both in terms of community contribution and selecting suitable leadership in terms of governance. Since the need for approval is more acute than the Good Dog's (again, through no fault of their own), they're unlikely to be discerning with respect to news and corrupt activity of any malignant narcissists which have been elected into office. The worst case scenario is that they will provide narcissistic leadership within the political, financial, and corporate sectors with narcissistic supply in order to be accepted. Otherwise, they'll simply rebel against that too and not care.

Because of the fear of Failure bestowed upon them, they may not have the patience or acumen to perform independent research into current events involving corruption. Healing for the Bad Dog is *fully* understanding the dysfunctional role they were pigeonholed in from the very start of their life. Specifically, pin-pointing the fears conditioned in them that they are Unlovable, a Failure, and Vulnerable to mistreatment and disrespect and challenging them are *crucial* to their recovery. *They literally have to "retrain" themselves.* "Barking" and "biting" both their Owner and the Good Dog will help them claim their violated dignity by those parties. Lastly, *they need to eradicate the notion that approval is needed from anyone in order to love themselves.* In fact, the Bad Dog should learn to "bite" those who don't treat them with love, care, and respect.

Otherwise, the Bad Dog will not "win" regardless of how hard they try to please. They'll also have next to no outlet for their righteous anger and frustration while still in the doghouse - that is, unless another dog is brought into the picture.

If you're second-born and reading this and the Bad Dog role is something you can identify with, you may wish to consider the roles which follow provided you've had no younger siblings. The "Lost Child" or Kick Dog role which comes next as well as others may be something you identify with.

Kick Dog

The role known to come next in the lineup of children within the dysfunctional household is "The Lost Child." Oh, if only this were always the case...

If this is the last child born into the doghouse, that child is probably going to *wish* they were lost, because being born into a doghouse with a malignantly narcissistic owner and two older, dysfunctional siblings is a recipe for a variety of types of abuse and mistreatment. Now, there's more "shit rolling downhill" - the Owner's plus *two dogs* - and the hill is taller.

Especially if the Lost Child is the same gender as the malignant parent, this child is brought in at the worst disadvantage yet: the Owner sees nothing wrong with his ability to "train dogs" since the first was able to follow rewards-based orders and "got it." But now, thanks to the Owner's unhealed Entitlement and/or Abandonment issues being exacerbated by the Bad Dog's perceived "defectiveness," the Owner is more frustrated than before. In addition, here comes another pup who is likely to pale and fail in comparison to the first dog which conjures more negative feelings within the Owner thanks again to the Abandonment and/or Entitlement issues he has. Besides: the reason he "adopted" these dogs in the first place was for them to *anesthetize* his issues of Abandonment and Entitlement, not make them worse! They're supposed to make *him* feel good!

The *new* dog - just like the Good Dog and the Bad Dog - yearns to be loved and cared for as a puppy. But, because to *the Owner,* his feelings are facts and his feelings are other people's responsibility (again, projection), love, care, and respect are the last thing on the horizon for the new dog.

Since the Owner expected love, care, and respect to go in one direction only - toward *him* - from the start and has received the opposite outside of the Good Dog's performance, the newly "adopted" puppy is at an even greater disadvantage than the dog that would become the Bad Dog. The unfulfilled expectations of the Owner for these dogs to poo-poo his fears of Abandonment and/or Entitlement has led to the Owner's *increase* in negative feelings. And, since the Owner is narcissistic or has

ASPD, *projection* is the way these negative feelings are "managed."

The new puppy, vulnerable and perceptive, readily sees the anger and frustration in his Owner from an early start. Both frightened and wanting love, care, and respect that any young creature *needs* at this developmental stage, the puppy does the only thing a puppy knows to do in this case: he cries.

This reaction is the diametric opposite the Owner desires and this new puppy is now a "bad puppy" in his eyes. To the owner, *every puppy* should be happy and disregarding of his negativity - his "issues" are other someone else's fault, after all. So, the blame and ridicule the Bad Dog received at a later stage in his development is now subjected to the new dog at an earlier stage.

The very fact that the puppy is crying makes it a Failure to the Owner. The "Bad Puppy" is now subjected to abuse, which could be akin to the kind the Bad Dog received in the form of verbal or psychological negative feedback, humiliation, or physical abuse - anything to get that damn puppy to fall in line. Anything but positive reinforcement.

Because the new dog appears to be even less competent that the second dog, not to mention more vulnerable since the Good Dog has grown in size and age since the appearance of the Bad Dog, the Good Dog capitalizes on this as yet another source of ego-treats he's become accustomed to. To build on its narcissism which is the surrogate for self-love, the Good Dog will exploit the new dog *more* than the Bad Dog! Hell, since the Owner's doing it, there can't be anything wrong if *he* does it. Plus, the Owner already projects onto the Bad Dog and doesn't seem to mind when the Good Dog does it either! The Owner *might* even hold the Good Dog in higher esteem and approve of the Good Dog *more* if he joins in or mimics the Owner's behavior!

And the *Owner does!*

Seeing that the Owner *approves* of the new puppy's abuse and mistreatment now that the Good Dog has joined in and approves of the Good Dog's participation, the Bad Dog figures he will be approved of too if *he* joins in as well!

And the *Owner does!*

And *now* the Bad Dog *finally* gets the approval from the Owner he's been so desperately waiting for *all his life! Finally! An ego treat!* Who needs love, care, and respect now! "I can get my Owner's *approval by tormenting my younger sibling too!"*

If this goes on for a prolonged period of time - and it will - both the Good Dog and the Bad Dog will be effectively trained to *project* their baggage onto others, namely the Kick Dog, while all three are still the house - actually, four when including the Owner who got this whole dog shit-show started. After a while, the Good Dog and the Bad Dog will become just as malignant as their Owner.

The abuse and maltreatment the Kick Dog receives as a result is the worst in the doghouse. Not only in terms of severity, but frequency and plurality as well. *Three assholes are shitting down the hill now - simultaneously, in pairs, or on their own.*

Anyone who refers to this role as a "Lost Child" has limited awareness to the torture those who inhabited this role may have endured while growing up. Being an actual "Lost Child" - that is, lost and alone - would have been a holiday for these kids.

To provide a real life example of the abuse and humiliation such young children may receive, one can look at the case of the "FamilyOFive" channel which was terminated by YouTube in 2018. This channel aired a series of videos of the parents physically and emotionally abusing their young children. In one, the eldest son was instructed by his step-father to slap his step-sister's face after she performed a bottle trick incorrectly. In another, the father and his stepson threw the father's youngest son through a doorway and into a bookcase, leaving the child with injuries on his face. The channel received *176 million views: that's over **half** the population of the United States.* (Sickening.) After the two youngest were removed from their custody and placed in the care of their biological mother, the "FamilyOFive" parents, when issuing an apology, made the claim that they were a "loving, close-knit family." [1]

These children likely to be "Lost Adults" when they get older since their *family* joined *in tandem* to inflict verbal, psychological, and physical torture upon the most vulnerable amongst them while they were very young. The "issues" they inherited as a result are as follows and in chronological order *and at the very least: Abandonment, Unlovability, Vulnerability, Mistrust, Failure, Subjugation, Exclusion.*

"Lost child" is the best case scenario. The best moments of these kids' childhoods took place *when they had the chance to be alone*. And this was rare. More frequently, they were ridiculed, excluded, blame-shifted, *scapegoated (more than the Scapegoat!), subjugated, beaten, insulted, and ostracized.*

If this is the last child born into the family, it's likely that they'll take on the next role as well:

[1] https://en.wikipedia.org/wiki/FamilyOFive

Trick Dog

After the Lost Child is brought into the family, the next in line will be the "Mascot" or the "Jester." The nickname for this child is derived from the propensity for this role to engage in humorous or animated behaviors for two reasons. First, it is to "lighten things up" or diffuse the fear factor within the household. This role finds that if they can make the Owner and the other dogs laugh, the child will have value and learns that this is the only way they will derive any sort of attention. The second reason is as a defense mechanism: amusing the Owner serves as protection from receiving the same sort of abuse that the Lost Child receives.

But it is the very fact that the Owner now has his very own Jester that the child becomes the Trick Dog. Like the other dogs in the household, the purpose of the Trick Dog, in the eyes of the Owner, is to make the owner happy. Again, the reason the dogs are there as far as the Owner is concerned is to make the Owner feel good, not the other way around. Nor should the narcissistic Owner be expected to make the dogs feel good because, again, love, care, and respect only go in one direction - toward the Owner.

If the Trick Dog falls short of providing the Owner care in the form of entertainment - that is, when the love, care, and respect stop flowing toward the Owner - the Trick Dog can and will receive the opposite in return. This is where the Jester image becomes poignant: if the child is unable or unwilling to "perform" for the "King," the King takes it out on the performer. Thus, the Trick Dog will be abused, ridiculed, humiliated, and so on by the Owner when the Owner's imperial narcissism isn't indulged and he isn't made to "feel good."
 Otherwise, when the Trick Dog *does* make the Owner laugh, the Owner sees the "dog" as a "good dog."

Again, like any narcissist in a relationship, not only are others are responsible to make him feel good, it's their fault when they don't and the love, care, and respect only go towards him.

Stray Dog

Wait a minute! *"Stray Dog?" That role isn't in the dysfunctional family!*

Exactly. The "Stray Dog" escapes the dysfunctional family, sheds whatever role it played, and doesn't get involved in anything resembling the dysfunctional family it belonged to because *it truly loves itself*. The dysfunctional family is in the rear-view mirror, uncared about without resentment, and this dog pursues life, liberty, and happiness.

The Stray Dog lets the dysfunctional family members continue their dysfunctional behavior amongst themselves and doesn't get involved.

The Stray Dog distances himself from the dysfunctional family's antics both logistically and psychologically. If interaction with said family is necessary, the Stray Dog will practice "observe, don't absorb" but mainly go no contact and get his ass on the road to life. No more drama.

Now, a good Stray Dog will practice a combination of detached compassion, disgust, and indifference for the other dogs and the Owner - especially the Owner - if and when they enter the dog's stream of consciousness. By understanding that the Owner himself was spoiled or had Abandonment and neglect issues, a combination of rejection and forgiveness toward the Owner comes easily. Eventually, the Stray Dog may even develop a relationship with the Owner which is based on mutual love, care, and respect.

Dog Whisperer

I figured I'd take a moment to describe how a "good" or *functional* Owner would behave considering the gross, near-inanimate treatment of children by a narcissistic, dysfunctional parent described earlier.

First and foremost, a functional parent *should* have relationships based on *equality* with their children; that is, love, care, and respect go in both directions. Unlike the Owner in the previously described scenarios, a functional "Owner" would not simply put "food in the dogs' dishes" and a roof over their heads and call it a day while ordering the dogs around while they do what the Owner wants them to do. A functional Owner would teach his dogs that healthy relationships involved both parties being considerate of both parties: *"I'm okay, you're okay."* In healthy families, everyone is considered, everyone receives the same treatment, and everyone abides by the same rules and is afforded the same rights. A healthy "Owner" would also talk *to* his dogs and not *at* his dogs. Again, these are children in real life, not dogs. The narcissistic parent does not behave this way: just because he or she is *older* does not mean he or she is *better*. This reflects the "I'm okay, you're not okay" attitude many narcissistic people personify. Many times children "don't' listen" is due to the fact that they know the adult isn't treating them with the same respect that they would wish to receive. The fact that they rebel and "don't listen" is precisely due to this.

Second, aside from providing food and shelter for his dogs, the functional Owner would interact with them. This rarely happens in dysfunctional households. But in functional households, the Owners who play with and love their dogs are likely to be happy as well as their dogs, who develop self-confidence and social skills as a result. It's also a great way to promote cohesion within the family as well.

Third, although everyone in a functional household matters and has the same rights
and abides by the same rules (and the Owner *must* lead by example here), the Owner respects each dogs individuality and uniqueness and develops a personal relationship with respect to each dog based on those differences. But never will the Owner "play favorites" and give the impression that one dog is preferred over another. Kind of like Cesar Milan, he'll ensure that all of his "dogs" are regarded the same.

Fourth, a good Owner will "train" his dogs much like a functional company would its employees: when a new dog is brought in, the dog will receive much supervision and few responsibilities, increase supervision while the amount responsibilities increase, decrease supervision as responsibilities plateau, then eliminate supervision as the dog flies solo. *Every* dog brought into the house should be provided with the same "training"; just because a dog is "brought in" later than others does not mean it should be trained less or trained by other dogs.

11

"The Holy Dysfunctional Family"

"I'm afraid, based on my own experience, that fascism will come to America in the name of national security."

- Jim Garrison

In 2012, authors Drs. Joseph P. Farrell and Scott D. DeHart produced *Apocalypse Theatre: Yahweh the Two-Faced God.* In this book, the authors examine the behavior of Judeo-Christian god "Yahweh," noting that the character of this deity is that of an abusive parent. The authors challenge the reader, regardless of whatever theological explanation they may have to offer coming from whichever religious denomination they're affiliated with, to reconcile with the fact that they could never justify themselves engaging in the same sort of behavior as this "god" let alone consider such behavior "moral" if they or others emulated it - in fact, just the opposite.

While writing the previous chapter on dysfunctional family "dogs" roles, this image of Yahweh as proposed by Farrell and DeHart calcified for me: *when considering the Yahwist or "Abrahamic" religions and the order in which they chronologically appeared, it became clear to me that each one corresponds to a dysfunctional "dog" role described in the previous chapter with Yahweh in the "Owner" role.*

Examining the behavior, character, and actions of the subsequent religions born out of the Yahwist tradition and their resemblance to dysfunctional family roles will be the focus of this chapter. If you're religious and prefer not to have your faith questioned or challenged, I suggest you bypass the remainder of this book.

Otherwise, I sincerely believe many members of the groups and organizations I'm about to describe sincerely have the best intentions both for themselves as well as others and a true desire to honor what they perceive as God as much as possible. There's no way I would find fault in anyone with that.

Going back to the dysfunctional roles children inherit thanks to a narcissistic parent in the home, they are, in chronological order: The Hero/Golden Child, the Rebel/Scapegoat, the "Lost Child", the Mascot/Jester.

For the sake of this Chapter, I'm going to use my prototypes but add the two featured in the previous chapter: Good Dog, Guard Dog, Bad Dog, Kick Dog, Trick Dog, and Stray Dog.

For each of the Abrahamic religions, it's possible to assign each to a dysfunctional family childhood role with "Yahweh" being the malignant father but before doing this, it's worth reiterating what was discussed in *TSOA*, namely that dysfunctional families and cults are one in the same; the latter is simply larger. *Within cults, the following happens:*

- Power, control, and knowledge is consolidated at the top (or with whom anyone is heading the cult) or the leadership clams to have special privilege, abilities, or knowledge.
- The leadership is authoritarian who commands loyalty, obedience, and allegiance from the group.
- The leadership is never to be held accountable from those within or outside the organization.
- The group displays unwavering loyalty to its leader (whether dead or alive.)
- A system of hierarchy is usually established.
- Rising within the pyramid structure depends on capitulating to the "capstone."
- The organization (regardless of size) is to display excessive commitment to its leader.
- The leader dictates to the organization what it is to think, believe, and feel and how to act, sometimes in great detail.
- Questioning, skepticism, and dissent is discouraged or punished. Independent or critical thinking is chastised or prohibited.
- The organization, as a whole, has an "Us versus Them" mentality and may cause conflict with external society or other organizations.
- Fear and ignorance is dispensed toward the bottom if the organization is hierarchal.
- What is promoted as "facts" or "doctrine" cannot be substantiated or verified.

- Fear, shame, and guilt are common tactics employed to control members. Abuse is used when the leader deems fit.
- The organization is pre-occupied with bringing in new members.
- Making money/gaining power is a pre-occupation of the organization.
- An "ends justifies the means" mentality is promoted, at least within an "inner circle" close to the leadership.
- Members are coerced into providing tithes, money, property, or labor contributions to the organization.
- The capstone surrounds itself with others who will protect it, defend it, and not *challenge* it.
- The conditions at the pyramid's bottom are worse than that of the capstone.
- Dissidents, objectors, and detractors are smeared, attacked, or marginalized.
- Members are encourage to only interact or live with other members of the cult.
- Maintaining a positive public image is an ongoing imperative, even if it is contrary to the organization's internal reality.
- Any "secrets" are to stay within the organization, contained within the leadership if possible.
- Leaving or attempting to leave brings a fear of reprisal.

Referring back to Chapter 10 and the objectives of the narcissistic parent, which are based on **what they do for him, their loyalty, and the way they "make him feel," the objectives of the cult leader - the capstone - are the same.**

Some of the above characteristics may be considered to be abusive, if not, dysfunctional. Additional traits which are indicative of an *abusive* cult are:

- Brainwashing: conditioning members to believe things which aren't true (gas lighting.)
- Isolation.
- A double Standard dichotomy between the leadership and the members.
- A solid, pyramid-structure is in place.
- Charismatic/convincing leadership.
- Strong control is exercised over the members.
- Cult members adopt a new personality/identity.

The predominant "Abrahamic," "Hebraic," Jehovah-based religions in order of chronological appearance are: Judaism, Catholicism/Christianity, and Islam. Each one of these four can be assigned a dysfunctional family role. If the roles in order of appearance align with the religions in order of appearance, we have:

> The Hero/Golden Child (Good Dog) = Judaism
> The Rebel/Scapegoat (Bad Dog) = Catholicism/Christianity
> The Lost Child (Kick Dog) = Islam

I do not enjoy attributing a "dog" moniker to any of these religions; the only reason I do is to incorporate the Guard Dog and Stray Dog roles as well:

> Guard Dog: Secret Societies, Mystery Schools,
> Stray Dog: Catharism and other "Gnostic" religions
> Mad Dog: The Church of the SubGenius, "Nonsense religions"

Judaism

Starting off Yahweh's dysfunctional clan is, of course, Judaism, whose people are regarded by Yahweh as his "Chosen." Whether Yahweh deliberately referred to the Israelites as his "Chosen People" to designate his "Golden Child" or not, the following passage from Deuteronomy 7:6-8 is the first where this is expressed:

"For you are a holy people to the Lord your God; the Lord your God has chosen you to be a people for His own possession out of all the peoples who are on the face of the earth. "The Lord did not set His love on you nor choose you because you were more in number than any of the peoples, for you were the fewest of all peoples, but because the Lord loved you and kept the oath which He swore to your forefathers, the Lord brought you out by a mighty hand and redeemed you from the house of slavery, from the hand of Pharaoh king of Egypt."

The origin of Judaism has conflicting accounts: the current historical view places it some time during the Bronze Age (3300-1200 BC) whereas the first Greek records to reference Judaism as a religion appear during the Hellenistic period (323BC-31 BC.) Other religious literature tells the story of the Israelites going back to at least 1500 BC.

It is not my objective to canvas the entire background, details, or history of this religion or to examine offshoots such as Kabbalism or

Zionism *at this time except to say Judaism has had offshoots or appendages*. For now, note the following regarding Judaism: 1) The occupation of the Holy Land by the Roman Empire (for reasons which will be evident in the next section); 2) The fact that not all the above traits listed as cult characteristics apply to Judaism (perhaps offshoots such as Zionism; I don't know); 3) The descendants of Abraham's grandson Jacob being enslaved in *Egypt*; and 4) The subsequent inclusion of the Old Testament with the New Testament in versions of the Bible used by Catholics, Protestants, and other Christian denominations.

As far as the character of Yahweh, the book of Genesis (22:2-8) we have the story of the "Binding of Isaac" in which Yahweh commands Abraham to sacrifice his young son on one of the mountains in the land of Moriah as a "burnt offering."

The next morning, obedient Abraham sets out with the unsuspecting Isaac, two young male servants, and a donkey with the chopped wood and a fire to a mountain top in Moriah to carry out Yahweh's orders. On day three of the journey, Abraham sees Moriah and instructs the two servants to wait with the donkey as he and Isaac proceed with the wood, the fire, and a knife to the mountaintop. On the way, poor, confused Isaac asks his father where the sacrifice is - pointing out that they have the wood, fire, and a knife, but no animal. His father responds to his son that "God himself will provide a lamb for a burnt offering."

After they reach their destination, Abraham builds an altar, lays out the wood, binds

Isaac, and places him on the wood. Then, Abraham takes the knife, gets ready to slay his son and -

An Angel (in disguise?) pops in and says, "No need. God just wanted to check to see if you would do it. He just wanted to know if you *feared him* or not. Carry on." Then, a ram shows up - well, it locked horns with a bush and the bush won - so Abraham kills it instead.

So, in this story - just because Yahweh wanted to *see* (wouldn't he already *know* if he were God?) if Abraham would be obedient - or to *test* the degree to which Abraham would *be* obedient to him - he instructs Abraham to a three day long trip to a mountain top to threaten the life of his child: *Just to see if he would do it.*

This sort of behavior is more aptly called a *mind game* and, as many of you already know, it's something narcissists are prone to engage in. Isaac, from this point on, has *every reason* to second guess the word of Yahweh since Yahweh just demonstrated that he doesn't mean what he says nor does he say what he means.

What's the objective of this exercise? If it's to "test" Abraham's loyalty, aren't there other ways to accomplish this without potentially traumatizing a child? Yahweh *could* have asked Abraham to do something Yahweh actually wanted him to do in order to assess this.

Not here. Yahweh instead commands Abraham to murder his own son to test if Abraham *fears* him - *fears* him enough to do anything Yahweh asks him to do regardless of how heinous it might be. This is reminiscent of the narcissistic tendency to expect a partner to "prove their love" or "fight for" the relationship discussed earlier (along with the reasons narcissists tend to do this…as well as the absurdity to do such a thing.)

This scene clearly depicts Yahweh's issue of *Entitlement* - testing the extent to which Abraham will do what Yahweh wants him to do for him….*out of fear*.

Another story, from the *Book of Job,* is undeniably intriguing both in content and how anti-climatic and nebulous its ending is.

Here, the focus of the story is Job, a resident of the land of Uz, who's introduced to the reader as having a life blessed with abundance and good health. For this prosperity, Job's character is *not* narcissistic or entitled; rather, he displays his gratitude for what he has by being pious and righteous.

The scene then shifts to Heaven where God has a conversation with Satan (who art also in Heaven?) about Job's piety, which Satan claims is only there because of his good fortune. God then gives Satan permission to remove his wealth and kill his children and servants to see if he will still be pious.

I'm going to pause right here. So, despite Job displaying *gratitude* for what he *has,* Yahweh decides to *test* Job (even though Job has already "passed the test" by displaying his gratitude for what he has) by making his life a living hell in order to see if he will still continue to be pious and grateful. Okay. Satan removes Job's wealth while his children and servants are killed.

But Job passes the "test!" He *continues* to be pious and even *praises* God. Okay! We got our answer.

Except we apparently didn't since Yahweh continues to allow Satan to wreak more havoc on Job's life by afflicting his body with boils. Such is the reward for passing the test.

Job's life clearly doesn't get better and he expresses regret for his very existence and resents being born. His wish for a "final exit" isn't granted either. To make matters worse, he's visited by three "miserable comforters" (ie., "concern trolls") who add insult not only to injury but patient, pious, behavior by asserting - inappropriately - that's Job's suffering is due to his sins. (Perhaps the three were sent by Satan as well?)

Maybe if Job behaved like an Adult-toddler and had a tantrum earlier in the game - or had been *ungrateful and corrupt* from the start - his fate may have been different and wouldn't have been tested in the first place?

Yeah. Makes sense.

Thanks to the irony of his "support system," Job *finally* cops a nutty. He now sees both God and his shitty "support system" as intrusive and suffocating (7:17-19) assholes, fixated on punishment (10:13-14), and hostile, destructive, and unforgiving (7:20-21) - for things he never did wrong in the first place. He then shifts his focus from his own unjust suffering to take note of the unfairness of Yahweh's governance of the world, noticing that the wicked have taken advantage of the poor and helpless but no punishment strikes them. (24:1-12)

I sincerely hope the relevance of Job's observation to modern-day is apparent…

Yahweh finally addresses Job toward the end in the form of a "whirlwind" in speeches which clarify *nothing* - not Job's suffering, injustice, or Job's assertion of his innocence. Instead, Yahweh poses the irrelevant question: "Where were you when I laid the foundations of the earth?"

How this is pertinent to Job or Yahweh's decision to revoke "the good life" from him is confusing if not irrelevant since Yahweh's decision to do so took place *during the course of Job's life, **not*** when Yahweh supposedly "laid the foundations of the earth" (which I personally doubt he did.) If it sounds like the "word salad" commonly dished out by narcissists, it probably is.

But nevertheless and for reasons *completely unbeknownst to the reader*, Job (as described in 42:1-6) confesses his lack of knowledge "of things beyond me which I did not know," his eyes have seen, and he retracts and repents (for what?) "in the dust and ashes." What that is, the reader never finds out.

It actually does have a "happy ending" in Chapter 32 as Yahweh informs Job's inept support system that they didn't represent whatsoever and tells them to make a burnt offering to Job because "for only to him [Job] will I show favor." Job wins the showcase showdown and his health, wealth, and family (huh? they're *dead*) are restored.

Yes, I know my descriptions are cynical (they deserve to be) - they get worse in the next section with regard to "Catholicism," so heads up. To me, though, the story of Job really has no meaning at least as it pertains to Job himself. The guy doesn't have a "victim mentality" - he has a "victim reality." A victim mentality involves something like crying about being Abandoned when there's someone there or feeling Unlovable after people have tried to show you love. Worse, it involves exploiting such beliefs in order to get something (unjustifiably) in return or projecting such negative feelings onto others.

Note that Job doesn't do *any* of that. Also note that his unjust circumstances not only are undeserving but don't change until he displays *righteous anger*.

The story of Job is akin to a dog Owner who has treated his dog well. The dog is well-behaved, pleasant, and responsive with appreciation. The Owner begins to wonder if the dog will still be behaved if his toys and puppies are taken away. But why? It's like an *experiment* - testing how far or what conditions the behaved dog will face before it stops being loyal to its Owner. Even with the toys revoked and the puppies killed, the dog is still *loyal*. Even when the dog's health is compromised, the dog is still loyal. It's when the dog is *taunted and blamed unfairly for his circumstances - when this "Good Dog is branded a "Bad Dog"* - that the dog starts to bite. But this is all for Yahweh's edification.

But note what the story of Job *does* have in common with the Abraham/Isaac Sacrifice story: *In both cases, Yahweh is testing his subjects' LOYALTY to him - to theextreme. With Abraham, it's "Will you do whatever I say?"; With Job, it's "Will You Put Up With Anything I put you through?"*

With respect to Abraham, Yahweh is flexing his own <u>Entitlement</u>, with Job, it's <u>Projection.</u>

How "good" of a "Good Dog" will this Good Dog be and how much can I kick the Kick Dog, respectively.

This is huge, because this ably creates a personality profile for this Entity, *because only a personality with Abandonment Issues is going to conduct experiments and TEST to see how far they can push someone or if they can be pushed before they become disloyal - that is, "ABANDON THEM."*

"WILL YOU BE WITH ME (OBEY ME, STAY LOYAL TO ME) 'NO MATTER WHAT?'"

INSTEAD OF BEING UNCONDITIONALLY LOVING *HIMSELF*, YAHWEH IS TESTING TO SEE WHETHER OR NOT

OTHERS WITH BE UNCONDITIONALLY LOVING WITH RESPECT *TO HIM.*

Oh ho ho…quite reminiscent of the "Dog Owner" described in the last chapter…who had NPD or M-Based ASPD or was co-morbid for both.

This aside, and without going through the *whole 593-page Old Testament* and performing a bit-by-bit psychoanalysis or character synopsis, author Richard Dawkins writes in *The God Delusion:*

"The God of the Old Testament is arguably the most unpleasant character in all fiction: jealous and proud of it; a petty, unjust, unforgiving control-freak; a vindictive, bloodthirsty ethnic cleanser; a misogynistic, homophobic, racist, infanticidal, genocidal, filicidal, pestilential, megalomaniacal, sadomasochistic, capriciously malevolent bully." [1]

This isn't the first time such a commentary has been expressed. From my standpoint, the above psychoanalysis *actually* provides some hope - odds as it seems: If there *is* such an entity as Yahweh and he ("it?" Oh fuck it) *does* have Abandonment issues and the conditioned described in this book as Maternal-based ASPD, all he really needs is for others to be *present for him*. Otherwise, if his condition arose form being *over-indulged, enabled, or spoiled* as described back in Chapter 2 under Narcissistic Personality Disorder, it's going to be a bit more of a challenge. We'll look into this more later on.

But, if Yahweh is displaying Abandonment issues, it would need to have be Abandoned. And if it's been Abandoned…*how could it be God?*

[1] Richard Dawkins, *The God Delusion*, Great Britain: Bantam Press, 2006, 31.

Catholicism/Christianity

Being raised "Bi-Catholic" in that I was baptized in the Byzantine Rite, schooled in the Roman Rite, and attended mass in *both* rites on a regular basis, I always *knew* something wasn't "right." Very rarely did anything actually seem *spiritual* to me with liturgies of *either* rite. I was an altar boy with the former rite for years.

In truth, I liked the Byzantine Church. Despite its traditional, regimented reputation, the church was actually quite progressive and open. The parish I belonged to even had a weekly adult group where members could openly question church dogma and discuss controversial topics. During the meetings I attended, adults young and old could have mature, open discussions with others who kept an open mind.The church also had a wonderful sense of community and was a great social outlet; it felt like a large family. In many ways, the "family" I had at church made up for the dysfunctional one I was raised in.

And the denomination itself can be credited with preserving the ethnic culture and customs tied to it, which came from a part of the world with a tumultuous history. And some of the priests and nuns who served this parish were the most lovely people I've ever met.

But the term "Lamb of God" always seemed strange to me - the "Sacrificial Lamb" that is supposedly Jesus of Nazareth - that "God" sent his "only son" to "die for our sins." The *Scapegoat* who *rebelled*…it never sat well with me. We'll see why in a bit.

First, let's examine the details of "early Christianity" up to and including the establishment of Catholicism (*meaning "Universal"*) as an Abrahamic religion.

Jesus "of Nazareth" was born in Judea in 4 BC according to most scholars. Some like John Paul Meier, American Catholic Priest and biblical scholar, place his birth year at 7 or 6BC. Others place it at 3 or 2 BC. [2] Regardless of the precise year Jesus was born, he was born into a region which was under Roman occupation, which lasted between 27 BC - 476 AD, before it's devision between Roman and Byzantine headquarters.

The death of Jesus is estimated to have occurred between 30-33 AD.[3] The number of apostles, according to the New Testament, numbered *twelve*. According to accounts in the New Testament, they faced opposition with other Jewish schools of thought as well as Roman officials. The supposed persecution of Jesus of Nazareth is reported to be officiated by Pontius Pilate, the Roman governor of Judea, with the approval of the Jewish community, also according to New testament records.

The "Early Christians," according to New Testament accounts, were Second-Temple Jews who were persecuted by the Pharisees (a Jewish social group and "school of thought") who opened Jerusalem to the Romans out of opposition to the Sadducean faction who were also persecuted.

Assisting the Pharisees was Saul of Tarsus (5 AD [4] - 64-67 AD [5]) before his own supposed conversion. Saul, who became the "Apostle

Paul," never met Jesus in person but rather, according to the Book of Acts, had a "vision" where the resurrected Jesus appeared to him in a great, blinding light, deactivating his vision for three days thereafter. Paul himself is reported to have established Christian communities between the mid-30s and mid-50s AD. [6]

King Herod (or Agrippa) continued the persecution when he became king of the Roman client state of Judea in 41 AD, during which the apostle James (the Greater) lost his life and the apostle Peter almost lost his. [7] After Herod's death, high priest Annas II took advantage of a power vacuum to further the persecutions, taking the life of James the Just (or, literally in the texts, "James, the Brother of Jesus." "Half-brother of God?") who was a leader of "Christians" in Jerusalem. It's worth mentioning here that Second Temple Judaism ended with the destruction of Jerusalem due to the Great Jewish revolt in 70 AD, which was instigated by the Roman killing of 3000 Jews and accompanied by the extinction of the aristocratic Sadducees.

The next report of Christian persecution occurred under Nero when, in 64 AD, a great fire broke out in Rome which decimated the ecumenical health of the Roman population. Some believe Nero himself was responsible, which may have accounted for his subsequent persecution of the Christians in Rome, as documented by Roman historian and politician Tacitus in The *Annals of Tacitus*. Whether or not Nero blamed or *blame-shifted* has been contested.

The next major recorded persecution occurred in Roman Gaul in 177 AD. According to this account, "Christians" were mass slaughtered in Lyon by Roman officials for refusing to renounce their faith. In Eusebius of Caesaria's *Ecclesiastical History,* Book 5, Chapter 1, Christians - Greeks from Asia and Gallo-Romans - were supposedly thrown to wild beasts, yet this account was written in Egypt in the 4th century by Eusebius. It's based on a letter supposedly sent from the "Christians" who were about to be martyred to Irenaeus (130 AD - 202 AD), a Greek Bishop.

The largest recorded Christian persecution and most well-known was "The Great Persecution" or the "Diocletian Persecution." During the first fifteen years of his rule, Diocletian, who reigned from April 1st, 286 to May 1st, 305, rid the army of all Christians and condemned all *Manichaeans* to death as well (keep this in mind, because we'll revisit this later.) He also surrounded himself with an anti-"Christian" clique. The persecution began with a series of four edicts from Emperors Diocletian, Maximian, Galerius, and Constantius.[8] On February 23, 303 AD, the cathedral in Nicodemia was torn down, followed by an edict enacted the next day to destroy all "Christian" church buildings, *confiscate and burn all sacred writings, confiscate all sacred items used in meetings,* and outlaw all worship gatherings. Another edict calling for the arrest of all clergy was issued a few months later, with the volume of arrests so high prisons were overcrowded to the point of having to cease the arrests. In early 304, "Christians" were require to make sacrifices to the Roman Imperial Cult or face death. Later, Galerius, who succeeded Diocletian, escalated the persecutions until his death in 311. [9] According to Eusebius, men, women, and children were burned, drowned, beheaded, starved, and crucified. HE VIII.8-9

We're going step away from proceeding with early "Christianity" timeline, first to recap. Provided there *was* a historical figure who can be designated as "Jesus of Nazareth" (and I believe there *was* for what it's worth), **whatever he was doing or promoting was met with opposition both during and after his life as well as his apostles' who knew him in person** - *per the content of the New Testament itself.* **This persecution continued off and on for nearly three centuries,** either by certain schools of Jewish thought or by mandate from high-ranking Roman officiates, **with the last persecution being the most pronounced, involving mass extermination as well as the destruction of pertinent texts and records - a mass "book burning."**

As we will see, it is very much worth mentioning that on December 25, 274 (which is the Winter Solstice as well and,coincidentally, what would be regarded as the birthdate of the historical Jesus of Nazareth) Roman Emperor Aurelian (who reigned from 270 to 275) made **Sol Invictus** (meaning "Unconquered Sun") an official cult alongside other traditional Roman Cults as "Sol Invictus" became the official Sun God of the Roman Empire and a patron of soldiers. [10] Priests of Sol were now pontificates and member of the *new college of pontificates* instituted by Aurelian. *Every pontifex of Sol was a member of the Senatorial Elite, indicative the Sun Cult's status.* [11]

Guess who else has a birthdate of December 25th, aka the Winter Solstice? *Mithra!* The pre-Zoroastrian Iranian Sun God. It's also a god of War. Prior to Zoroaster's influence in Iran during the 6th Century AD when polytheism was observed, with Mithra being the most important amongst their gods. He was the god of *contracts ("DEALS") and mutual obligation.*

During the 2nd and 3rd centuries CE, he was known as "Mithras," whose worship was indulged by the likes of Emperors Commodus (180–

192), Severus (193–211), and Caracalla (211–217). But wait! There's more. Guess who dedicated an altar to Mithras at the Roman Fortress Carnuntum in 307 AD as commemoration as their Empire's patron deity? None other than…*Diocletian.* [12]

So, again, whatever Jesus was practicing and/or promoting during the time he was alive brought him agita as well as his apostles who joined him - death in many cases - and those who practiced or followed their beliefs or practices were also met with death as well as the destruction of their texts and records and confiscation of their religious items.

But Constantine is on the way, right? He's going to legalize Christianity and support the establishment of the Catholic Church *and convert himself, right?*

Well, let's think about this: now that the texts pertaining to this movement have been destroyed and the prominent leaders deactivated through murder, imprisonment, or in some other fashion, the movement doesn't really exist much anymore - at the very least, in terms of leadership and documentation. Plus, with the bulk of the meat and potatoes eaten, the movement is now easily compromised.

So, even if/though Constantine I becomes Caesar on July 25, 306 AD and agrees to treat "Christians" benevolently within the Roman Empire by means of the Edict of Milan *six-and-a-half years later* in February of 313 AD…what's left?

How about a coin featuring the bust of Constantine with "Sol Invicto Comiti" on it and an image of the Sun God on the back side from circa *315 AD?:*

Dang. Well, that doesn't mean Catholicism stopped paying attention to *Jesus of Nazareth* after *The Council of Nicea, in 325 AD right?*

Well, the images and artwork of the subsequent churches and cathedrals suggest it's actually a "Sun" God and not the real-life Jesus. Here's an image from outside the Cathedral of St. Michael and St. Gudula in Brussels, completed in AD 1519. Take note of the bas relief images in the corners of the window: A Bull (Taurus), a Lion (Leo), an Eagle (Associated with Scorpio), and a Human (Aquarius) - The Four Fixed Signs of the Zodiac - supposedly associated with the four archangels Michael, Raphael, Gabriel, and Uriel:

Here's another image of a facade from a cathedral I couldn't identify:

Human (Aquarius), Lion (Leo), Bull (Taurus), Eagle (Scorpio)

And here's a picture of a fresco from the Svetitskhoveli Cathedral located in Mtskheta, Georgia, featuring the whole cast of characters circumambulating the "Son" - *no* - make that **Sun** of "God":

Here's two "Mutables" - Gemini and Pisces - making an appearance:

If the reader feels like it, make a trip to Chartres Cathedral in France and check out its stained-glass windows: same thing; more astrological representations.

So, no, I don't think it's the case that Constantine I was a convert. He was probably a *pervert*. By that, I mean think he simply took the Sun God baton and it carried on to the council with the *intention of exploiting what remained of "Christianity" and then co-opted it as best as possible and rebranded it to resemble the Sun Cult in order to curtail whatever "Christians" remained.* He helped to *pervert* that which the authentic Jesus of Nazareth *was doing.* Whatever wasn't accomplished could be hashed out later.

Even *if* the Mithraism or Sol Invictus *weren't* the one of the cults "Christianity" was co-opted and/or rebranded to *mimic,* most Catholics and Christians *are not* under the impression that the "Son of God" they've been manipulated into observing and, in some cases, *worshipping* is actually the *Sun itself* - The **Sun** of "God" - and *not* Jesus of Nazareth *himself!*

Curiously, dedications to Mithras *supposedly* ceased after Constantine's victory at Milvian Bridge on October 28th, 312 AD [13]... *A maximum of a mere* **four months** *before the Edict of Milan and* **over six years** *after he became Caesar.* Some sources claim it was due to his winning this battle under the "sign of the cross." [12] Others say it was under the Chi-rho symbol. [13] Even if this were true, the term "christos," abbreviated "chi-rho" after the first two letters, is the Greek translation for the Hebrew "Masiah" or "messiah" meaning "one who is anointed" and appears in the Greek Septuagint (the Koine Greek translation of the Hebrew Bible) in reference to *kings.* It seems more likely that the early "Christian" movement or practice has been subverted enough to make it "okay" to exist in the Roman Empire. "Let it feel safe and trusting, then manipulate it after it does." Then, stick that frog in the pot and turn up the heat...

Thus, there probably are kernels of truth in the Gospels as far a historical validity, but with the stories of the Sun of God being orbited by twelve "apostles" (or constellations), who knows how authentic they are.

The number of attendees at the Council of Nicea varies depending on the source; the following were apparently present:

- Eusebius of Caesarea (260-340) = > 250 [14]
- Athanasius of Alexandria (296-373) = 318 [15]
- Eustathius of Antioch (?) = c.270 [16]

I include the birth and death years for each to show that at least two-hundred years had transpired between the birth of any of those present at the convention and the death of Jesus of Nazareth. The Council of Nicea convened about 300 years after the death of Jesus.

But even the notion that the historical Jesus of Nazareth was the literal "Son of God" is not only unnecessary as we shall see, but *extremely* unlikely. The story of the "Immaculate Conception" - that the virgin Mary Mother of Jesus became pregnant with God's child who turned out to be the historic Jesus of Nazareth...this doesn't happen. To the straight or the bisexual guys reading: say you're involved with a young woman - you're dating - and she claims to be a virgin. After a year, she starts to "show," you *know* it's not gas and, knowing you didn't "help her out with that," you ask her: "What's up?" And, without everything around you appearing mythical and romanticized like a Hollywood film production, "your girl" replies back to you in a quasi-Shakespearean accent: "*My betrothed: I am carrying the Son of Our Lohd. He is nigh...*" Would you buy it?

The "Virgin Mother" motif dates back to God knows when and possibly before because the birth story of Horus, also a *Sun* and *War god,* who was also born to a Virgin - *Isis-Meri* - on December 25th - the Winter Solstice, yet again. He had twelve disciples which traveled around him and known as "The Truth," "The Light" (this is important!), and "God's *Anointed* Son" - *The "Christ."* According to the mythos, he was crucified, buried for three days, then resurrected. [17] During the Winter Solstice is when the Sun appears to stop moving south in the Northern Hemisphere for three days - December 22nd, 23rd, and 24th, - then comes back up on the 25th: *Christ*-mas. "The cross" the sun "dies" on is "The Southern Cross" or the "Crux" constellation which appears above the sun as it hangs low:

Then, toward the end of every Sunday Mass, Jesus gets eaten. I'm not trying to be a smart ass here: this is what happens - according to the religion's own doctrine. Yes, I know it's a communion wafer but this is the doctrine. While I was in Catholic school, more than one teacher or nun told the students that, when the priest performs the sacrament, the wafers *literally* turn into Jesus' body and the wine (if there is some) is *actually* his blood. If that's not mock cannibalism, it has to be *something*. But if you're a Catholic eating this, you're told you're ingesting Jesus during "Holy Communion" or the "Sacrament of the Eucharist."

Don't get me wrong: if there *is* a valid reason for co-opting a movement - whether it's social, spiritual, cultural, or whatever - and replacing it with a astrological Sun-God themed Cult, I'm all ears. If the "masses" needed to be duped in order to jump on board, why is that? Personally, I have nothing against astrology, but what I *don't* like is the underhanded and subjugating takeover behavior behind all this. Why the shell-games? *Was the practice of whatever was behind "Early Christianity" a threat of some sort to this cult?*

The good news is, if you've been a practicing Catholic or Christian and aligned with the teachings of Jesus, you were most likely observing the same god as he. The New Testament gospels seem legitimate save the Pauline texts, which appear to manipulate those "Christians" at the time to comply with and appease the ruling Elite. However, it would appear that the historical Jesus was teaching his students how to access the Divine *personally and on their own* as depicted in many of the gospels now labelled as "Gnostic" despite their authenticity. This makes sense, because the resulting organization that is known as the Roman Catholic Church created and profited from a monopoly on God since it conditioned its members to regard its clergy as an essential intermediary between themselves and "the Divine."

Plus, the canonical gospels (and probably more which were omitted from the New Testament or destroyed) appear to be authentic; therefore the words and teachings of the historical Jesus seem to have been preserved to some extent within the New Testament. This would make sense: if Jesus' practice/movement was in fact co-opted and rebranded to resemble a sort of religious front company that was actually a sun-worshipping cult, at least the "veneer" is real. A "convenience store" front camouflauging a drug-peddling operation still sells Smart Water.

However, I sincerely hope that what I've written is taken into consideration by those who consider themselves Christian because if it is true that the "Christ" role applied to the historical Jesus of Nazareth is actually representative of some Sun God - a "Savior in Disguise" - of a covert cult, then the "second coming of Christ" may not be a revisitation of the historical Jesus of Nazareth in actuality, but the Sun God who goes by many names.

But the resulting organization that is the Roman Catholic Church has since behaved *precisely* like the Roman Empire itself: a cross between a front-company and a cult. A "*Sun* of God Cult." Both are hierarchal organizations. Both are "Sun of God" Cults. Both have capstones: Caesar and the Pope (who may or may not be the actual "capstone," but that would require another chapter which I'm not writing.) And you can't have female Caesars just like you can't have female popes. Both have high-ranking members who've exonerated themselves for the same crimes or sins they chastise their subscribers for committing. Both are expansionistic (again, "Catholicism" means "Universal.") Both have satellite representatives. Both, ostensibly, worship the Sun unbeknownst to most of those who *actually support the existence of the organization.*

The thing with hierarchal organizations - religious, corporate, or otherwise - is that they're *insatiable:* they constantly need *fuel* in order to survive. Always. Whether that "fuel" is a burn 'em and turn 'em "Human Resource," "Natural Resources," "Unnatural Resources," "Recruitment for 'Human resources,'" or "Mergers and Acquisitions," or "Cutbacks in order to conserve the 'fuel.'" Whenever the fuel runs out - or when the leadership is so narcissistic they are *utterly convinced* they know what they're doing what they actually *have no idea* - the pyramid collapses. It happens over, and over, and over, again. Otherwise, it gets usurped by another pyramid.

Even Paul of Tarsus is reported to have clashed with Peter and James; since he worked with the Pharisees, it wouldn't surprise me in the least if he were a mole or conditioned to be one.

Anyway, after that long-winded diatribe, the historical Jesus *may* have been scapegoated in real life by means of execution, but whatever practice he *was* involved in *most certainly was* executed when his movement was subjugated and quashed by a cult to the Sun God.

It is the author's belief that whatever the historical Jesus *was* doing was stamped out the moment he kicked the bucket - with very little accurate documentation surviving or existing to this day. Whatever *does exist* is liable to be under the auspices of the Vatican - which operates a central bank as untouchable as its artifacts and manuscripts.

Oddly enough, after nearly a decade of research *and experience* which led me to this conclusion, this was substantiated while perusing *The Book of the SubGenius,* a 1983 publication which emerged from the "nonsense religion" the "Church of the SubGenius":

"According to the Coloring Book Version, Jesus died so that we'd be born Good Guys and only become Bad Guys by *choice.* No doubt today He'd be *real damn pleased* to see HIS FAN CLUB using HIS NAME to help the Conspiracy take that choice *away.* Yeah, the Con infiltrated Early Christianity *the second He bit the dust and lost no time in converting it into* 'a form, a CEREMONY, *A RITUAL.*' **We Hear and Obey. We Hear and Obey.**"[18]

Amongst other confirmations and revelations, this book - despite it's parody status - strangely makes the most sense. And it would benefit anyone who's aware of the Orwellian "War is Peace, Freedom is Slavery, Ignorance is Strength" conditioning going on currently which we were warned about earlier - by Orwell, Eisenhower, Kennedy, and more.

However, despite its confirmation about what I suspected about Paul of Tarsus, I still question *every* material I come across including this book - I *have* to apply critical thinking to *everything* - but it *does* have a lot of useful advice to say the very least. One thing I question though: the primary deity of the Church or the SubGenius is…Jehovah/Yahweh! He might be the lesser of two evils, for all I know.

Back to Yahweh and "Christianity": one thing that gives me pause is the inclusion of the Old Testament with the New in the Catholic and Christian Bibles. So, this is either Yahweh co-opting the already co-opted Christian Sun-Cult or this is the undercover Sun Cult's attempt to co-opt Judaism and it's adherents - which may have already been co-opted!

[1] https://www.myjewishlearning.com/article/halakhah-the-laws-of-jewish-life/

[2] *Finegan, Jack (1998). Handbook of Biblical Chronology, rev. ed. Hendrickson Publishers. p. 319.*

[3] *Humphreys, Colin J.; Waddington, W. G. (1992).* "The Jewish Calendar, a Lunar Eclipse and the Date of Christ's Crucifixion"

[4] "Saul of Tarsus: Rooted in Three Worlds". *In the Footsteps of Paul. PBS. 2003.*

[5] Brown, Raymond Edward *(1997). An Introduction to the New Testament. Doubleday. ISBN 978-0-385-24767-2.*

[6] Sanders, E.P. *(December 27, 2019).* "Saint Paul, the Apostle". *Encyclopædia Britannica.*

[7] Wand, John Williams Charles *(1990). A History of the Early Church to AD 500. Routledge. p. 320. ISBN 9780203131145.*

[8] https://en.wikipedia.org/wiki/Diocletianic_Persecution#Manichean_persecution

[9] http://www.churchhistory101.com/century4-p3.php

[10] Manfred Clauss, *Die römischen Kaiser – 55 historische Portraits von Caesar bis Iustinian,* ISBN 978-3-406-47288-6, p. 250

[11] For a full list of the pontifices of Sol see J. Rupke (ed.), *Fasti Sacerdotum* (2005), p. 606. Memmius Vitrasius Orfitus lists his priesthoods as pontifex of Vesta, one of the quindecimviri sacris faciundis, and pontifex of Sol, in that order (*Corpus Inscriptionum Latinarum* vol. 6, 1739–1742). In a list of eight priesthoods, Vettius Agorius Praetextatus puts *Pontifex Solis* in third place (*CIL* VI, 1779).

[12] https://www.britannica.com/topic/Mithraism

[13] https://en.wikipedia.org/wiki/Battle_of_the_Milvian_Bridge

[14] Eusebius Pamphilius, *The Life of Constantine [Vita Constantini].*

[15] Athanasius of Alexandria, *Ad Afros Epistola Synodica*

[16] Theodoret of Cyrus, *The Ecclesiastical History of Theodoret*

[17] *Zeitgeist: The Movie.* Dir. Peter Joseph. YouTube. YouTube, 14 Apr. 2014. Web. 9 Feb. 2015. https://www.youtube.com/watch?v=pvKkR0-d83k

[18] *Dobbs, J.R. "Bob" (1983) The Book of the SubGenius. p. 93.*

Islam

I'm not going to go into excessive detail about Islam's "Lost Child" or "Kick Dog" status or an extensive examination into its history or texts. This chapter is already long enough and its purpose it's to correlate the Abrahamic religions which were created by Yahweh to the dysfunctional families roles which emerge from the parenting of a malignant narcissistic parent.

Next in line is Islam which would inhabit the "Lost Child" or "Kick Dog" role and boy does it. Islam emerged in 610 AD when Mohammed (570 - June 8, 632 AD) reported having revelations from God (Allah) delivered to him from Archangel Gabriel while meditating in a cave. These revelations were memorized, recorded, and provided the content for the Quran, the central religious *604-page* text used by many Muslims.

Reminiscent of the "Lost Child" role in its best case scenario, Islam is somewhat off on its own - or at least wishes it were courtesy of the ongoing flack it's received for nearly twenty years straight. Like the previous two, it's observant of "Yahweh" but the deity is, of course, referred to as "Allah." Also, although the Bible is regarded as a holy book in this religion, it's central text is, again, the Quran. And, although Islam regards both Abraham and Jesus (Issa), it's chief prophet Mohammed.

The primary prophet of Islam, Mohammed, is also "excluded" and representing his image is very contentious in the "Muslim community." The poor guy - the "Lost Child" representative - is himself in hiding.

Trust me, Mohammed knows what he's doing.

So, with this third religion, we have the use of a different book, a different name for God (although it's the same God), and its "poster-prophet" avoids posters and literally tries his damnedest not to be seen. Yep: "Lost Child."

But, throughout history, Islam has also taken on the Kick Dog status. Especially in modern history, with predominantly Muslim nations such as Iraq, Afghanistan, Pakistan, Libya, Syria, and Somalia being invaded by the "Christian" nation the United States with support from its ally Israel, it becomes even more apparent how the Good Dog (Judaism) and the Bad Dog (Christianity) gang up on the Kick Dog (Islam) and quite possibly with the help, encouragement, and direction of the Owner ("Yahweh") as depicted in the previous chapter. Apparently, countries are now synonymous with religions (because feelings are facts!) and to criticize the policies of one means to criticize a religion.

Thanks to the Holy Dysfunctional Family, the Islamic Kick Dog gets the crap beaten out of it. Like the "Lost Child," the antagonism Islam faces is shoved right back in its face claiming it has a "victim mentality" - plus it's *blamed and blame-shifted upon* - when it was truly a victim reality. I can only hope Yahweh's "Cinderella" finds her "Prince Charming" and lives a life of "happily ever after." Otherwise, if the drumbeats for war with Iran escalate, it's going to find its "glass slipper" coming from the molten sand of one of her nuked deserts.

Hopefully, by now it's becoming evident that, not only is Yahweh/Allah a dysfunctional, "patriarchal" "God," but the "children" which he has produced have adopted the dysfunctional roles as well. My heart goes out to Islam. Coexist my ass unless the "family" gets cohesive, affordable therapy and functionalizes itself.

Mormonism

As mentioned in the previous chapter, the next dysfunctional role performed is the "Mascot/Jester" - the child who yearns to be seen and given any attention - even if it's humiliation - despite never being taken seriously or gaining the prominence of the dogs who came before it. Mormonism might fall under this category - but instead of accepting "Yahweh" or "Allah," it's "God the Father" or "Elohim." Like Islam, they accept Jesus not just as a prophet but as "God the Son" or, curiously, sometimes referred to as "Jehovah." The "Holy Ghost" is observed as well. The three, observed as separate beings, together make up "the Godhead." Quite interestingly, however, both the Father and Jesus have perfected, glorified bodies in Mormonism.

Anyway, it's not my intention to lampoon any religion under this category; my mentioning of this role is simply to point out that it exists within the Holy Dysfunctional Family.

Before we leave Mormonism, it's worth looking into its origins. According to its history, on September 21, 1823 while living in upstate New York, Joseph Smith reported that the Angel Moroni appeared to him and directed him to a book written on golden plates buried on Cumorah Hill in Manchester, Ontario County which detailed the religious history of an ancient people.[1][2] In March 1830, Smith published what he claimed was a translation of these plates as "The Book of Mormon" which was named after "Mormon," the ancient prophet and historian who wrote the book. One month later, Smith founded the "Church of Christ" which Smith, by the assistance of missionaries, sent out to proselytize. [3]

I'm not going to proceed into its history, but you might be wondering: "Where are the plates today?" Gold is one of - if not, the most - durable, stable, and reliable elements in existence. We don't know. In all fairness to Smith, a testimonial was provided by a group of eight witnesses who saw the plates and described them as having "an appearance of gold" and not *specifically* gold itself. The original authors ("Mormon" plus others?) simply said they engraved their writings on "plates." [4]

The Golden Plates themselves are reported to have weighed 30 to 60 pounds, were gold in color as well as thin and metallic, and engraved with hieroglyphics on both sides of the sheets (how?) and bound with three D-rings. [5] Smith claims that the book was buried in a stone box and was prevented by Moroni from taking the plates but instructed him to return to the same location in a year. Such was the case until September 1827 when he returned home with the plates during his fourth annual visit, where he forbade anyone to see them until he translated the content from its original "reformed Egyptian" language, and this translation became the Book of Mormon. The translation process, according to witnesses, involved Smith using a "seer stone" which was akin to modern day glasses. [6] After eleven men provided eye-witness testimony over the plates' existence [5], *Smith claimed the plates were returned back to Moroni so that they could not be examined.* [5]

Although some critics have made the claim that Smith himself manufactured the plates or that the testimony of the witnesses was based on "visions" rather than physical experience [5], I'm not going to jump to any conclusions here but will say that I find the following details of this story interesting:

1)   The original content of the Book of Mormon was engraved on gold or gold-colored metal.
2)   The golden plates' discovery were assisted by an "Angel."
3)   The engravings allegedly on the plates themselves were described as hieroglyphics or "reformed Egyptian."

[1] *Bushman, Richard Lyman (2008). Mormonism: A Very Short Introduction. New York: Oxford University Press.*
[2] Either one-third or two-thirds; accounts vary: http://www.sidneyrigdon.com/

dbroadhu/IL/mischig.htm#101781 Archived 2013-11-14 at the Wayback Machine &
http://www.sidneyrigdon.com/dbroadhu/NY/wayn1830.htm#031931 Archived
2013-11-07 at the Wayback Machine [*unreliable source?*]

[3] *O'Dea, Thomas F. (1957). The Mormons*

[4] https://www.churchofjesuschrist.org/study/history/topics/gold-plates?lang=eng

[5] *Vogel, Dan (2004), Joseph Smith: The Making of a Prophet, Salt Lake City:
Signature Books*

[6] Bushman (2005, pp. 71–72); Marquardt & Walters (1994, pp. 103–04); Van
Wagoner & Walker (1982, pp. 52–53) (citing numerous witnesses of the translation
process); Quinn (1998, pp. 169–70, 173) (describing similar methods for both the two-
stone Urim and Thummim and the chocolate-colored seer stone). Smith's use of a
single stone is well documented (Van Wagoner & Walker 1982, pp. 59–62), although
Smith said that his earliest translation used a set of stone spectacles called the Urim
and Thummim which he found with the plates (Smith et al. 1839–1843, p. 5). Smith's
mother, Lucy Mack Smith, was the only known witness of the Urim and Thummim,
which she said she had observed when covered by a thin cloth (Smith 1853, p. 101).

Secret Societies

Just as described in the previous chapter, the Father of the Holy
Dysfunctional Family has a Guard Dog. Most likely, it's more than one.
It's probably a pack.

As described previously, the Guard Dog is so close to his owner,
it may as well *be* his owner - or at least the instrument by which the
Owner has trained to "hear and obey" so diligently, he carries out orders
with unwavering loyalty. The "treats" such dogs must receive on account
of doing so…*chez gourmet*...

Since the Owner himself is clandestine and hidden (perhaps even
in physical form as suggested by Mormonism), so will be his Guard
Dogs. We know they exist - understandably with more evidence than the
Owner himself - but, like the Owner, they operate in "secret."

"Secret Societies," "Mystery schools," and the like… Since their
loyalty is even greater than the Good Dog, it's highly likely that *some
predate Judaism, "Yahweh's" Good Dog*…

Since the Catholic "Bad Dog" branched off from Judaism's "Good
Dog," one could reasonably consider that Judaism's Good Dog emerged
from the Guard Dog…which is:

Egypt - ancient Egypt, which the Old Testament itself details in
Exodus.

Yes, that's right. Just as Early Christianity crossed paths with

Judaism two-thousand years ago, Judaism itself had a brush with the Ancient Egyptians and its "mystery schools." Just like "Christianity" has its cross-pollination with Judaism, so does Judaism have with the "Mystery Schools."

These Mystery Schools may include the following: The Freemasons (meh, potentially), the Illuminati (most likely), Opus Dei, the Rosicrucians, the Zionists, the Jesuits, The Hermetic Order of the Golden Dawn, Ordo Temple Orientus, Skull and Bones (maybe), Vril Society, Knights Templar, Teutonic Knights, and the Merovingian Bloodline (which I highly doubt are descendants of the historic Jesus and Mary Magdalene, but would be surprised if they're descendants of *something*), Sol Invictus, Mithraism, and *Aryanism (Nazis.)* The list probably goes on, but a common theme amongst them, is the Sun, Light, a Cross (which could be *hooked)*, with the exception of Skull and Bones (well, actually, there are some *crossbones* there…) Many of these claim to have their origins - or at least possess information pertaining to - the mystery schools of Ancient Egypt - perhaps to the priesthood itself.

Now, we've already seen evidence of Sun-observation in Christianity. One of the supposed objectives of the Council of Nicea was the relationship between God the Father and the "Son" (or Sun, in real life), specifically, are they one in the same. Another is the celebration date of Easter (or "Pascha") which, curiously, is based on the first Sunday after the first full moon on or after the March equinox (which lands in the sign of Aries = "Lamb" of God - *oh God*...), and the *practice of the Liturgy.*

Catharism

Now, we get to the "Stray Dog" - or the Dog who breaks away from its Owner to live a free and independent life…until it's killed by its previous "Owner." It's not the only "dog" in history who tried to break away, either. The Cathars were a "Christian" dualist and probable "Gnostic" revival movement which appeared in the 11th century and thrived in some areas in Southern Europe (particularly Northern Italy and the Languedoc region of France) between the 12th and 14th century ***until its extermination by the Catholic Church during the Third Crusade.***

Cathar (or "Cathari" or Albigensian) cosmology involved a dualism between two opposing deities: the Good God of the New Testament (the creator of spirit) and the Evil God of the Old Testament (who reigned over the corporeal world.) [1] The latter was considered by the Cathars to be *Satan*, also identified as "King of the World" ("King of Kings?" "Lord of Lords?"), "The Demiurge," or "Rex Mundi." Thus, the God of Judaism, "Yahweh," was regarded by the Cathars as either Satan or Satan's *father*.[2] God, on the other hand, was a disincarnate being; a God of love, order, and peace.

The Cathars regarded human beings to be angels who were seduced by Satan during a war in heaven against the army of Archangel Michael, after which they would have been *forced to spend an eternity in Hell in Satan's material realm.* [2] The Cathars maintained that reincarnation would ensue until the human soul renounced the material world completely; otherwise they would continue to reincarnate to live on the corrupt Earth - or *Hell.* [3] The concept of the "Resurrection of Jesus" - that he "rose again on the Third Day" - was rejected by the Cathars who instead perceived this as simply Jesus of Nazareth's reincarnation. The "Christian" symbol of the Cross was seen as an instrument for torture and evil. [2]

Like the Bogomils, their neo-Gnostic predecessors who originated in the 10th century, the Cathars believed that *Satan had been the Good God's true servant before rebelling against him.* [4] ***It's highly worthwhile to note that the influence on the Bogomils' belief systems can be traced back to the Manichaeans [5][11] - the same Gnostic group which was exterminated by the Sun God-worshipping Diocletian as mentioned previously - the same Diocletian who persecuted the Early "Christians" starting on February 23, 303 AD.***

Also worth noting is that the Cathars *rejected the Sacrament of the Eucharist, or "Holy Communion," claiming the impossibility that it could be the actual body and blood of "Christ."* They also rejected the Sacrament of Baptism. [6]

The Cathars *did not have an hierarchal system;* they had a flat structure. [7] Since "spirit" was prioritized and "matter" eschewed, women could hold roles as equally as men, since spirit was regarded as genderless and immaterial.[3] The Cathars also rejected the Catholic priesthood, labeling its members, including the Pope, as unworthy and corrupted. [8]

One sacrament observed by the Cathars and *possibly* unique to them was *Consolamentum* which took the place of Baptism. Instead of receiving baptism by water, Consolamentum involved the laying of hands - reminiscent of Reiki or the hands-on healing performed in Spiritualism today. It was only administered twice in a lifetime: upon confirmation of the faith and upon impending death. Once Consolamentum was received, the member was referred to as a "Bon Homme" (or "parfait" or "perfect" from outside the faith.) [9] After becoming a "Parfait," members were required to be celibate, vegetarian, and dedicate their lives to spreading Cathar doctrines. Although Catharism had a "flat structure," its "parfaits" became leaders in Cathar communities. [10]

In some Cathar communities, death by suicide was acceptable. This was possibly due to its belief that the Earthly existence was equivalent to Hell, but also observed in the ritual of "Endura" as a rational and dignified response under certain conditions.[11] Russian-born French historian Zoé Oldenbourg compared the Cathars to "Western Buddhists" because she considered that their view of the doctrine of "resurrection" taught by Christ was similar to the Buddhist doctrine of reincarnation and rebirth. [12] The correlation between the Cathars and Buddhists is important; as we shall see, the Gnostic concept of "Gnosis" or "to know" may be the same concept as Enlightenment - or accessing the Divine from going within.

Like the Manichaeans before them and probably the "Early Christian" movement itself, the Cathars were exterminated (Catholicism had a "Catharsis") mostly during the Albigensian Crusade, which was carried out between 1209-1229 AD. Any remaining practices or adherents to Catharism were quashed during the Inquisition established in 1234 AD by Pope Gregory IX. By 1350, all known remnants of the movement had been extinguished. [13]

[1] *Sibly, W. A.; Sibly, M. D. (2002). The History of the Albigensian Crusade. Boydell Press. pp. 10–11.*

[2] *Peters, Edward, ed. (1980). "The Cathars". Heresy and Authority in Medieval Europe.*

[3] *O'Shea, Stephen (2000). The Perfect Heresy: The Revolutionary Life and Death of the Medieval Cathars. New York: Walker & Company.*

[4] *Barber, Malcolm (2000), The Cathars: Dualist heretics in Languedoc in the High Middle Ages, Harlow: Longman*

[5] https://en.wikipedia.org/wiki/Bogomilism

[6] *Burr, David (1996), Bernard Gui: Inquisitor's Manual, Internet History Sourcebooks Project, New York City: Fordham University, retrieved 25 May 2013*

[7] *Johnston, William M (2000). Encyclopedia of Monasticism.*

[8] *Costen, Michael D. (1997). The Cathars and the Albigensian Crusade. Manchester and New York: Manchester University Press.*

[9] *Johnston, William M (2000). Encyclopedia of Monasticism. Fitzroy Dearborn*

Publishers.
[10] *Emmanuel Le Roy Ladurie (1975). Montaillou: The Promised Land of Error. Random House/editions Gilmard*
[11] https://www.ancient.eu/Cathars/
[12] *Maseko, Achim N. (2008), Church Schism & Corruption, South Africa: Lulu.com, p. 482,*
[13] Strayer, Joseph R. *(1971). The Albigensian Crusades. New York, NY: The Dial Press.*

"Gnosticism"

By now, not only have the Cathars been exterminated, but the Manichaeans and "Early Christians" as well - and at the hands of what appears to be the same organization, just that the organization rebranded itself in the early fourth century (and possibly before.) Other dualist or "Gnostic" movements include the Paulicians, which had its roots begin around 660 AD. Paulicianism, also influenced by the Manichaeans, was founded in present day Armenia by one Constantine-Silvanus. [1] Its name, according to medieval Byzantine sources, is derived from 3rd century Bishop of Antioch Paul of Samosata while other sources claim its name is derived from the Apostle Paul, or Paul of Tarsus. Their doctrines are unclear, but it is believed that they were dualistic, non-trinitarian, and regarded the Demiurge the same way as the Cathars as well as the existence of a "Good God." [2] The Paulicians faced persecution as well.

Some of the early groups considered to have a "Gnostic" doctrine are:

- *Basilidians:* Emerging from Basilides, who taught in Alexandria, Egypt between 117 - 138 AD, claims to have inherited his teachings from the Apostle Matthias (died c. 80 AD) in the *Gospel of Basilides*. Matthias supposedly replaced Judas Iscariot after his betrayal of Jesus of Nazareth as described in *Acts I*. But this is strange: he was either a pupil of Simonian teacher Menander (who studied under Simon Magus) according to Eusebeus of Caesarea's (260/265 - 339/340 AD) *Ecclesiastical History* Book IV, Chapter VII or a disciple of *Saint Peter's* named Glaucias according to Clement of Alexandria's (c.150 - c.215) *Stromata* Book VII Chapter XVII. **This is both befuddling and important considering the contention between Simon Magus and Saint Simon Peter as depicted in Acts 8:9-24. Whereas Magus is portrayed as someone who "practiced sorcery," Peter and John "placed their hands" on people while in Samaria and**

"they received the Holy Spirit." What Peter and John were doing, according to *Acts,* was reminiscent to the Cathar sacrament of *Consolamentum*. Also, considering the sources, Clement was closer in chronological proximity to Basilides than Eusebeus. Clement himself writes that his teachings are intended to make his students"Gnostics." [3]

- *Valentinians:* Emerging from Valentinus (c.100-180 AD), born in Egypt and schooled in Alexandria (The "Great Library" of which was destroyed in 48 BC) where the Gnostic Basilides taught, yet Clement of Alexandria (c.150 - c.215 AD) claims he was taught by the Gnostic Theudas (dates? There's a problem with this: if it's the same Theudas featured in *Acts,* it would have been impossible since that Theudas died in c.46 AD a disciple of the Apostle Paul. [4] His teaching career reached its height between 150 - 155 AD while in Rome. [5] According to early Church Father and apologist Irenaeus (early 2nd century - c.202 AD), the Valentinians weren't Gnostics themselves but profoundly inspired by the Gnostics.[6]
- *Sethians:* 2nd and 3rd Century AD.
- *Mandaenism:* Persian.
- *Cainites:* Eastern Roman Empire, 2nd Century.
- *Carpocratians:* Emerging from Carpocrates of Alexandria during the first half of the 2nd century.
- *Thomasines:* Emerging from Saint Thomas the Apostle, 52 AD [7] and established in the state of Kerala in India. Thomas' trip to India was reported by 3rd and 4th century historians such as Ambrose of Milan, Gregory of Nazianzus, Jerome, and Ephrem the Syrian.[8] Although the *Acts of Thomas* has complete Greek and Syriac versions as well as fragments, the Greek versions suggest to scholars that the Syriac version are original, which place him in Edessa, Syria. The text itself, however, describes Thomas in "India" and the service of Indo-Parthian King Gondophares who ruled from 19 - 46 AD. [9] The Indo-Parthian kingdom existed between 19 - 224/5 AD occupying areas of present day Iran, Afghanistan, and northwest region of the Indian subcontinent.[10] Thomas, according to tradition, is believed to had been martyred in Tamil Nadu which is closer in geographical proximity to Kerala which is along the southern tip of the Indian subcontinent. [11]

It's worth mentioning that most of what we know about the early

"Gnostic" sects comes from Irenaeus of Lyon and Clement of Alexandria. Again, the above list is partial, and delving into the particulars of each would be material for a separate book. Suffice it to say, the "Gnostic communities" or schools which emerged after Jesus' death did not survive with the exception of Mandaenism, although resurgences of similar doctrines appeared in later movements such as Catharism.

Since the materials pertaining to the Cathars, Bogomils, Manichaeans, and - especially - the "Early Christians" were purged, there's no true way to discern which tenets
 or beliefs were held by the "Early Christians" at the time. For all we know, they may have been what's referred to as "Gnostics." Most of the Gnostic groups mentioned previously claimed that they observed or were trying to restore the practices and beliefs of the historic Jesus of Nazareth. I'll let the reader decide on that.

For now, and considering that "Gnosticism" isn't a single standardized system of beliefs, let's list some common themes these groups share in terms of belief systems and practices:

- The presence of a "Demiurge," often equated with the Old Testament God and/or Satan and correlated to the corporeal world.
- A dualistic cosmology, involving the Demiurge and a "Good God" representing peace, love, and order; or "good" versus "evil."
- An overall flat structure as opposed to an hierarchal organization.
- An emphasis on "Spirit," commonly referred to as "Sophia."
- The concept of "Gnosis" or internal *intuition* or "knowing"; the awareness of Divine presence coming from within, reminiscent of Buddhism's Enlightenment.
- The tendency to be perceived as "heretics" by the organization which persecuted them (if applicable.)
- Non-trinitarian.
- A rejection of the veneration of Mary mother of Jesus.
- Taking human life is considered abhorrent.
- A rejection of iconography such as the Cross and certain rites and sacraments.

Despite many movements considered "Gnostic" disappearing or being disappeared throughout history along with their materials, the finding at Nag Hammadi, Egypt in 1947 of numerous manuscripts provides some insight into their belief system. At the very least, the grouping of the various documents as a collection provides insight into a possible "Gnostic" ideology, at least within the region itself.

The finding itself includes fifty-two treatises grouped in twelve codices which most scholars believe date back to *the 3rd or 4th centuries AD* with the exception of the written text of the *Gospel of Thomas,* the *Gospel of Truth,* the *Gospel of Judas,* and the *Pistis Sophia* which are believed be dated *to the 2nd century.* [12] Also, the fact that these manuscripts were found *buried and sealed* in a clay jar is interesting. [13] Considering these details, and this of course is speculation, but it's almost as if these manuscripts were buried to ***prevent them from being discovered and destroyed*** *- especially when considering* ***they were buried around the time of the "Great Persecution" of the "Early Christians" under Diocletian.***

If this is the case, it absolutely supports the concept that "Gnosticism" or "Gnostic" beliefs were pertinent to "Early Christianity" and that "Early Christianity" was *Gnostic in nature - or at least whatever movement existed prior to the early 300s AD.* This is not to suggest that the contents of the New Testament should be refuted, but that there were numerous other Gospels and texts in circulation which were extinguished before the time of the Council of Nicea convened. A list of the texts along with their translations can be found at http://www.gnosis.org/naghamm/ nhl.html if the reader is interested.

What's also peculiar is the fact that Paul's letters - coming from someone who had previously assisted the Pharisees in their persecution of Jesus and his followers and whom never met Jesus in person - were *included* in the New Testament while texts attributed to apostles whom interacted directly with Jesus were omitted or destroyed before it's compilation. Plus, some content from Paul's letters endorsed acquiescence to Roman authority as featured in the Book of Paul's letter to the Romans:

Romans 13: Let everyone be subject to the governing authorities, for there is no authority except that which God has established. The authorities that exist have been established by God. [2] Consequently, whoever rebels against the authority is rebelling against what God has instituted, and those who do so will bring judgment on themselves. [3] For rulers hold no terror for those who do right, but for those who do wrong. Do you want to be free from fear of the one in authority? Then do what is right and you will be commended. [4] For the one in authority is God's servant for your good. But if you do wrong, be afraid, for rulers do not bear the sword for no reason. They are God's servants, agents of wrath to bring punishment on the wrongdoer. [5] Therefore, it is necessary to submit to the authorities, not only because of possible punishment but also as a matter of conscience.

^{6} This is also why you pay taxes, for the authorities are God's servants, who give their full time to governing. ^{7} Give to everyone what you owe them: If you owe taxes, pay taxes; if revenue, then revenue; if respect, then respect; if honor, then honor.

Whether the "authority" are "God's servants" or not, he was right about them bringing wrath upon those who rebelled since they were persecuted for nearly three centuries afterward any time they did, apparently.

Also of note is the contention between Paul and James, the Brother of Jesus which some researchers and scholars have taken on as subject material. [14] In Acts 15 and 21, tension is depicted between the two.

The concept of "Gnosis" refers to a "knowledge" or insight into man's true nature as divine. When this is accomplished, this releases one from the constraint from the earthly condition. [15] Again, the term "Gnostic" was not self-applied to groups or movements, but referred to the access of the divine within or internal "knowledge" *(gnosis)* rather than by faith *(pistes)* which differentiated between communion with the highest God within (or intuition) versus the Demiurge or God of the corporeal realm. "Gnosis" was obtained through an internal awareness, introspection, and meditation. [16]

On the surface, the concept of "Gnosis" resembles that of Enlightenment in Buddhism. Both involve meditative practices, internal awareness, and stilling the mind. It appears Manichaeism, originating in Persia and having cross-pollinated with "Early Christianity" within the Roman Empire, was also influenced by Buddhism. [17]

The "constraints from the earthly condition" may not only refer to breaking the cycle of reincarnation after achieving gnosis or Enlightenment, it could also refer to the development of psychic senses in additional to the five physical senses as described in *Toxic States of America,* Chapter 13. In *Buddhism and Gnosis,* Buddhologist Edward Conze draws parallels between Mahayana Buddhism and Gnosticism. [18]

The quote from the Gospel of Thomas - considered "Gnostic" material - reflects this concept:

"Rather, the **kingdom** is **inside** of **you**, and it is outside of **you**. When **you** come to know yourselves, then **you** will become known, and **you** will realize that it is **you** who are the sons of the living father. But if **you** will not know yourselves, **you** dwell in poverty and it is **you** who are that poverty."

How would Jesus of Nazareth factor into this? There's been speculation that the historical Jesus was a member of the *Essenes,* a Jewish sect which flourished during the Second Temple Period throughout the Roman-occupied Judaea between the 2nd century BC **to the first century AD.** Their numbers were fewer than the Pharisees and the Sadducees, the two major sects at the time, and they lived a communal life. The earliest documentation of the sect comes from Roman writer Pliny the Elder (died 79 AD) in *Natural History* (published 77 AD) where he writes that the Essenes had no money, had existed for thousands of generations, and their priests whom he referred to as **"Contemplatives"** do not marry. He writes that they were located **somewhere** *above* **Ein Gedi and next to the Dead Sea.** Ein Gedi, a nature reserve on the west side of the Dead Sea, is located less than 50 miles southeast of Jerusalem and **24 miles south of Qumran** - where the Dead Sea Scrolls, a collection of ancient Jewish manuscripts from created around 408 BC to 318 AD discovered in 1946/47 - 1956, were found.

The Essenes, as described by Romano-Jewish historian Josephus (37 - 100 AD) and Jewish Philosopher Philo of Alexandria (c.20 BC - c.50 AD), were also communal, tended to be celibate and had collective ownership, and typically elected a leader who attended to the group and whose orders they were to obey. They also refrained from sacrificing animals [19] and controlled their temper. [20] They did not have slaves but rather served each other. [21] This sort of lifestyle is what is clearly depicted with Jesus and his disciples in the New Testament as well as gospels considered to be "gnostic."

Here's where things get interesting: early Church Leader Epiphanius of Salamis (c.310-320 - 403 AD) makes a distinction between two sets of Essenes in the *Panarion,* written in 374-75 AD:

"The Nasaraean—they were Jews by nationality—originally from Gileaditis, Bashanitis and the Transjordan... They acknowledged Moses and believed that he had received laws—not this law, however, but some other. And so, they were Jews who kept all the Jewish observances, but they would not offer sacrifice or eat meat. They considered it unlawful to eat meat or make sacrifices with it. *They claim that these Books are fictions, and that none of these customs were instituted by the fathers.* [Italics mine.] This was the difference between the Nasaraean and the others..." (1:18)

After this Nasaraean sect in turn comes another closely connected with them, called the Ossaeans. These are Jews like the former... originally came from Nabataea, Ituraea, Moabitis, and Arielis, the lands beyond the basin of what sacred scripture called the Salt Sea... Though it is different from the other six of these seven sects, it causes schism only by forbidding the books of Moses like the Nasaraean. (1:19)"

So, is it Jesus "of Nazareth" or Jesus "the Nasaraene?" Most Christians know that Jesus was not born in Nazareth according to Scripture, but in Bethlehem - which is actually much closer in proximity to Ein Gedi and Qumran than Nazareth (which is about 90 miles farther away.)

The above passage is interesting because it suggests that the Nazarenes "claim that these Books are fictions" and that "none of these customs were instituted by the fathers." Considering they "acknowledged Moses and believed that he had received laws - not this law, however, but some other," it's questionable about which "Books" the Nazarenes refuted. But with the numerous examples cited in the New Testament regarding the friction Jesus had with the Pharisees, it seems there was some disconnect with respect to beliefs as well as the concept of God. As seen in John 8: 39-44:

39 They answered and said to Him, "Abraham is our father." Jesus said to them, "If you are Abraham's children, do the deeds of Abraham. 40 "But as it is, you are seeking to kill Me, a man who has told you the truth, which I heard from God; this Abraham did not do. 41 "You are doing the deeds of your father." They said to Him, "We were not born of fornication; we have one Father: God." 42 Jesus said to them, "If God were your Father, you would love Me, for I proceeded forth and have come from God, for I have not even come on My own initiative, but He sent Me. 43 "Why do you not understand what I am saying? *It is* because you cannot hear My word. 44 "You are of *your* father the devil, and you want to do the desires of your father. He was a murderer from the beginning, and does not stand in the truth because there is no truth in him.

Whenever he speaks a lie, he speaks from his own *nature,* for he is a liar and the father of lies.

"You are of *your* father the devil…" That's a pretty charged statement, not to mention a sharp similarity to the Cathar belief doctrine described previously. Whether or not Jesus is referring to Abraham or the God of the Old Testament is unclear, but it does reflect the content of Epiphanius' passage from the *Panarion* provided earlier.

But even this can be countered by the discovery of the Dead Sea Scrolls found at Qumran, many of which where copies of books found in the Old Testament, so make of that what you will. Regardless, this sentiment - "you are of *your* father the devil…" - may very well be the subject material of the following movie...

[1] *"Constantine-Silvanus". Encyclopædia Britannica. Retrieved 1 March 2019.*

[2] *"Paulician". Encyclopædia Britannica. Retrieved 1 March 2019.*

[3] https://gnosticismexplained.org/gnostic-sects/

[4] *Roukema, Riemer (1998). Gnosis and Faith in Early Christianity.*

[5] *Filoramo, Giovanni (1990). A History of Gnosticism.*

[6] Brakke, David. 2010. *The Gnostics: Myth, Ritual, and Diversity in Early Christianity.* Harvard University Press. p. 30.

[7] *Fahlbusch, Erwin; Bromiley, Geoffrey William; Lochman, Jan Milic (2008). The Encyclodedia of Christianity.*

[8] *Frykenberg, Robert Eric (2008). Christianity in India: from Beginnings to the Present. Oxford University Press.*

[9] https://en.wikipedia.org/wiki/Acts_of_Thomas

[10] *Gazerani, Saghi (2015). The Sistani Cycle of Epics and Iran's National History: On the Margins of Historiography.*

[11] *Farmer, David Hugh (2011). The Oxford Dictionary of Saints, Fifth Edition Revised (5th ed.). Oxford: University Press.*

[12] *Bock, Darrell (2006). The Missing Gospels. Nelson Books. p. 6.*

[13] Marvin Meyer and James M. Robinson, *The Nag Hammadi Scriptures: The International Edition.* HarperOne, 2007. pp 2-3.

[14] https://www.vision.org/james-and-paul-why-conflict-312

[15] *Kurt Rudolph (2001). Gnosis: The Nature and History of Gnosticism. A&C Black. p. 2.*

[16] https://englishgnosisusa.us/

[17] *Foltz, Richard (2010), Religions of the Silk Road (2nd ed.), Palgrave Macmillan,*

[18] *Conze, Edward (1967), "Buddhism and Gnosis", in Bianchi, U. (ed.), Origins of Gnosticism: Colloquium of Messina, 13–18 April 1966*

[19] Philo, §75: ου ζωα καταθυοντες [= not sacrificing animals]

[20] Josephus (c. 75). *The Wars of the Jews.*

[21] Josephus (c. 94). *Antiquities of the Jews.* 18.21.

12

<u>"Satan Claus"</u>

"The very word "secrecy" is repugnant in a free and open society; and we are as a people inherently and historically opposed to secret societies, to secret oaths and to secret proceedings...Our way of life is under attack. Those who make themselves our enemy are advancing around the globe...no war ever posed a greater threat to our security. If you are awaiting a finding of "clear and present danger," then I can only say that the danger has never been more clear and its presence has never been more imminent...For we are opposed around the world by a monolithic and ruthless conspiracy that relies primarily on covert means for expanding its sphere of influence–on infiltration instead of invasion, on subversion instead of elections, on intimidation instead of free choice, on guerrillas by night instead of armies by day. It is a system which has conscripted vast human and material resources into the building of a tightly knit, highly efficient machine that combines military, diplomatic, intelligence, economic, scientific and political operations. Its preparations are concealed, not published. Its mistakes are buried, not headlined. Its dissenters are silenced, not praised. No expenditure is questioned, no rumor is printed, no secret is revealed."

- President John F. Kennedy, April 27, 1961 [1]

Eyes Wide Open

In 1999, Stanley Kubrick produced his what would be his last and final film, *Eyes Wide Shut,* which he co-wrote and directed. The storyline is based on Arthur Schnitzler's 1926 novel *Traumnovelle* or *"Dream Story."* Two key storyline differences involve the setting of *Eyes Wide Shut* being transferred from Vienna to New York City and that the events taking place in *Eyes Wide Shut* are during the days leading up to Christmas - December 25, the day the sun rises during the Winter Solstice - whereas in *Traumnovelle, this is not the case.*

The story centers on married couple Bill and Alice Harford, a well-to-do small family with one child. The film begins with Alice, a former art gallery curator, and Bill, a physician, preparing for a night out at a holiday gala hosted by one of Bill's patients, Victor Ziegler, and his wife Illona. Shortly after their arrival the couple separate and Bill is reunited with his college friend, Nick Nightingale. Nick, a hired pianist for the event, informs Bill that he's visiting and will be playing at a Jazz Club later that night if Bill wishes to catch up later. Later during the gala while both are separated, Bill and Alice are seduced by other parties; Bill, by a pair of "models" and Alice by an older Hungarian gentleman by the name of Sandor Szavost. Both Bill and Alice indulge in flirtatious activity. Alice, after being propositioned by Sandor to look at Victor's private art collection upstairs, turns down both Sandor and his offer, referring to her marital status. Bill, on the other hand, starts to grow uncomfortable as the women start guiding him surreptitiously to an undisclosed location. When Bill asks where it is they're going, the models inform him, "where the rainbow ends." Now confused and uncomfortable, Bill's noticeable reluctance is interrupted by Ziegler's butler, who asks for Bill's assistance.

Displayed at the gala are elaborate and extravagant holiday light decorations, such as this one behind Alice and Sandor while they're dancing:

The eight pointed star featured throughout this scene is, along with a lion, a symbol associated with ancient Mesopotamian goddess Inanna [1], the goddess of sex, war, justice, and political power. While originally worshipped in Sumer, she was later observed by the Akkadians, Babylonians, and Assyrians under the name Ishtar. Referred to as the "Queen of Heaven" and associated with the planet Venus [1], she was worshipped in Sumer at least as early as the Uruk Period (c. 4000 BC - c. 3100 BC.) The cult of Inanna-Ishtar may have been involved with sexual rites within those civilizations. She influenced the Phoenician goddess Astoreth and the Greek Aphrodite. She appears in more myths than any other Sumerian deity [2][3], many of which involve her *taking over the domains of other deities*. She was described as young and impetuous and constantly striving for more power than she had been allotted.[4] The most prominent myth surrounding Inanna is her attempt to descend and conquer the Underworld ruled by her older sister Ereshkigal but is instead found guilty of hubris (narcissism/ego) and stuck dead by its seven judges (the Anunnaki.) Here's Ishtar on an Akkadian seal, the eight-pointed star in the upper-left corner, the lion in the bottom-left, dated 2350 - 2150 BC:

The goddess is also correlated to the demon Lilith featured in the Talmud, who was Adam's first wife and coupled with fallen Archangel Samael, who enjoyed commitment-less sexual pleasures with men. Lilith is also featured with lions as well as owls as in the "Burney Relief," featured below, from Babylon c.1750 BC [5] Take note of Ziegler's wife's name:

Illona, which may be a contraction for "Inanna" and "Lilith":

Moving right along, Bill is taken to an upstairs bathroom by the butler to meet with a panicked Ziegler, who was concerned about a young woman named Mandy with whom he was having sex until she had overdosed on a speedball. Bill resuscitates the young woman.

The next evening, while the couple is smoking pot in their bedroom, they confront each other about the flirtatious behavior each was involved in the night before. This leads to an argument about temptation during which Bill claims women are less likely to succumb to due to their propensity to be more faithful than men. To counter this, Alice admits to a temptation she *would* have indulged during a family vacation made previously to Cape Cod, claiming she would have risked her marriage, motherhood, everything, if she were given the chance to have sex with a naval officer she had seen there. Bill, now feeling betrayed and insecure, immediately receives a phone call from the daughter of a patient who had just passed away. He leaves their home to pay his respects, during which the daughter of the deceased patient tries to seduce him.

After his visit and still angered and insecure, Bill attempts to retaliate against his wife's disclosure by accepting the advances of a prostitute. Before the two can engage in her services, Bill receives a phone call from his wife which prompts guilt and he leaves the situation.

Bill then meets with Nick who is finishing up a set at a Jazz Club. Nick informs him of a peculiar engagement where he's been hired to play piano while blindfolded yet in the company of incredibly beautiful women. Curiously, the table lamps at the club look like little suns:

Nick informs Bill that the event requires a mask and a black cape to attend plus a password which Nick reveals is "Fidelio." Bill, intrigued by this, goes to a costume shop to rent the items and proceeds to the event which is held at a gated, opulent mansion outside of the city.

Upon arriving, Bill is greeted by two attendants who grant him access after he provides the password. He is then shuttled to the mansions' entrance where his coat is taken and he dons his mask and cloak:

Notice the two statues flanking the entrance of "Light Bearers." (If you were to watch the film and look carefully, around the moment the above action takes place, you will see what looks like a demonic face of red light appear on Bill's lower body.) When Bill proceeds to the main hall, he sees the beginning of a ritual in progress:

The ritual involves a man dressed in a red cloak and wearing a gold mask fumigating incense in a distiller while walking counter-clockwise in a circle surrounded by *twelve* masked women who are cloaked in black on a red carpet. The surrounding congregation is also masked and robed in black. Soon, the twelve women rise in unison and disrobe.

The red-cloaked man subsequently pounds his staff twelve times, each time in front of one of each of the women as they're dismissed from the circle. As each is dismissed, they pair themselves up with a member of the surrounding congregation and walk off. One of the women pairs up with Bill and, as they walk away, warns him that he is in grave danger, will be found out, and needs to leave as soon as possible. He ignores the warning and remains to witness sexual acts performed by members of the congregation within the mansion's many rooms.

His impostor status is discovered by the group as the red-cloaked leader confronts Bill while he is surrounded by the masked congregation. The leader instructs Bill to remove his mask and, after he does so, his clothes as well. Before he does, the same masked woman who took him away reappears, offering to be taken instead of Bill. She is subsequently taken away by a man wearing what appears to be a plaque doctor mask and Bill is allowed to go, but strongly warned not to mention what he witnessed to anyone, or else the most dire consequences would befall him and his family.

Oddly enough, after this scene, any temptations which come Bill's way either backfire or don't pan out. But, when he returns home and enters his apartment, a red-colored eye can be seen moving across his back in the film version:

Red eye for the straight guy. Anyway, he finds Alice laughing in her sleep and wakes up. It turns out the dream wasn't funny, but a nightmare involving her betraying Bill while fornicating with the Naval Officer amongst others while laughing at Bill.

Bill attempts to visit Nick the next morning at his hotel, only to be informed by the desk clerk that he's gone and was escorted out by two large men earlier that morning, appearing to have been bruised. The clerk, being gay and finding Bill attractive, flirts in vain with Bill. Later, Bill finds out at the costume shop that the mask he rented is missing and is subsequently charged for it. Then, he goes back to the mansion only to be given "the slip" - actually, a pre-typed letter addressed to him telling him to give up his inquires which are useless. He then goes back to his office and, still miffed at Alice now for her dream as well as her disclosure, calls his dead patient's daughter to exact a revenge fuck, but her husband answers the phone. *Click*. Bound and determined to cheat, he then goes back to the prostitute's apartment only to find out she isn't there. Her roommate is, though, and she tells him that she's been diagnosed with HIV.

Then, Bill sees that he's being stalked around the streets of New York by a large man in a trench coat so he grabs a newspaper and ducks into a coffee shop where the following devil's horn decorations can be seen:

The paper he's purchased (which has the headline "Lucky to be alive") features an article about an ex-beauty queen by the name of Amanda who died of an overdose. He visits a morgue to see if "Amanda" is Mandy, the same woman whose life he saved at Ziegler's party - and it is. He then confronts Ziegler on this at his home, which Ziegler passive-aggressively denies. It seems like Ziegler could be lying at times while telling the truth during others. Kubrick helps the viewer out with a prop - a newspaper - that keeps disappearing and reappearing on a side table while the conversation is taking place. Ziegler also makes mention of the fact that the attendees at the masked ritual are people in high places. *This* coincides with the beliefs expressed by Paul the Apostle in Romans 13 provided earlier under *Gnosticism* with respect to the divine right of rulers and their appointment by God.

Upon Bill's return home, he finds Alice sleeping again, but this time the mask he "lost" has been placed on the pillow next to her. He breaks down and spends the rest of the night filling her in on what he's experienced for the past few days. The next morning, Bill, Alice, and their daughter visit a toy store for Christmas. When Bill asks Alice "What should they do?", their daughter Helena holds up a Barbie Doll dressed like a fairy or an angel (a real one):

Soon after, while Bill and Alice are conversing, two men who could be seen earlier at Ziegler's party approach Helena from behind and we don't see her again. The story ends with Alice telling Bill that she does in fact love him (despite thinking he's a pussy, consciously or subconsciously) and that they should be grateful to be where they're at after all they've been through and that it can't be the end all be all.

…tell that to Helena…

The moral of the story is: if you have "issues," whether conscious or subconscious (hence, "Eyes Wide Shut"), the Black Sun-cult consisting of highly egotistical people with narcissism like Inanna's (perhaps Lucifer's as well) is going to conjure demons to make your life hell - either by pointing them out or tempting you to act out on them with dire consequences.

The film is saturated with symbology; to get into it in detail would be lengthy to say the least. The imagery not only involves Inanna/Ishtar/ Lilith, but also Lilith's partner Samael - the "horns" featured earlier, but also the Sun or "Son of God" since Samael is a "fallen" archangel. But the "sun lamps" at the jazz cafe would certainly allude to this. In light of this (no pun or sun intended), if Samael is also synonymous with Lucifer, it would explain the "Light bearers" seen earlier at the mansion where the dark arts were being practiced.

In some Gnostic cosmologies, Samael became synonymous with the Demiurge - a concept that would fit right in considering the opulence and wealth of the unnamed secret society featured in *Eyes Wide Shut* and the Demiurge's link to the corporeal world.

Before anyone gets worked up let's take a moment to understand where this is coming from by revisiting Chapter 2. Samael - *if this is Samael* - doesn't love people who don't love themselves - or at least him in the form of *loyalty*. If you don't, it's taken personally.

Remember, the password was "Fidelio."

But the adage, "God only helps people who helps themselves" doesn't apply to God; it's actually Samael. And if it's you're expected to help yourself and you *do so,* then you really don't need any help from others, so it turns out to be a farce.

And if it's the case that you *do* help others who are like Samael, that's worthless and only proves to be a drain of your energy: whatever you give will be taken for granted, taken advantage of, or given little back in return - they think they're *entitled* to it after all. It doesn't come back to you in the form of "good karma" either - just regrets for giving it in the first place and the realization that you're "too giving."

But, if the information presented in Chapter 2 is accurate, then compassion for these types is possible if they had experienced abandonment or neglect - *or rejection, if that is the case*. Different schools of mythos, of course, paint different pictures. The Bogomils maintained a dualistic story between God's two angelic sons, the elder Satanail (Samael) and the younger Michael in which Satanail rebelled and became an evil spirit. According to the story, Adam was allowed to till the ground on condition that he sold himself and his posterity to Satanail, the owner of the Earth. [6]

Why the falling out, I don't know or even know if this is true to begin with. (Hell, it's a pain in the ass trying to keep track of "who's who" when a deity, archon, "god," or "angel" has a name change with every new pantheon.) One could speculate that it's akin to what happens when a spouse or parent has a child and the love which was exclusively bestowed upon the other spouse or child respectively is now *to be shared*. This was described previously with males with respect to their wives or mothers: if the wife gives birth to the son, the father may become jealous of the attention his wife gives to the son since it all used to be for him. If a mother (or father) produces a second son, the first son may resent both the parent and his younger brother for the disruption of the love he used to receive, perceiving quantity as quality. If this is the case, Satanail/Samael would not just have felt abandoned and neglected, but *betrayed* as well - which would compel anyone to seek *loyalty* out in others going forward as a result, which may reflect in "Yahweh's" (aka Samael's) character as depicted with Abraham and Job. It would also account for any narcissism: the affront the being felt after being betrayed would have this sort of psychological backlash. "I thought you though I was 'the Best!' I *am* 'the Best!' Why did you need another kid?" So, he seeks out others who make him feel as though he is "the Best" since they do the same thing with others and can relate: it is *in fact* "their God." No, I do not mean this pejoratively; *only with great care and compassion.*

Despite some Christian schools designating him as a fallen angel, Samael is considered to be a member of the heavenly host in Talmudic texts, associated with destructive duties, and the father of Cain in addition to being the partner of Lilith. [7] He's described as the "Severity of God" in Arthur Edward Waite's *The Holy Kabbalah.*

In texts considered to be Gnostic, such as the *Apocryphon of John, On the Origin of the World,* and *Hypostasis of the Archons* (all found within the Nag Hammadi Library), "Samael" is one of three names applied to the Demiurge, the other two being Yaldabaoth and Saklas. Here, Yaldabaoth *claims chief divinity for himself* (reminiscent of "no other god except me") whereupon Sophia refers to him as "Samael" due to his ignorance. In *Hypostasis of the Archons* as well as the *First Epistle of John,* he's claimed to be the first sinner. [8] He is depicted as a *lion-faced* serpent [9] as represented as a relief on a Gnostic gem:

The reason I include this image is speculation that there might be a correlation to the lion motif depicted next to Ishtar/Lilith and/or the Sphinx of ancient Egypt.

The *Book of Enoch,* which was found amongst other books at Qumran which suggests its association with the Essenes and most likely Jesus himself, *may* have in turn influenced Early Christianity (which may itself have been "Gnostic.") The *Book of Enoch* was lost since the 8th century (how convenient) and reintroduced to Europe in the late 18th century by James Bruce, who had obtained the most complete copy of the manuscript to date during a trip to Ethiopia (Abyssinia.) The copy obtained by Bruce was written in Ge'ez, and ancient Semetic language used in southern Eritrea and northern Ethiopia, and translated to English during the 19th century.

Enoch, whom identifies himself as the book's author in its content, comes from the Antediluvian ("Pre-Flood") Period. Believed to be Noah's great-grandfather, Enoch is referred to in the New Testament *Epistle of Jude* as "Enoch the Seventh from Adam" (Jude 1:14-15.) [10]

The *Book of Enoch* is divided into five distinct sections. In the first, the *Book of the Watchers* devotes much of its attention to the "watchers" (also called "Gregori" per the *Second Book of Enoch*) who have fallen - angels dispatched to Earth to watch over humans who instead lusted after mortal women and at the encouragement of Samyaza (Samael) who instructs them to "mate" with them:

"And Semyaza, who was their leader, said unto them: "I fear ye will not indeed agree to do this deed, and I alone shall have to pay the penalty of a great sin." And they all answered him and said: "Let us all swear an oath, and all bind ourselves by mutual imprecations not to abandon this plan but to do this thing."

The offspring of the watchers and humans are referred to a Nephilim - savage "giants" who pillage the earth and endanger humanity. Samyaza and his associates subsequently teach their targets developments in weaponry, cosmetics, mirrors, sorcery and the "forbidden arts," celestial "secrets" or "mysteries" amongst other things. In Genesis 6:1-4, these "watchers" are referred to as *"sons of God."*

We see in *Eyes Wide Shut* a visual reference made to watcher/human relations in the Ziegler's foyer when the Harfords first arrive:

The two men seated beneath the statue are the same two men who appear to have abducted Helena during the last scene at the toy store. But the statue clearly depicts an angel loving a woman a little too much. Next to this image, I've included a picture of the 1923 marble sculpture *The Sons of God Saw the Daughters of Men That They Were Fair* by Daniel Chester French at the Corcoran Gallery of Art in Washington, D.C.

Most contemporary English translations of Genesis 6:1-4 and Numbers 13:33 have translated the Hebrew *"nefilim"* as "giants" when *"nefilim"* literally translates as "the fallen ones." The translation of "nefilim" as "giants" appears to have occurred with the Septuagint, the earliest version of the Hebrew Bible translated into Koine Greek during the 3rd or 2nd century BC. This choice influenced the subsequent Latin translation, the Vulgate, during the 4th/5th century AD. [11] This makes more sense, since they're no evidence of actual "giants" or their remains but plenty of "fallen ones."

It's worth noting that the *Book of Enoch* makes a distinction between fallen angel chieftain Samyaza and Azazel, whom Samyaza is under incidentally. This is interesting considering that in Leviticus 16 there's an account of a sacrifice of two males goats: one to "Yahweh" and one which is sent out into the wilderness "for Azazel." In the *Book of Enoch*, he writes:

The whole earth has been corrupted through the works that were taught by Azazel: to him ascribe all sin. 1*Enoch 10:8*

If Azazel and Samyaza are two separate beings, can they be correlated to Satan and Lucifer, with the latter being the "light bearer" who brings the "Nephilim" knowledge pertaining to warfare, the dark arts, etc.?

According to both the *Book of Enoch* and the *Book of Giants* (before 2nd century BC and also found at Qumran which also recounts a similar story), 200 "fallen angels" along with their leader Samyaza (referred to as "Shemihazah" in *Giants)* originally organized their secret society on Mount Hernon, which is on the Lebanon/Syria border.

The "fallen angel" theme is further represented in *Eyes Wide Shut* once again in the decorations found at Ziegler's gala. The five-pointed star, if point upright, is an angelic symbol; if inverted it's referred to as a "pentagram" which is often associated with demons. At the gala, star lights mimicking a descent-like motif as the stars become inverted are in display:

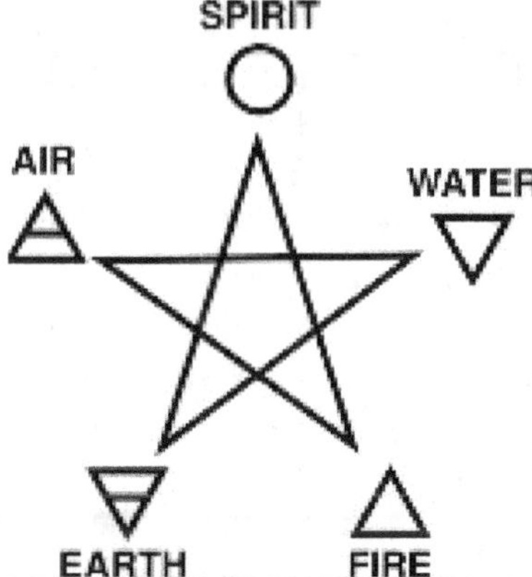

"Lucifer," meaning "Light-bringer" is a Latin name for the planet Venus and is often used for mythological figures associated with the planet. Due to the movements of the planet itself and its discontinuous appearances in the sky, the mythology surrounding these figures often involved a fall from the heavens to the Earth or the underworld. In classical mythology, Lucifer was personified as a male figure bearing a torch. The Greek name corresponding to Lucifer is Phosphorus ("light-bringer") or Heosphorus ("dawn-bringer".)

"Lucifer" as a moniker is confusing. For instance, correlating "Lucifer" with Inanna or Ishtar is inaccurate since the Greek and Roman correlations to these goddesses are Aphrodite and, well, *Venus* respectively. Thus, since "Lucifer" and "Venus" are both Latin, it stands a great chance that they may not refer to the same thing - in this case, referencing a pre-cursor goddess named Inanna, Ishtar, or Aphrodite. Nevertheless, some sources do cite Lucifer as the "Devil" or "Satan" or something akin to it, and it's most likely in error. For instance, in the book the *Gospel of the Secret Supper* observed by the Bogomils and the Cathars, Lucifer is a glorified angel and older brother of *Jesus* who fell from heaven to Earth and started his corporeal kingdom as the Demiurge, much like the Bogomil story of Satanail/Samael being the archangel older brother of *Archangel Michael* mentioned earlier. It could be the case of disorganized semantics where "Lucifer," being the Latin male counterpart name for Venus, was instead used as Aphrodite's/Ishtar's/Inanna's *partner* which was Samael in Bogomil cosmology. To my knowledge, no pantheon or mythos correlated Samael/Satanail with the planet Venus - more like Saturn.

The Bogomils, according to some sources, *did* perceive Michael as being sent in the form of the man who would become *Jesus*. Satanail or "Lucifer" trapped souls from Heaven in the world of matter, his domain. Michael was then sent in the form of a man, Jesus, who was sent to liberate the captured souls. [12] If this holds any validity, this *would* make Jesus of Nazareth a "Son of God" since his soul was literally angelic.

Other books depicting the fallen "Watchers" who seduced mortal women to produce the nephilim are the *Genesis Apocryphon*, the *Book of Jubilees* (both found at Qumran), the *Testament of Reuben*, *2 Baruch*, *Josephus*, and the *Book of Jude*.

What's *highly interesting* is that in the Ethiopian Orthodox Church's canonical Amharic version of the *Book of Jubilees* states that these "angels" were the rebellious offspring of *Seth* (Deqiqa Set) and the mortal females were the daughters of *Cain*. [13] The problem with this interpretation is that if the "Seth" in reference is regarded to be the third son of Adam and Cain as Adam's second son, this would have Seth's children reproducing with their cousins. But, more conspicuously, Adam's son Seth and his offspring were reputedly just as mortal as Cain and his. Plus, Enoch himself is reported to be a descendant of the Old Testament "Seth," son of Adam which, of course, would be contradictory.

However, if "Seth" (Greek: Σήθ) is actually a reference to the *Egyptian god Set* (Greek spelling also Σήθ), this makes more sense since a *deity* is producing offspring. This insinuates that it's possible that the Old Testament narrative of Adam/Eve/Abel/Cain is a re-telling of the

Egyptian Atum (Ra)/Isis/Osiris/Set (or *Setan)* mythos especially when considering that Set killed brother Osiris much like how Cain killed brother Abel. Also, just as Eve, Abel, and Cain were begotten from Adam, Isis, Osiris, and Set were begotten from Atum. (Let's face it: "Adam" and "Atum" sound quite similar.) Horus, also begotten from Atum according to some sources while others claim it is Osiris, this might be equivalent to Old Testament Seth. [14] This is all conjecture, of course, but keep in mind the enslavement of the Israelites by the Ancient Egyptians and the potential of adopting some Egyptian mythos. After all, Moses was adopted into the Egyptian royal family. Yet, even this would suggest that *Cain* is the equivalent to *Set:* which would still make sense in a way since the Nephilim are considered descendants from both in the *Book of Jubilees,* except that it is implied that Cain was mortal.

Whatever the case may be, it's evident that the "Lucifer" alluded to in *Eyes Wide Shut* isn't an honest, altruistic one.

But, before we leave this chapter, let's take a brief look at what actually happened in *Eyes Wide Shut*. Prior to the gala, when the audience is introduced to the Harfords, the couple appears to be getting along and living a reasonably secure life - mentally, physically, and financially. Their marriage, at least on the surface, also seems stable and secure. Both Alice and Bill appear confident and secure in themselves as well.

However, it's after the gala during which both reject sexual propositioning that "the ball gets rolling." The next night, when the two are getting high, is when *fear* is introduced to Bill's awareness when Alice confesses her willingness to jeopardize their marriage for the sake of a one night stand. After this, Bill feels betrayal - specifically the fears of Unlovability, Mistrust, Abandonment, and Failure as a man and a husband. The resulting anger which emerges from the sense of hurt and betrayal causes him to want to exact revenge by being unfaithful to his wife, which could lead to dire circumstances such as contracting HIV. Later, he attends a dark arts ritual which, apparently, is performed to summon demons.

So, the fact that both Bill and Alice rejected the advances of members of this "elite" group is reminiscent of the rejection stories of Lilith and Samael, both seemingly due to hubris. It's possible that, because of this rejection, the dark arts magic of this group tempted Alice to catalyze this feeling of unlovability and betrayal in Bill, which led to Bill's quest to seek out a "revenge fuck" that would have cost him his life.

This sort of practice is reflective of malignant narcissism. Because Sandor and the "models" didn't get *what they wanted* and *were rejected,* this stimulated the core issues behind malignant narcissism which are, respectively, Entitlement and Abandonment. Thus, the black magic practice this group participates in is *projection* - or retaliation against those who neglect, abandon, or don't give into their demands. The "demons" produced by the rituals are *fears* - in Bill's case, Unlovability, Mistrust, Abandonment, and Failure.

But it's because Bill is now insecure - that he no longer "loves himself" or is secure within himself - that he is in peril. What made both Bill and Alice attractive to these "nephilim" originally was their self-love, and it is when these "nephilim" or psychic vampires or whatever you'd like to call them didn't get to "feed" off the couple's self-love that they retaliated.

This is precisely how malignant narcissists operate: they do not have self-love; *they instead need to feed off narcissistic supply or some "food" that those who have self-love or can give love give.* If the malignant narcissist does not get what he needs which is that which he cannot provide on his own - *self-love* - from potential hosts, he retaliates in some fashion, which is *projection*.

So, "Where the rainbow ends" is where the life-energy of a person - the multi-colored chakra system - is drained dry by these types.

"Vampires."

Like the "fallen angels" Samael and Lilith, they became reliant on Spirit's light and, when rejected (or abandoned), they needed to siphon it from others as opposed to learning how to providing it on their own.

Regardless, exactly *how do* or *how would* these "angels" mate with humans if this is even remotely true?

[1] *Black, Jeremy; Green, Anthony (1992), Gods, Demons and Symbols of Ancient Mesopotamia: An Illustrated Dictionary, The British Museum Press*
[2] *Wolkstein, Diane; Kramer, Samuel Noah (1983), Inanna: Queen of Heaven and Earth: Her Stories and Hymns from Sumer, New York City, New York: Harper&Row Publishers*
[3] *Penglase, Charles (1994), Greek Myths and Mesopotamia: Parallels and Influence in the Homeric Hymns and Hesiod, New York City, New York: Routledge*
[4] *Vanstiphout, H. L. (1984), "Inanna/Ishtar as a Figure of Controversy", Struggles of Gods: Papers of the Groningen Work Group for the Study of the History of Religions, Berlin: Mouton Publishers*
[5] http://analogicalplanet.com/Pages/ContentPages/Sidebars/BurneyRelief.html
[6] *"1911 Encyclopædia Britannica/Bogomils". 1911. Retrieved 20 October 2018.*

"Bogomils taught that God had two sons, the elder Satanail and the younger Michael"

[7] *Patai, Raphael (2015). Encyclopedia of Jewish Folklore and Traditions. London: Routledge. p. 463*

[8] Ingvild Sælid Gilhus *The Nature of the Archons: A Study in the Soteriology of a Gnostic Treatise from Nag Hammadi (CGII, 4)* Otto Harrassowitz Verlag 1985

[9] Ivry *Perspectives on Jewish Though* Routledge 2013

[10] Barker, Margaret. (2005) [1998]. *The Lost Prophet: The Book of Enoch and Its Influence on Christianity*. London: SPCK; Sheffield Phoenix Press.

[11] *Kosior, Wojciech (22 May 2018), "The Fallen (Or) Giants? The Gigantic Qualities of the Nefilim in the Hebrew Bible", Jewish Translation – Translating Jewishness, De Gruyter, pp. 17–38,*

[12] Michael C. Thomsett *Heresy in the Roman Catholic Church: A History* McFarland 2011

[13] Ethiopian Orthodox Church's canonical Amharic version of *Jubilees*, 5:21 – archived here: https://web.archive.org/web/20110614225402/http://good-amharic-books.com/images/PDFs/3-apoch-2-cr.pdf#

[14] https://www.ancient.eu/isis/

Ancient Aliens in Disguise

So, if Enoch's story and that of *Eyes Wide Shut* have any validity, how do these "fallen angels" "mate" with mortals? What exactly is meant by "mate" because, if the belief that these beings *actually* produce fallen angel/human hybrids, wouldn't they look different? Or have some "angelic" DNA?

I doubt it. You'd have better luck creating a monkey/human hybrid since monkeys actually *have* DNA. I think the answer comes in the fact that these angels were sharing ideas in the form of developments with respect to warfare, the dark arts, the "mysteries," etc. Did they involve themselves with a kind of sexual activity with mortals? It's possible. But it's more probable that the answer comes from information provided by former psychic spy and remote viewer for the US Army Lyn Buchanan in the following quote:

"After the military, I was asked by a branch of the government to do a paper, a study paper to compare and contrast ET psychic ability to human psychic ability. The study that I did was because I was given access to many of the things that never made it into project grudge or the blue book or anything like that because they couldn't be denied. So anyway, in studying these, I found out that we can take the ET's of all different kinds and species and all that and put them into four main categories. We've got those who are more psychic than us and those that are less psychic than us. In each of those two categories we've got friendly to us and unfriendly to us, the unfriendly non-psychic ones tend to not come here. They don't like us, they don't want to be around us. The non-psychic friendly ones come here for trade. The psychic friendly ones actually want to help us develop our abilities and become stronger at it. And the unfriendly psychic ones want us wiped off the planet, they want us dead, period, no questions asked." [1]

So, if we have "aliens" who ("that?" I dunno) have psychic abilities, part of their psychic abilities *most likely* would involve being able to communicate *telepathically* to humans. Part of being able to communicate telepathically would involve communicating by sharing feelings and thoughts *("clairsentience")* as well as through visual imagery *("clairvoyance")* by psychic means. Fortunately, there exists a *Third Book of Enoch* which pertains to Watchers whom have not fallen. Since the "aliens" have psychic ability, not only would they be able to transmit psychic information as well, but they ostensibly would be able to receive it.

Yet, since the above quote suggests the existence of both "friendly" and "unfriendly" psychic aliens, it would appear that either are capable of taking note of our thoughts and feelings and acting accordingly. Another question arises which is: "How long have these 'aliens' been around and *exactly how long have they been interacting with humans?"*

Yes, I'm proposing that these "Watchers" - if they exist - may be the "aliens" Mr. Buchanan is referring to - if they exist. The "good" ones are going to convene with others who have "good energies" while the "bad" converse or "mate" with those mortal who have "bad energies."

What's depicted in *Eyes Wide Shut* is the mortal/"alien" interaction when both sets of beings have malignant narcissistic characters and how they behave as a result. Both have grandiose senses of self, a sense of entitlement, an expectation for others to be "loyal" *to* them (narcissistic supply), and a penchant for those who are insecure and target them as a result. Again, this is due to their own issues of Entitlement and/or Abandonment. Again, it's not their fault they're like this (maybe it is?), but it is our problem unless they consider it to be theirs.

According to Buchanan, the psychic ability of some of these aliens is stronger than those of humans, but humans have a farther range in terms of distance and time. This is interesting, considering the ability to project strong clairvoyant images and clairsentient sentiments might be behind this Marion Vision phenomenon, such as that at Fatima and Lourdes. If this is relevant, determining which "aliens" such "visions" are coming from is difficult. However, if they're appearing to children, I'd say it's likely that they're from the "good" aliens.

This could also be behind the mythos pertaining to the appearances of angels to the like of Mohammad, John Smith, and so on. I'd say it would depend on their respective characters whether or not they saw angels or "angels in disguise..."

Parlaying this to the apostle Paul, one has to wonder: considering "Jesus" appeared to him during the time when he was actively involved in assisting the Pharisees to persecute Early "Christians," who may have been projecting that image?

The Book of the SubGenius has something to say about this sort of "Watcher" activity on pages 103 and 104:

"The Watchers manipulate people and nations in many ways...A random list of manipulatees and other running-dogs of the saucer imperialists would include Joan of Arc, Joseph Smith (founder of Mormonism), Moses, Mohammed, Nostradamus, Edgar Cayce, Imhotep, Socrates, Erik Von Daniken, Benjamin Franklin, Dr. Philo Drummond, John Wilkes Booth, Leonardo da Vinci, Helen [sic] Blavatsky, the masterminds behind the Kennedy assassination, the founders of the FreeMasons, the Rosicrucians, and the Thule Society; Hitler, Idi Amin, Paracelsus, Bo and Peep, John Rockefeller, Uri Geller, Wilhelm Reich, Timothy Leary, King George III, Giordano Bruno, John Lilly, John Dee, Sirhan Sirhan, Mark Chapman, Nikola Tesla, Charlie Manson, Admiral Byrd, Bo Derek, Jack Ruby, and Jonathan Winters."

" In 2000 B.C. a Japanese king had 'flying sun discs' for advisors. King Minos of Crete was given the Rules for Torture by Volcano Demons. just as Hammurabi got his Conspiracy Rulebook from a UFOnaut named Shamash. Sodom and Gomorrah were nuked by "Angels" for not being perverted *enough,* and Knossos was microwaved for *no reason at all.*"

"(Meanwhile the ancient Bible Prophets were having Close Encounters right and left.) Most of the kings of Babylon had "winged advisors"; there's no telling how many lesser religions were started by the Satanic 'saucer gods.'"

"Their work in religion is spectacular to this day. The UFO that appeared before tens of thousands and instantly dried up a muddy field during the "Miracle of Fatima" in Portugal spoke to its three little girl mediums [one was a boy] in Catholic jargon, and gave secret messages that the Pope was to reveal to the world in 1968 (he didn't, after his audience with "Bob".) Their "bright cloud" of blinding light converted Saul to Paul on the road to Damascus."

Yes, this is from a nonsense religion book. But if your of the belief that modern-day reflects Orwell's *1984* world of opposites where "war is peace, freedom is slavery, and ignorance is strength," "nonsense" may not be nonsense after all.

Let's just hope Enoch was right about there being "friendly" Watchers. *Eyes Wide Shut* seems to suggest as much when Helena promotes Angelic Barbie. Just remember that his books were left out of the Old Testament.

A moment ago, I expressed my skepticism that these "Watchers" could have *actually* mated with human women. However, this peculiar quote comes from the *Genesis Apocryphon (Col.2), also* found at Qumran:

"She said to me: O my master and [brother, recall for yourself] my pregnancy. I swear to you by the Great Holy One, by the Ruler of Hea[ven] that this seed is yours, that this pregnancy is from you, that from you is the planting of [this] fruit [and that it is] not from any **alien**, or from any of the Watchers, or from any heavenly being."[2]

In the context in which the above quote is given, it is the response of Bath-Anosh to Lamech, Noah's father. Here, an exasperated Lamech is concerned and questioning whether or not Noah is his child or fathered by one of the Watchers. But, obviously, the word "alien"is used. Clearly, "alien" can refer to more than one thing, but I'll allow the readers to rely on their own context clues.

Personally, I consider anything written or spoken to be anecdotal evidence since anything written or spoken can be fabricated with relative ease, but the above quote is peculiar to say the least.

[1] https://www.collective-evolution.com/2019/04/12/skilled-army-remote-viewer-reveals-details-about-the-et-presence-on-earth/

[2] https://pages.uncc.edu/john-reeves/course-materials/rels-2104-hebrew-scripturesold-testament/translation-of-1q-genesis-apocryphon/

The Celestine Calamity

In 1993, James Redfield authored *The Celestine Prophecy,* a New-Age thriller involving the quest of an ancient manuscript by its lead protagonist. Redfield, himself a former therapist and student in Eastern Philosophies, quit his job as a counselor to produce his fictional work. In it, he describes four main "roles" that people play in order to extract energy from each other, which are: *The "Intimidator," The "Interrogator," The "Aloof,"* and *The "Poor Me."* Interacting with one of these types is liable to leave one feeling drained and depleted energetically.

The dysfunctional roles presented in *The Celestine Prophecy* are self explanatory. The "Intimidator" "drains" people with intimidating or threatening behavior, the "Interrogator" by putting people on the defensive, the "Aloof" by behaving in an emotionally unavailable way, and the "Poor Me" by inspiring others' pity.

One role typically produces its opposite in others if played over time: the "Intimidator" role creates the "Poor Me" role and vice versa whereas the "Interrogator" role produces an "Aloof" role and vice versa. Part of the content of the first half of this book describes how the malignant narcissists and "psychopaths" are created from excessive and/or extreme exposure to "Aloof" and "Poor Me" behaviors.

What we see here from the emergence of these four roles are two camps: "Aggressive" versus "Passive." In various Schools of Thought, this can be correlated to the "Left-Hand Path" versus "Right-Hand Path," respectively:

Left-Hand Path (Aggressive)		**Right-Hand Path (Passive)**	
Intimidator	Interrogator	Aloof	Poor Me

The Left-Hand Path and Right-Hand Path are going to have conflicting viewpoints with respect to each other. First and foremost is the perception of the figurehead of "God": the "left" is prone to perceive God as a glorious patriarch, a reprimanding disciplinarian, someone to be feared and obeyed, powerful, glorious, and whose "love" is approval and based upon obedience. We see this with most if not all of the Abrahamic religions.

The "right" is prone to perceive God as matriarchal, someone who is loving and nurturing, and unconditionally loving as observed by religions considered "Gnostic" in nature, an example being the "Sophia" observed by the Cathars and similar preceding sects or what many refer to today as "Spirit." This is completely understandable since the Left-Hand path seeks a deity which staves off the sense *Abandonment (which could be neglect, rejection, or betrayal - hence the reason "secrets" are kept by this "Hand": it confuses the loyalty with love since what it loved betrayed it.)* This Abandonment is also the culprit behind the Left Hand perceiving the "Aloof" and "Poor Me" personalities as "bad." Meanwhile, the Right-Hand seeks the comfort to counter the *abuse* they received (or perceived, depending on your perspective) from "Intimidators" and "Interrogators" by honoring a "Good God" of love, peace, and order.

In light of this, it's no wonder such Gnostic religions go extinct: by rejecting a "Left-Hand" God, they're committing the ultimate act of Abandonment - *Betrayal - in the "eye" of the Left-Hand*. They're thus seen as "heretical" since all the pain and suffering the Left-Hand path has experienced in life is attributed to such feelings of rejection, neglect, and abandonment. The "Right-Hand God" the Left-Hand path *desperately wants but* inwardly resents is leaving them, much like a child wants his mother but ends up hating her for not being there for him - first put on a pedestal only to be left on the pedestal.

The Right-Hand path seeks a peaceful, equality-based environment *due to* the abuse they received at the hands of those who extract energy by mans of intimidating or interrogating. This is not to say they won't "fight back" either. If a "Right-Hand" Pather is pushed too far, they may actually turn the tables and abuse their abusers. The abuse in this case, however, is more like "wrath" - actually, it *is* wrath.

"Spirituality" is likely to be defined differently between the two camps as well. Whereas the Left-Hand Path will regard this as "will-power" or "mental strength," the Right-Hand Path will regard it as "kindness, compassion, and empathy." The Left-Hand Path is about *Control* while the Right Hand is about *Care*.

So, not only does there emerge a schism between the two versions of God but also its structure: the Left-Hand Path will naturally gravitate to, form, and support *hierarchal organizations* which are regarded by the Right as "patriarchal" or even "the Patriarchy." This is to be expected since the Left-Hand perceives "loyalty" as "good" precisely because "loyalty" is sought to alleviate the participants' experience with Abandonment, thanks to the Aloof and Poor Me upbringing they were exposed to as children. Thus, obedience and acquiescence to authority are seen as "good" and such authority therefore has a right to be angry or upset when it doesn't receive it - and they feel this way *because they can identify with it*. They can also identify with authority's belief that it has a *right to project* when it's not capitulated to because of this very abandonment. So, shit rolls downhill - in this case, the side of the pyramid - because it "*deserves*" to be rolled downhill. Because it *deserves* to be rolled downhill, they will assist in *pushing* it downhill especially when those downhill *don't demonstrate their loyalty in the form of capitulating performance*.

The Right-Hand Path, on the other hand, will seek out *flat structures* - hopefully - otherwise, it's no structure at all. As far as religious institutions, they'll take on a similar communal appearance like that of the Cathars or the Essenes or another sort of commune. Fellowships, unions, and profit-shares are other examples of Right-Hand Path conglomerates. The groups may have a "leader," but the leader is held accountable to do what's best for the group as a whole. If the leader shows signs of self-interest and being dominated by the ego, he or she runs the risk of being removed from their position by the group. I'd go as far to say that the United States actually started off this way - "for the People, by the People" - but has now morphed into a patriarchal system as described in detail in *The Toxic States of America*. Whereas the "loyalty" of the Left-Hand pyramid is expressed as hero-worship of its capstone-leader and obedience to orders given by the tiers above, the "loyalty" of the Right-Hand flat structure is applied to each other and the group as a whole.

Another ostensible difference is basic cosmology: Left-Hand religions such as the Abrahamic ones mentioned earlier tend to be *monotheistic* and observe one God who is to be obeyed whereas Right-Hand religions tend to recognize a *dualistic* cosmology between a "Good" God and an "Evil" God such as Zoroastrianism and the "Gnostic" religions mentioned previously with the "Good" God taking precedence despite the dualism.

The problem is, it's when these roles become more prevalent that we see hierarchal organizations become more prominent. "Poor Me's" and "Aloofs" are going to produce more "Intimidators" and "Interrogators" and vice versa. Since the abandonment the "Intimidators" and "Interrogators" faced which caused their "roles " to emerge is going to push them into roles where they seek power and control - or at the very least *support* it - this is to be expected. The propensity to exert power and control emerge from the psychological backlash of being abandoned or neglected as early as childhood. Thus, with the increase in "Intimidators" and "Interrogators" increases the likelihood that hierarchal systems of organization will emerge as religions, governments, financial systems, militaries, educational systems, corporations, media outlets, etc.

It appears that the "New World Order" seeks not only to establish one pyramid for each through various mergers and acquisitions, but to create a "grand pyramid" where the capstones of these pyramids cross-pollinate. We can already see evidence of this considering former investment bank CEOs have become Treasury Secretaries, former Secretaries of State have moved on to positions within academia, and corporate CEO's are now dictating national policies.

The thing is, **the pyramid structure is going to face two "structural problems"** *especially if the capstone of the pyramid has Abandonment and/or Entitlement issues*. **First**, every member of each tier would have to experience "loyalty" toward the tier above it if not the capstone itself. If Entitlement is present within the leadership, they're not only going to have to get used to not being able to question the directives being handed down, but also carry out such objectives even when they're counterproductive, flawed, unfair, or unethical.

Otherwise, this "loyalty" to the tiers above it or the capstone itself can emerge from the members within the tier being able identify with Abandonment issues of the tier above it in that they can *sympathize* with it *themselves or* out of maturity and subsequent *empathy* for the Abandonment issues present in the tier above it. Otherwise, the tier above will find it necessary to "motivate by fear" by means of Intimidation or Interrogation up to and including "termination."

The latter is usually what ends up occurring within pyramid structures. If "Poor Me's" or "Aloof's" feel like the only reciprocity they're receiving is a paycheck (if this is a job we're talking about) - and nothing in terms of morale or being heard - they're not likely to stay or last long. Nor are they likely to stay if they feel like they're being short-changed. If they feel they're being "motivated" by intimidation or interrogation or that the fear factor is high, they're likely to leave. Chances are, the work they're putting in is not worth the paycheck they're receiving (if this is a job situation we're talking about) and the workplace conditions they're in a are in fact toxic. If not all members of every "tier" perceive "loyalty" as good and do their job by following orders, they're going to need another incentive. If a positive workplace culture isn't in place - at least being happy to go to work if this is a job situation - they'll just "go through the motions" to get by. There's also the chance that the "Poor Me's" and the "Aloofs" may just have poor work ethic because of their internal and seemingly incurable resentment.

This is not to say that pyramid organizations *can't work*. They actually *could* and *have worked*. If the dynamics at play involve starting at the bottom and working upwards through performance, merit, and the ability to work cooperatively with others and being *promoted* on account of it, these types of organizations can be quite successful not to mention *functional*. This sort of career-path resembles a series of apprenticeships where mastery of one level leads to the advancement to the next. Successive leadership is likely to be successful because they have a working knowledge of the everyday realities of those working within the tiers below it.

While I think this *has* been the case with pyramid organizations in the past, theory and practice diverge especially when the inclusion of malignant narcissists enters the organization. Advancement in this case is *not* based on performance and merit, but also on manipulation, projection, and motivating through fear - specifically, intimidation and interrogation. "Politics" enter the equation when such individuals blame-shift, scapegoat, take credit for others' accomplishments, "throw others under the bus," fabricate results, subject their employees to unreasonable demands and expectations, act as spin-doctors, and more. Oftentimes, these individuals are brought in from outside the organization and placed in high-ranking positions with the belief that the results they've achieved within other organizations will be replicated. However, such persons are likely to have oversold themselves during the hiring process.

It's when the organization is led by leadership which is devoid of empathy and has a grandiose sense of self that problems arise. If they do not have an idea whether or not the conditions, demands, and expectations imposed onto those within lower tiers - especially the base, the furthest removed from the capstone - are *reasonable* they can, and should, expect their organization to crumble. Chances are, they wouldn't be able to satisfy the demands they place on others and, literally, the "Left-Hand" has no idea what the "Right-Hand" is doing or going through. Just like the "dysfunctional family," its microscopic version, it's called dysfunctional for a reason - it breaks down and stops working. If their grandiose self is overindulged and their ego is inflated to the point where they don't think it's possible for them to make a poor decision - "to big to fail" - their hubris is going to come back and bite them in the ass.

That being said, *even if* the members of the pyramid's base or within lower tiers *have* a sense of loyalty to their "superiors" up to and including the capstone due to being able to *sympathize* with the psychological issues behind the need for control, power, and loyalty displayed by their superiors, this loyalty is subject to erosion if the poor conditions they face outweigh their sense of loyalty.

The second structural problem I just mentioned - the potential for the capstone to have a grandiose sense of self (inflated ego) and/or a lack of empathy - leads to *Entitlement*. If Entitlement and Abandonment issues are a part of the capstone's psychology, it's a guarantee that the organization will need *fuel* and will not be by itself *self-sustainable. This is precisely due to these two "issues": they cause a NEED for external resources to compensate for the entitlement and abandonment.* Consequently, the salaries of upper management or its "board" (if it has one) are insatiable and profits need to accommodate this. "Profit" can be anything from revenue, to new members (for which missionaries or recruiters - same thing - are required), and increase in real estate in terms of "branches" or "churches" or "stores," availability of physical resources, availability of natural resources, cycling through human resources to avoid pay raises, tithes, donations, mergers, acquisitions, annexations, buyouts, foreign government takeovers, and so on. Read Naomi Klein's *Shock Doctrine*. The need to "grow" the pyramid becomes as necessary as a narcissist's need for narcissistic supply. "Profit" simply means "increase for self." We hear many political groups talk about "sustainability." *Very few things that require profit can be sustainable. Like the narcissist himself, they are usually parasitic.*

So, whether it's due to the lack of foundational loyalty due to unreasonable demands or insatiability due to the "capstone's" Abandonment and Entitlement issues, implosion is going to look like this:

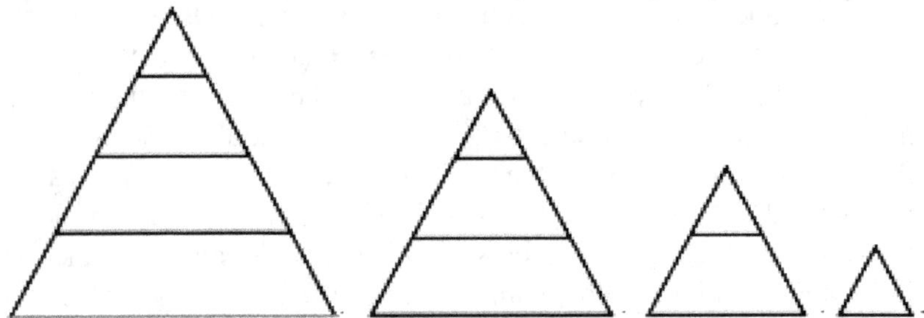

First to go is the "Poor Me" followed by the "Aloof." We've already seen ample evidence of this with the 2008 "bailout," mortgage crises, Enron, and China's suicide in the workplace. (Any time suicide is going on in a population - especially to this extent - that should be a red flag.)

Actually, you wouldn't need to be either a "Poor Me" or an

"Aloof" to develop the desire to leave. If the capstone's pathology is acute enough - overly demanding with unrealistic expectations and little to no consideration for the tiers below - no mentally healthy or self-loving personality is going to tolerate such conditions for long. The "best" are actually going to be the first to leave since they're know better than to indulge this melodramatic horseshit to begin with.

After that, it's only Left-Hand aggressors remaining using offense mechanisms and it's like putting cats in a bag. The "Interrogators" will lose out, then the "Intimidators" will be left to hash it out amongst themselves and cannibalize each other.

Think of it this way: if the capstone has abandonment issues, it's going to need *someone* to project onto. If it's narcissistic or entitled, it's going to need a *source to consume from. It can't do either with itself.*

Plus, it's possible to build pyramids with limestone. Building pyramids with people? Maybe not. Limestone doesn't have feelings, dammit :(

I hate presenting problems without posing solutions. I recommend that the Left-Hand Path show the Right-Hand love and empathy while the Right-Hand be compassionate and attentive the Left-Hand's issue of Abandonment. It can't be only one hand shaking or else it isn't a hand-shake. Otherwise, these sorts of organizations *will be too big for their britches*.

In contrast, flat-structure organizations are not only non-expansionist, they tend to last longer (provided their existence isn't threatened by a pyramid organization) and they're more self-sustaining: that is, they require less of the "fuel" mentioned earlier and tend to give back. The only reason they would need to grow or increase their "power" is to avoid being usurped by a pyramid organization. I've heard some speakers (some I have a good deal of respect for) claim that hierarchal structures and civilizations now called "the Patriarchy" is all our species has ever known and therefore must be accepted. This, however, is not true. There *have* been matriarchal civilizations which have been long-lasting in the past, history just hasn't acknowledged them. I referred toone in *The Toxic States of America* which existed between c. 5000/4500 BC - 2500 BC in present day Eastern Europe called the Cucuteni-Trypillian Civilization. It was non-aggressive, had no social stratification or system of hierarchy, and had the largest city-states at the time.

Lastly, take note that within Left-Hand Path religions, it's typically only men who can hold positions of ecclesiastical authority whereas in Right-Hand organizations such as Catharism, women can also hold such positions. It's almost as if the feminine is being both rejected and subjugated in Left-Hand denominations - like someone who has Mommy issues.

What's my personal take on all this? I think both sides are short-sighted and only seeing the world through their "eye." The Right-Hand path would benefit from empathizing with the Left-Hand's abandonment psychology while holding steadfast that it is spoiled and hypocritical, setting boundaries while adamantly enforcing mutual respect.

If the Cathars had a modicum of this perspective, perhaps they would probably still be in existence because at least the Left-Hand God would know He was still cared about to some extent. Instead, the Cathars rejected Him for their own reasons (which they obviously deemed valid.) But, to the Left-Hand God, this was like Mommy yelling at the kid for feeling neglected, telling him he was "bad," and then walking away completely. To a kid, this is sort of abandonment is life-threatening, so the kid - in his mind - has every reason to perceive "Mommy" as bad - *the worst,* actually - and that *she should* die for being willing him to be left alone to die. And that's the reason the Cathars were seen as "heretics." In the Left-Hand God's defense with this situation, He did make efforts to maintain some sort of contact. Specifically, Pope Innocent III attempted a peaceful conversion of the Cathars after his ordination in 1198 AD to no avail. [1]

The Left-Hand path would benefit from imagining a small child coming into this world where Daddy was either absent or, when he was available, was threatening to the child's physical and emotional wellbeing. The child wasn't loved whatsoever, but instead humiliated, ridiculed, violated (trust or bodily), screamed at, threatened, ostracized, intimidated, abused, etc. There was *no love: only abuse.* The child was expected to love and respect itself *and* the parent without ever receiving either in return. This is how the Right-Hand path views the Left-Hand God: an evil, secretive, draconian, tempestuous, volatile, selfish, and emotionally unavailable whopping hypocrite to the point of utter completion, expecting to receive love, care, and respect but giving the exact opposite."Do as I say!", "Obey me!", "Bow down and worship me!" without ever giving the child the impression that it was cared about or considered let alone loved. The child is also transparent to the parent while the parent is opaque to the child. (Again, narcissists *love* to invade others' privacy while remaining highly secretive themselves and the skeletons in their closets grossly outnumber those whom they're spying on.)

As such, whether imaginary or real, the loving Right-Hand God provides the child with what he needed but never received. If the Left-Hand God had emulated this to the slightest degree, the Cathars probably would have accepted Him to some extent and not abandoned Him.

This template, of course, is predicated solely on the basis of the root psychological foundations behind the Left-Hand path versus the Right-Hand path as described earlier under this section. However, if the mythos behind the belief systems of the Cathars, the Bogomils, *Eyes Wide Shut,* and other sources are correct, it's not just an Abandonment issue the Left-Hand God is carrying around: it's hubris as well. But, since we're here, let's look at other myths.

But, to reiterate before proceeding, it's imperative to clarify what is going on here: The Right Hand is to love, care for, and respect itself *and* the Left Hand while the Left Hand takes advantage of this love, care, and respect - even demands it at times - and doesn't give much if any in return.

So, here's the deal with the Left-Hand/"Sun God" Cult - whatever that is at this point:

You not only have to "love yourself" but you're also expected to love them or else they will harm you if you don't. Whether or not you "love yourself" and them as well, they are not going to love you back (they may do the opposite) - instead, they're only going to continue to make it about them. Plus, they're dependent on the love you give them in order to feel good about themselves.

What I've just written is precisely the dynamic at play in Narcissistic/Codependent relationships: *your hand gives, their hand takes. Period.* End of story. **This is a psychological scam.** But, here's the problem:

If the Left-Hand God *is malignantly* narcissistic, and the prognosis that Entitlement and Abandonment issues (rooted in abandonment, neglect, or rejection) are behind this condition, then there's no way it can be "god" - something else would have been required to over-indulge, spoil, or enable it as well as abandon it in some fashion, whether that is through neglect, rejection, or actual abandonment.

Whether it's Entitlement, Abandonment, or both, *something* considers itself to be "god," so let's review who this "god" might be:

[1] *Alphandéry, Paul Daniel (1911). "Albigenses" . In Chisholm, Hugh (ed.). Encyclopædia Britannica. 1 (11th ed.).*

Will The Real "Sun of God" Please Stand Up?

The first scenario is that the "Son/Sun of God" *is* actually Yahweh or the Sun/Son of Yahweh - the almighty, all-powerful, all-knowing god of the Old Testament which was subsequently connected to the New Testament sometime after the death of Jesus of Nazareth or, according to many "Christian" belief systems, the same God as that of the Old Testament and Jesus was literally his son. "God the Father."

The second involves what was covered in the previous subheading "Eyes Wide Open" and the Bogomil mythology about the fall of the Archangel Satanail (or Samael.) This scenario involves Satanail being the older brother of the Archangel Michael. The reason behind the falling out occurred is not explained in the available Bogomil literature, but it was speculated earlier that it could have been due to a sibling rivalry or hubris on the part of Satanail.

This scenario is, of course, reflected in various sects deemed to have Gnostic roots, such as the Cathars, Bogomils, Paulicians, and possibly the Manichaeans. The "fallen angel" meme is certainly the one expressed in *Eyes Wide Shut,* possibly depicting Satan (Satanail/Samael) as the deity observed by the Sun Cult and/or his "son/sun" Lucifer.

This would make sense as far as the "Holy Dysfunctional Family" template presented earlier, with the Patriarch of the Abrahamic religions being malignantly narcissistic. Like Yahweh in the Old Testament earlier, the Sun-God of *Eyes Wide Shut* expects *loyalty ("Fidelio")* and obedience. Like the malignant narcissist, it also inflicts pain and suffering on those who demonstrate bad karma on account of having "issues" or a lack of self-love.

This also dovetails on the third "son of God" scenario, the Talmudic version of Samael, the Archangel correlated to Satan. While sometimes being identified as a fallen angel, he's otherwise seen as not necessarily evil since his functions involve punishing or destroying sinners - which is odd considering what his worshippers are supposedly capable of.

Whatever the case may be, I'll let the reader arrive to their own interpretation. The purpose for including this whole analysis with respect to dysfunctional families, the patriarchal Abrahamic religions, the "Gnostic" cosmology, and the storyline presented in *Eyes Wide Shut* is to demonstrate the potential malignant, narcissistic characteristic of a being that considers and presents itself as "God."

If this is the case - that the being which is regarded by many as "God" truly exists and is, in fact, a malignant narcissist - it's reasonable to attribute the "wag the dog" news, the black operations, and the consolidation of wealth and power to a preposterously small fraction of the human population to be emblematic of the gas lighting, scapegoating, and selfishness respectively seen in malignant narcissism and could be that of a narcissistic being whom is regarded by many as "God."

It would also explain why those who are deceptive, devoid of empathy and compassion, selfish and miserly, hypocritical, scheming, and highly narcissistic comprise the ruling elite of this Earth and not those who are beneficent, fair-minded, and lead by example.

Of course, it's also possible that such behavior and activity is the result of the general public's poor karma as well, sort of an amplified version of the scenario the character of Bill Harford faced in *Eyes Wide Shut* - that is, acting out inappropriately on account of one's "issues" leads to dangerous consequences.

In both cases, like the malignant narcissist himself, "God" would have no reservation against engaging in the gas lighting, mass manipulation, and punitive, retaliatory behavior due to feelings of neglect, abandonment, betrayal, or disobedience - in his mind, he has a right to do so.

But, if the establishment of the "New World Order" as referenced by President George H.W. Bush's speech on September 11th, 1990 [1] is to be headed by the "Sun-God" that is Yahweh/Samael/Satanail/Lucifer or what have you and this being is in fact malignantly narcissistic, what we can expect as a result is precisely the "Boot stamping on the human face forever" as predicted by George Orwell [2], who described the future as being a world in which there are "no emotions except fear, rage, triumph, and self-abasement" - precisely the only emotions felt within the dysfunctional family. Forget about mutual respect. Or love. Or joy. It's equivalent to the work environment where "the Boss" rules from the office and not the front, motivates by fear, and everyone in the department is anxious, constantly feels like they're being watched, walks on eggshells, and is miserable.

This is the sort of world that has been coalescing and the mechanics behind this are dissected in detail in *The Toxic States of America*. This is not going to be a pleasant world for anyone to inhabit nor would it surprise me in the least that the already escalating suicide rate will increase as time goes on, much like a "burn 'em and turn 'em" work environment.

Living an autonomous, independent life outside of this system is going to be next to impossible. As Orwell forecasted, "there will be no loyalty except loyalty to the Party, but always there will be the intoxication of power." [2] We already see this formation occurring today with the masses' feverish and unfounded loyalty to whatever "party" or special interest group they endorse without any willingness to allow their associated ideologies or beliefs to be challenged and a propensity to vilify or engage in psychological brutality against anyone who is in disagreement.

Yes, the "New World" will involve the entire human race as a global dysfunctional family. Social fractioning, addictions, class struggles, and discord will go on indefinitely - that is, until the whole thing implodes. It is, of course, called "dysfunctional" for a reason.

Until then, the *ego* will reign supreme, *not* the conscience. (Perhaps *never* the conscience.) The ego appears precisely due to the issues of Entitlement and Abandonment mentioned previously: when the Entitlement is not upheld, the egotistical actions of power and control emerge due to fears of Abandonment of Self.

Of course, the ego is necessary for our protection - it allows us to set boundaries and say "no" to other's behavior which causes harm - that is, when the ego is healthy. Otherwise, it's wildly over-the-top and disproportionate to reality - oftentimes employed when no infringement on one's wellbeing has been made. Things go haywire due to the *Entitlement:* the individual's pedestal has been elevated due to being over-inflated, spoiled, or enabled in some way. Thus, the higher the pedestal, the more forceful the ego will be when it isn't upheld (Abandonment.)

The ego may also be hyperactive due to being *victimized* to a substantial extent: here, the individual plays the victim card so hard, they permit themselves to engage in excessive control, thirst for excessive power, or to be enabled in some fashion.

[1] https://www.weblinenews.com/september-11-george-bush-new-world-order/
[2] https://www.youtube.com/watch?v=JXm5hklbBsA

13

<u>*New Age and Pop Psychology Bullshit*</u>

"The most terrifying fact of the universe is not that it is hostile but that it is indifferent."

- Stanley Kubrick

Unfortunately, during this Orwellian Age where everything is turned on it's head and the masses are gas-lighted to the max, memes begin to circulate resembling some sort of New-Age brain-washing indoctrination with mottos that sound nice, reassuring, and refreshing, but really they're just about numbing and dumbing the public. Specifically, they are about conditioning the public to acquiesce to malignant goals described in *The Toxic States of America,* which are : 1) Creating a willing a docile victim, 2) Generating narcissistic supply, and 3) Enabling entitlement. Whomever came up with these, they're geared to manifest a mass public consciousness which is willfully ignorant, docile and apathetic, and conditioned to enable power and control to be usurped and consolidated to a small fraction of the global population. Specifically, they manipulate the ego. Lastly and most disturbing, they brainwash the public to welcome their own demise: "Get into the pot, frogs… don't worry, the bubbles mean it's a jacuzzi…"

Keep in mind that the origins of these memes are relatively recent; that is, none of them originate from any documentation by sages or imams from the days of yore. In fact, I'm quite confident that I'm older than most of them:

"Everything Happens For a Reason"/"Trust The Universe"

This sort of programming sounds nice, but this slogan conveniently overlooks the possibly that some things happen to teach us that some people and organizations mean us harm; that some people and organizations take our kindness, generosity, faith, trust, and goodwill for granted or take advantage of it. If everything truly happens for a reason, some of those things would be there to teach us *not* to trust the Universe.

At the time of writing this, the national debt of the United States is over *Twenty-Seven Trillion Dollars*.

This is where "trusting the universe" (in this case, our "elected" politicians who *are supposed to be working for the very public who put them in office)* gets you. Keep in mind that this exorbitant debt *is owed to someone*.

While this is a mystery (it shouldn't be) to the American public, only a fraction of its population has *done* something about it let alone acknowledge the reasons behind this disturbing detail. Thanks to a debt-based currency system established early last century and spending tax-payer dollars on the most privatized wars in human history for profit and profit alone (the spoils of which *do not* re-enter general economy, contrary to more brainwashing rhetoric spewed by corporate media outlets) this kind of shit "happens." The only thing "trickling down" is the urine from the Military-Industrial Complex onto the heads of the frogs boiling in the pot of water.)

"Everything Happens For a Reason" and "Trust The Universe" are the amongst the biggest lies spread to manipulate the masses to remain ignorant and passive - much to the detriment of future generations. This nugget of New Age bullshit helps the New World Order satisfy it goal of creating a willing and docile victim and preserves its entitlement. Why is this? We can thank the next passage:

Love Yourself

Of course, there's nothing wrong with loving yourself, having decent self-worth, and taking care of yourself. But, unfortunately, the "Love Yourself" meme floating around in today's "modern spirituality" is interpreted as a gateway to cultivate narcissism as opposed to true self-love. The former causes people to be self-involved, self-indulgent, solipsistic, critical, selfish, cold, entitled, demanding, snobbish, self-aggrandizing, egotistical, and, worst of all, dismissing.

This isn't "loving yourself": this is rude. This is very much a campaign of the psychological scam that is the Left-Hand path: "Take care of yourself so that you can take care of me and make me feel good while I give you nothing in return."

Obviously, this not helps the New World Order realize its goals of creating a willing and docile victim and maintaining entitlement, but permits it to amass power. The fact that it conditions its subscribers to become as narcissistic as itself, it conditions the public to find its own narcissism "normal."

True "self-love" means that your "self" becomes love. It also means being self-referring with respect to self-care and not trying to live up to someone or something else's ideals and being okay with that. It about being okay in one's own skin in a self-reliant manner.

However, "love yourself" has been adopted by many to be an excuse to turn away anyone in distress because it makes the individual *feel negative*. "You're bumming me out!" or "You're being negative" thus becomes the inner-monologue, permitting the conditions which create the circumstances to continue.

Seriously, how could - or *should* - anyone "love themselves" after they've enabled hundreds of thousands of civilian deaths, the displacement of their fellow citizens from their homes who work just as honestly and hard as they do - probably more, and a government system which has violated every Constitutional right imaginable thus leaving a tyrannical system for future generations to inhabit not to mention syphoned exorbitant amounts of money from all economies foreign and domestic? Do you think the citizens of Nazi Germany who enabled and endorsed Adolf Hitler "loved themselves" after they learned about the Holocaust?

Otherwise, yes: it's "Love Yourself." If you lose a loved one, don't expect that others might care about you or comfort you; care for and comfort yourself. If you find out the "house is on fire," don't ask for help; put it out yourself. If you're sick, tend to yourself. If you've lost your job and only source of income, support yourself. Need to someone to talk to? Talk to yourself. *Love yourself.*

Yes, this sort of mentality aptly describes the utter selfishness and spoiled behavior of many of those who subscribe to it.

If this is the expectation - that one should "love themselves" to the point where it requires an unreasonable amount of hermit-like self-reliance - in all fairness, the same expectation should be superimposed on those who expect this from you. Give them no consolation when they've lost someone close. If they're in a crisis, require them to face it alone. If they're sick, just tune them out since it's a fucking bummer. If they lose their job, tell them to trust the Universe. If they're upset and need to talk, throw them a sock puppet and run for the hills.

Basically, when they return looking for you to love them - in whatever way you used to or some way new: consolation, a support system, attention. self-esteem boosting, whatever. - deny them and require them to "love themselves." It would benefit them to understand what that's like through experience. .

"Love Yourself" has replaced "The Golden Rule" in terms of a general social ideology. Ideally, both should be given equal billing **but** you can't prioritize two things at the same time. You actually *do* need to prioritize yourself before anything else, but overly prioritizing "Love Yourself" over The Golden Rule can lead to the "Me Civilization" which arose during the 1980s, when "greed was good." The problem is, when people get accustomed to having consistent and surplus profit, others typically get subjected to consistent, surplus deficit - which leads to underpaying, menial, and destructive work conditions.

"We Only Learn Through Pain"

This meme proposes that pain and negative consequences for actions taken is the "only way" we as human beings learn life lessons. It's one I personally think is awful and I'll explain the reasons behind this.

What "learning" solely through negative reinforcement eventually teaches the student is to be fearful of trying at all since the "wrong move" leads to punitive results while the "right move" or a "good job" leads to no positive outcome at all.

Many studies have shown that negative reinforcement is the *worst* way to raise, train, or teach anyone, but instead of presenting those studies and their results, I'll rely on common sense. Referencing Chapter 10 and the "Dog Owner" metaphor, imagine a dog being "raised" by its owner is yelled at, kicked, slapped, etc. whenever it does something "wrong" in the eyes of its Owner. By "wrong," I mean anything from pooping in the corner to biting someone to leaving some drips outside of the water dish. If the dog's existence is a litany of experiences of such negative reinforcement, the dog will first begin to experience a life of anxiety followed by - at some point - resentment toward the Owner, rebelliousness and hatred toward the Owner and, if gone on long enough, rock-bottom stagnation. This resignation makes sense since "bad" behavior brings regret for doing *anything*, regardless of how innocuous the activity is while doing anything "good" makes no difference.

The worst case scenario is the dog *intentionally* performs the "wrong move" with the hopes that the negative consequences will shorten or end his life of abuse. Especially if the dog tried to do *and did* the "right thing" for so long with little to no positive reinforcement, the negative consequences convert to positive since the incentive for no life at all eclipses that of having a life of hell.

This sort of "raising" - whether it's a dog in their early years or a human being as they go throughout life - will have the same effect on any animal. "Learning only through pain" will cause the organism to become sociopathic, and by "sociopathic" I mean exhibiting the traits detailed in the Factor 2 category of the Psychopathy Checklist. The "dog" in this case is skittish, fearful, mistrusting, and possibly rebellious and aggressive toward others.

A more appropriate way to "teach" someone is to first *genuinely* have their best interest at heart. The student will be more receptive to any feedback provided they know this is the case. Explaining *why* such behavior is "bad" - with the "badness" being harm done to the student or others, and that the teacher *cares* about the student and how negative consequences their actions may adversely affect them - is imperative.

An example of this would be: "Don't smoke, because if you do it will ruin your health and shorten your life which will cause me to have less happy times with you" as opposed to being bitch-slapped, subjected to deprecating whining, or screamed at for smelling like a cigarette.

Otherwise, if the "dog" is never loved to begin with, they have nothing to value (even - and especially - Self) and thus no imperative to realize positive outcomes. Without being loved or cared about, there's really no incentive to live life, let alone choose options which preserve it.

"Teaching" without love, care, and respect for the pupil isn't "teaching," it's abuse. But this is precisely how narcissists "raise" their children. Parlaying this to a god or "Spirit" who behaves this way? Who needs Hell?

"Light Cannot Exist Without Darkness"

Take out a blank sheet of paper. Notice the color (white.) Notice what color *isn't there* (anything darker than white.) Basically, claiming that "Light" cannot exist without the "Dark" forces its adherents to accept and tolerate its existence. Obviously, this meme conditions it's believers to succumb to the presence of malignant narcissism.

"We're All One!"

Really? Then why do we have separate bodies and consciousnesses? This meme essentially promotes the "we're all in the same boat, like it or not" mentality, eschewing anything resembling dissension or a willingness to opt out of participation - thus reinforcing cult fortitude.

"What does not kill you makes you stronger."

Yeah? Not always. This nugget of New Age bullshit has sat around for a while and can be exploited to manifest the goals of creating a willing and docile victim as well as a sense of entitlement - provided the action causes another harm. Got robbed? Become less trusting. Someone cheated on you? Become even less trusting. Got blamed for you boss's mistakes? Suck it up and/or find a new job.

Lose custody of your child because your narcissistic ex lied profusely out their ass and fabricated evidence? "Now you have the opportunity to develop the emotional strength needed to overcome the pain of never being able to see your child again!" the New Age dipshits will champion.

"What does not kill you makes you stronger" conveniently disregards instances where what does not kill you can demoralize and weaken you for years to come or indefinitely - because some spoiled asshole wanted access to excessive control, elevate their narcissism, or reinforce their sense of entitlement.

14

The Psychology of Freemasonry

Cause we are living in a material world
And I am a material girl
You know that we are living in a material world
And I am a material girl."

- from Madonna's 1984(!) *hit* Material Girl

A few years back, I came across a lecture on Rosicrucianism delivered by Dr. Robert Gilbert at the Vesica Institute, during which he describes the three spiritual paths one could take based on the Kabbalistic Tree of Life, represented in the following diagram:

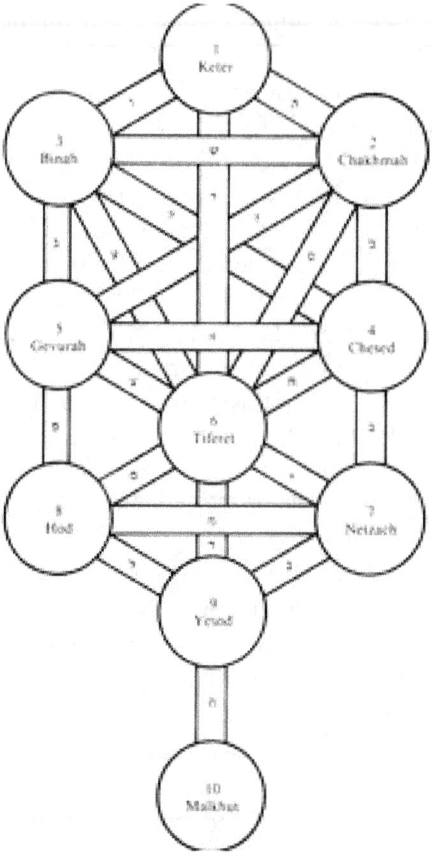

In his lecture, Gilbert remarks on the three pillars of this diagram: the left, the right, and the center - corresponding to qualities of Divine mercy, severity, and the middle, respectively. Historically, these pillars have corresponded to the different types of spiritual forces or beings. On one hand, you have spiral beings which do not understand the physical world, perceiving it as a place of unnecessary suffering and wish to end the cycles of death and rebirth. In the Western world, these beings were regarded as advanced spiritual beings and, since they were advanced and beings of pure love, they appeared as light beings. These are not "dark" beings; these are beings of tremendous light. The leader of this group was thus referred to as "Lucifer." To them, human beings are trapped in a realm of suffering and torture. People gravitating to this terminal tend to have excellent spiritual development, but their physical life takes a toll on account of it: their health, finances, and relationships tend to suffer. The sole focus on spirituality, however, can lead to spiritual perception that is illusory or hallucinogenic - thus warping the participants understanding of spiritual life.

The other polarity represents the complete opposite: a rejection of all things spiritual with a sole focus on the material aspect of life and thus deeply connected to matter. According to Gilbert, the first identification of the etheric beings associated with this polarity was first recorded in the Persian Zoroastrian texts and refer to as Ahrimanian and led by Angra Mainyu. Human beings who gravitate toward this terminal become completely materialistic and are not likely to believe that Spirit exists.

The Gnostics referred to the beings that gravitated toward this latter polarity as "Ahrimanic" and their leader, as mentioned earlier, as the Demiurge - the Dark Lord of this earth. In Egypt, this polarity was referred to as "Set." When the Israelites were led out of Egypt by Moses, who was initiated in the Egyptian Temples, "Set" was referred to as Ha-Setan (which evolved into "Satan") meaning "adversary" - an adversary to the welfare of human beings.

The Center Path, referred to by Gilbert as the "Christic" path, is what he refers to as the path with an "I am" awareness which allows for more grounded awareness. Think about living life in the present or "consciously." Below are some traits listed for all three categories:

Ahrimanic	**Christic**	**Luciferian**
Selfish	Considerate of Self and Others	Selfless
High Conflict	Appropriate Objection	Low Conflict
Ends Justify the Means	Contextual Morality	Dogmatic/Inflexible Morality
No Conscience	Appropriate Flexibility	High Conscience
High Boundaries	Appropriate Boundaries	Low Boundaries
Highly Disciplinary	Appropriately Disciplinary	Extremely Lenient
Inflated Ego	Balanced Ego	Weak Ego
Low Integrity	Honesty with Discretion	High Integrity

Narcissistic	Self-Loving Based in Truth	Self-Loathing
Miserly	Gives without Loss or with Strings Attached	Overly Generous
Highly Guarded	Cautious With Intimacy	Very Vulnerable
Low Work/High Pay	Medium work/Median Pay	High Work/Low Pay
Selfish/Only Receives	One Hand Gives/The Other Takes	Selfless/Only Gives
Self-interested	Mutual Consideration	People Pleasing
Overly Demanding	Balanced Give and Take	Overly Giving
Highly Disciplined	Adheres to Some Order	Low Discipline
Highly Secretive	Appropriate Intimacy	Open Book
Wealth Hungry	Provides for Self	Poverty-bound
Child Molesting	Child Rearing	Child Doting
Inflicts Suffering on Others	Dissolves Suffering	Self-inflicts
Close-minded	Open-minded but Anchored	Impressionable

Those of you familiar with the "Deep State" or the "Military Industrial Complex" or whatever you may call it, please review the characteristics it shares with the Ahrimanic category. Notice how the Catholic Church also resembles the Ahrimanic (and has for a while.) Notice how both take advantage of the Luciferian. Otherwise, I'd like for all of you to consider whether or not these traits became more apparent after the turn of the century.

Former Rosicrucian and founder of Anthroposophy Rudolph Steiner created a wood sculpture of Ahriman's head, the image of which is below:

Steiner also made the claim in a 1919 lecture that "a great part of mankind today is already under the control, from one side or another, of Ahrimanic forces of a cosmic nature which are growing stronger and stronger." [2]

He also claimed that Ahriman was an actual being, claiming that "The Ahrimanic impulse proceeds from a supersensible Being different from the Being of Christ or of Lucifer.… The influence of this Being becomes especially powerful in the Fifth Post-Atlantean Epoch. If we look at the confused conditioned of recent years we find that men have been brought to such chaotic conditions mainly through Ahrimanic powers."

Some "conspiracy theorists" claimed to have seen the image of a face emerge from the smoke of the World Trade Center attack on September 11th, 2001. Curiously, the face looks quite similar to the image of Ahriman depicted by Steiner:

Regardless, I should hope it is apparent to all readers how an emphasis on the physical has eclipsed that of the spiritual in today's "Western Civilization," especially since the turn of the century. In fact, things have become so *artificial* - from food to social interaction to currency systems to "news" to wars to human bodies to music to personalities to history to organisms themselves to *intelligence itself*. I'd hope this gravitation toward material mania is apparent to everyone reading.

The late George Carlin remarked:

Now, this ain't just ranting and raving. This ain't just blowing off steam. I got a little evidence to support my claim. It just seems to me seems to me, that only a really low IQ population could have taken this beautiful continent, this magnificent American landscape that we inherited… Well, actually, we stole it from the Mexicans and the Indians but hey, it was nice when we stole it. It looked pretty good. It was pristine. Paradise. Have you seen it lately? Have you taken a good look at it lately? It's fucking embarrassing.

Only a nation of unenlightened half-wits could have taken this beautiful place and turned it into what it is today, **a shopping mall**. A big, fucking shopping mall. You know that. That's all you got. That's all you got here, folks. Mile after mile of mall after mall. Many, many malls. Major malls and mini malls. They put the mini malls in between the major malls. And in between the mini malls they put the mini marts. And in between the mini marts. You've got the car lots, gas stations, muffler shops, Laundromats, cheap hotels, fast food joints, strip clubs and dirty bookstores. America the beautiful. One big transcontinental commercial cesspool. [3]

But now, even most of the malls are closed and converted to warehouses to online mega-retailers who engulfed smaller operations - in part *because they were allowed to by "the consuming public."*

Other cultural trends point toward a shift toward the Ahrimanic. The extent to which this great land has been developed and nature destroyed nature resembles a resentful child strangling its mother - Mother Nature in this case. The technology, instead of making things more convenient, is cumbersome, unreliable, and has only dehumanized our species by its indirect and impersonal application. It's also replaced a lot of jobs and proven itself incompetent in the process. It's actually less efficient in many cases.

Today, it's far easier to tamper with someone's email inbox without their knowledge than it is to access someone's physical mailbox or packages. And not just their inbox - personal computers can be hacked and accessed without the owner's awareness. I'm not sure what incriminating information such hackers are attempting to access especially considering it would pale tremendously in comparison to the crimes and transgressions their perverted minds are capable of committing.

Appliances are more short lived now, thanks to profiting off of planned obsolescence. Version 6.0 has the user wishing 5.0 were still around. And everything requires an upgrade sooner and sooner, which costs the "consumer" more money….to buy something they're not going to be able to keep in the long run.

Otherwise, it seems at times that technological advancements aren't made to really *improve* upon anything - it's more like they're just giving people something to do. Have touch-screen buttons made life easier or benefitted anyone more than a push button?

Even *assets and financial instruments* have become so exhausting on the material world, they're become hypothetical or based on something that based on something else which may or may not exist in the 3D - like the fiat US Dollar or derivatives.

"Love" is also under attack - that is, love that is considered considerate, warm, nurturing, and altruistic. This would be one case in an Ahrimanic society, especially considering that this mentality ostensibly arises out of "mommy issues." "Making love" has gone extinct; if not, it's endangered. Courtesy of the hook-up apps available, courtship and feelings are no longer associated with sex. While absurdly convenient, after a few texts arranging a time and place to screw have been sent, McFucking ensues and displaces relationships and sexual intercourse involving intimacy, trust, friendship and, well, love.

No wonder the kids are turning out fucked up. They have *no choice but* to be fucked up. *This is* fucked up.

Now, it's easy for many of us to vilify or demonize the Ahrimanic path, but we need to understand that sometimes it *is* necessary to increase our ability to exercise control, administer discipline, to stop "being nice" or too honest or becoming too generous. If we've been following the Luciferic path some pointers may need to be taken from the Ahrimanic path in order to get on the Christic. Either terminal in excess is going to led to destruction of self or others.

But, yes, an Ahrimanic environment is equivalent to Hell on Earth except for those who are demonic in character and those with psychologies resembling this side of the fence. But the question arises: if one *isn't* Ahrimanic and wishes to adhere to the Christic path…what do they do? Do they call out the bad behavior - the lies, the scams, the selfishness, the greed, the disaster capitalism, etc. (which is what I'm doing now by writing this book) - and set boundaries or do they simply acknowledge that it exists and throw it up to kismet? Is repetitively calling out the bad behavior equivalent to stewing in past transgressions to the point where it pigeonholes you on the Luciferic path? Especially when is seems that no amount of broadcasting, whistle-blowing, protesting, or otherwise does any good in terms of correcting bad character or setting boundaries?

I struggle with this. I suppose the answer lies in becoming aware but not *losing* oneself in victimhood, however understandable it might be. I really don't know. What I *can* say is that losing oneself in this situation - that is, becoming selfless to the point of dispersing one's own energy to the point where there's nothing left of the Self is something to be careful of. I think this could be the culprit behind the rise in suicide over recent years. When it gets to this point, it's almost as if the person has become a martyr. But if the greed, selfishness, and underhandedness so indicative of the Ahrimanic Age in existence today is not readily apparent to the reader, I'm not sure what it's going to take...

I think the only thing that will help the world outside of this is knowing that Fear cannot exist where there is Love. For the Left, Fear feels like rage and anger whereas the Right feels sorrow and anxiety. Again, to the Left, love equals loyalty; to the Right, it means *care*.

Whether it's abandonment, unlovability, or any other "issue" afflicting us, perhaps taking regular moments of solitude to feel a Presence that is both inside and outside of us to alleviate our "issues" will ground more and more of us to love ourselves and others in equal measure.

This is essential if anything resembling world peace comes to fruition.

Otherwise, whether the God of the Left-hand path is correctly identified as Yahweh, Yaldabaoth, Samael, Mithra, Ahriman, etc., its actual name is irrelevant. What it is, however, may be regarded as the Supreme Malignant Narcissist - a god which has no compassion or remorse but instead seeks glory, attention, manifestation, power, and control. It may be more aptly regarded as the God of the Ego or even Hubris.

Even though "the God of the Black Sun" may be utterly self-interested - up to and including harming the physical and psychological welfare of others in order to realize its goals - its psychological profile squares snuggly with the Cathar's cosmology. Provided it *does* have some sort of malignantly narcissistic pathology, this would be expected since the Cathar's "Good God" rejected it - branding an issue of Abandonment onto its self-concept.

If the fall of Samael also involved hubris as the reason for its expulsion, we can add Entitlement to its list of core issues. With Abandonment and Entitlement at its psychological core, it's reasonable to diagnose this deity as the God of Malignant Narcissism.

But does this Being exist for a reason? Perhaps it serves as a disciplinarian, reprimanding us for falling short in our duties due to self-pity or a lack of self-love - issuing repercussions for having such a lack to begin with.

If the latter is the case, **then it must be regarded as a hypocrite** - because this being itself, similar to those it targets, has a lack of self-love. Like the malignant narcissist himself, he needs to control and/or manipulate others *to do his self-loving for him - to parasitically siphon* *attention, accolades, resources, and narcissistic supply from external sources.* **There is no way it would achieve "greatness" otherwise.**

So perhaps the Cathars and those similar to them were correct in their cosmological assessment - Yaldabaoth *is* hubris incarnate. In all fairness, we haven't heard the Black Sun God's point of view so it would be unfair to reach a judgement. For all we know, it probably harbors resentment against "Sophia" for abandoning it after she exalted it, since it may be the case that she placed him on a pedestal only to leave him there for whatever reason.

Whatever the case may be, The Black Sun God cannot be the only god if it harbors abandonment and entitlement issues - someone or something else, of course, would have needed to abandon and over-indulge it in order for these issues to have manifested.

But is this "God?" I think that all depends on where someone is standing. If the "witness" also has some unresolved abandonment or entitlement issues, he or she is going to have similar narcissistic tendencies which may cause them to regard this deity as "God." Otherwise, the "witness" may have an adverse reaction.

Regardless, it appears this "deity of the ego" seeks to manipulate others to do its bidding by appealing to their ego as well. As such, those who succumb to its influence act out in similar fashion; that is, to control, elevate their own narcissism, and exonerate themselves from rules which others are mindful of.

What I find most disheartening about this situation - despite its manipulative, parasitic, and, frankly, annoying character - is that *no one truly loves this god.* That is, *no one truly has compassion for the rejection it endured let alone set boundaries and tried to stop enabling its grandiose sense of self.* People either worship it out of a vicariousness for glory and power, hold it in awe out of their own lack of self worth, or conspire with it due to issues in common.

One thing is certain: if it takes the helm of a global, hierarchal organization and appoints itself as "King of Kings," we can expect a global, dysfunctional family to emerge (if it hasn't already.)

As George Orwell described:

"In our world, there will be no emotions except fear, rage, triumph, and self-abasement. The sex instinct will be eradicated. We shall abolish the orgasm. There will be no loyalty except loyalty to the Party. But always there will be the intoxication of power. Always, at every moment, there will be the thrill of victory, the sensation of trampling on an enemy who's helpless. If you want a picture of the future, imagine a boot stamping on a human face, forever.

The moral to be drawn from this dangerous nightmare situation is a simple one: don't let it happen. It depends on you."[4]

Orwell tried to warn us about deconstructing narcissism before it deconstructed us. Sadly, I think we might be too late.

THE END

[1] https://www.youtube.com/watch?v=DZSRKNw-lTE&list=LL&index=113
[2]https://www.newdawnmagazine.com/articles/rudolf-steiner-secret-societies-the-ahrimanic-deception
[3] https://www.youtube.com/watch?v=41jCCyT5wuA&feature=emb_title
[4] https://www.youtube.com/watch?v=9k_ptxWsadI